Hiking Trails of New Brunswick

Hiking
Trails
of New Brunswick

4th EDITION

MARIANNE EISELT & H.A. EISELT

GOOSE LANE

Edited by Charles Stuart.
Cover image: "Mount Carleton, New Brunswick, Canada Day, 2016," copyright © 2016 by Kelci MacDonald.
Interior photographs by Marianne Eiselt and H.A. Eiselt.
Maps prepared by Todd Graphic, www.toddgraphic.ns.ca.
Cover and page design by Julie Scriver.
Printed in China by MCRL Overseas Printing.
10 9 8 7 6 5 4 3 2 1

We acknowledge the generous support of the Government of Canada, the Canada Council for the Arts, and the Government of New Brunswick.

Goose Lane Editions
500 Beaverbrook Court, Suite 330
Fredericton, New Brunswick
CANADA E3B 5X4
www.gooselane.com

Library and Archives Canada Cataloguing in Publication

Eiselt, Marianne, author
    Hiking trails of New Brunswick / Marianne and H.A. Eiselt. -- 4th edition.

Includes bibliographical references and index.
ISBN 978-1-77310-012-8 (softcover)

1. Trails--New Brunswick--Guidebooks.
2. Hiking--New Brunswick--Guidebooks.
3. New Brunswick--Guidebooks.
I. Eiselt, Horst A., 1950-, author II. Title.

GV199.44.C22N46 2018   796.5109715'1
C2018-902204-3

The authors have made every effort to ensure that the information contained in this book is correct. However, neither the authors nor the publisher accept any responsibility, implied or otherwise, resulting from the use of this book or the trails described in it.

Contents

"Only where you have walked, have you really been."
Johann Wolfgang von Goethe

Preface

The 4th edition of *Hiking Trails of New Brunswick* that you hold in your hands is the result of an effort of two years (2016-2017) that required travelling 14,000 km (8,700 mi) in the car to reach the trails and almost 800 km (500 mi) to walk them. The descriptions were accurate at the time of this writing, but changes occur all the time. The latter fact became painfully obvious when we compared reality with our descriptions in the previous edition. As a case in point, take the Fundy National Park. While national and provincial parks are typically very stable in the sense that their trail systems rarely undergo major changes, the last ten years have seen major changes in Fundy National Park, one of New Brunswick's two national parks and one of the premier hiking areas in the province. Along with minor work on some trails such as, for instance, the Coastal Trail, the Coppermine Trail has been closed altogether in order to be rerouted. A similar fate has befallen the Goose River Trail, an old cart road, which, while it provided relatively fast access to a river estuary on the Fundy coast, was admittedly somewhat boring to hike. It will be completely rerouted in the future and integrated into the Coppermine Trail. The construction of the Fundy Parkway caused closures of access roads, and some trails were abandoned, as the funds had been exhausted by the building of the road. There are many other changes that have occurred in New Brunswick's trail system. Some new trails have emerged, such as the interesting hikes in Meduxnekeag, Ganong Nature Park, and the trails on Ministers Island opposite Saint Andrews, just to name a few. On the other hand, trails such as the Gaspereau Heritage Trail, Marys Point Nature Trail, Mud Lake Trail, and others have fallen into disrepair and/or are no longer maintained.

When choosing which trails to include and which not, we were guided by the following principles. First of all, we chose to include only trails that offer some features that are of interest to the hiker. This rule was necessary to exclude all four-wheel tracks in the province, of which there are thousands of kilometres and whose inclusion would result in an unwieldy volume. After some deliberation, we also decided not to include multi-use trails, unless they offer outstanding features. Finally, we decided to no longer include walks in city parks, which are great for evening strolls but not for hikes. This leaves some trails somewhere on the borderline of hiking/strolling, for instance, the Killarney Lake Trail near Fredericton and the Irishtown Nature Park near Moncton (both of these trails offer some nice vistas), so we decided to include them in the present volume. And while we normally would not include very short trails, there were at least two exceptions. One is the White Rapids Trail, a short nature walk laced with sculptures that accesses the Gaspereau Falls, and another is a short walk across the compound of the former internment camp on the road to Minto. There are some city parks that could have made it into this book (Rockwood Park in Saint John, Odell Park in Fredericton, Centennial Park in Moncton, and the trails in Rothesay). However, we decided against it, as they are great places for locals to walk the dog, ride a bike, or run, but not places to hike and explore nature.

Whoever walks on any number of trails will have stories to tell, and we are no exception. As we were walking one of the lesser used trails in Kouchibouguac National Park close to dusk, a local fishing enthusiast hollered something to us. It was probably just a typical New Brunswick "How ya doin'? Fine day, isn't it?" but we did not take it that way. Having been robbed on the Camino Portugues in the same year, we walked as fast as we could until we were sitting in the safety of our car. While the items that were taken from us have long since been replaced, we will probably look over our shoulders for the rest of our lives. And speaking of pilgrims, we vividly remember taking members of the Fredericton chapter of the Canadian Company of Pilgrims, a local group interested in pilgrimages, on a hike to the new trails in the Woodstock area. Since we did not know the new Meduxnekeag trails ourselves at the time, we went a week earlier to check things out so that it would at least look like we knew what we were doing. A week later, we met the pilgrims, and things went well, even when they had to balance on a log across a gully (albeit with a guide rope) and perform similar feats. Then came the fording of a brook. No big deal, really, and we provided assistance to the individuals who needed it so that they could step safely from one boulder to the next. One lady had with her a walking stick. Sufficient support, one would think, but the male author of this volume grabbed and pulled her anyway. The result was that both of them ended up on the (mercifully dry) ground on top of each other. Luckily enough, the only real victim was the walking stick, which did not survive the fall.

Sometimes people pose as somebody who they are not, but more often they are just assumed to be somebody else. This happened to us in the Superstition Mountains near Phoenix, Arizona, when a number of people asked us all kinds of questions about the mountains and some of their natural features. Having been there a number of times, we could answer most of these questions, but we were astonished by the repeated interrogations. Then it dawned on us: we were both wearing olive shirts and were assumed to be park rangers! Closer to home, we hiked some of the Mount Carleton trails in the early fall of 2016. In order to provide up-to-date trails (at least in the first years after the publication of the book), we had decided to walk many of the trails separately. This required a bit of planning, but it allowed us to avoid having to walk back on linear trails and generally just about doubled our efficiency. One day, Marianne had hiked up the Mount Carleton trail, while H.A. hiked the Big Brook - Dry Brook Loop. The idea was to meet up near the summit of Mount Carleton. In order to arrange this, we had purchased walkie-talkies, knowing full well that their efficiency in the woods would be limited to a rather short distance. So there was Marianne, on top of the mountain, when her receiver rings and a crackling voice starts talking. Thankfully, the reception was bad, so the other hikers on top of the mountain could not understand what was said in our private conversation. Again, people wondered whether they were in the presence of a ranger.

Then there was our three-day trip on the Dobson Trail from Moncton-Riverview to the northern boundary of Fundy National Park. As we always do, we drive our vehicle to the end of the trail and then get a shuttle to the trailhead. That way, we can arrive at the end of the trail whenever we want, and our own transportation will be waiting for us — provided it has not been stolen or vandalized. (Neither of these happened on any of the trips for this edition.) Our plan was to meet an acquaintance in Moncton, drive with her to the trail end on the Shepody Road, and then return to Moncton, where we had made a reservation at a bed and breakfast. The next morning would see us on the trail. Well, that was the plan. The part of driving with two vehicles to the trail end went without a hitch, even though seeing an eighteen-wheeler on the dirt road at night with the driver out and yelling something was somewhat disconcerting, to say the least. Anyway, we parked our vehicle, and off we were to Moncton. We drove to Alma first, as the trip had been longer than the lady expected and her vehicle was short on gas. No problem; we'd just make a quick stop in Alma, not much of a detour either. Unfortunately, this was late in the season, and the gas station in Alma — the only one for miles — was closed. Now what? Well, this is the reason we are members of the CAA. Marianne called, described the time and place, and then — nothing. After about an hour — it was around 10 p.m. now — she called again. "Oh yes, we did not quite understand where you were" was the response, or something like that. Fortunately, they found a local man with a big container half-filled with gas that we could purchase. And then we were on the phone again, as the poor couple in the Moncton bed and breakfast had been waiting . . . and waiting . . . They were really nice and they waited for us until 11:45 p.m., when we finally arrived. From that point on, things went smoothly, if we ignore (which is actually almost impossible to do) the constant drone of the multitude of wind turbines, a.k.a. bird shredders. Worse yet, they appeared to be always located in close vicinity of where we decided to pitch our tent.

Whatever the season, hiking the Fundy Footpath is always an adventure. For this edition, the plan was for one of us to hike the entire trail in three segments. While H.A. would walk one segment without a pack and just his camera, Marianne would hike some smaller trails and then pick up H.A. later in the day. Repeat three times, and the Fundy Footpath would be hiked. We've done it that way before and planned to proceed accordingly this time. Come the Fundy Parkway. The extension of the existing parkway caused the closure of all kinds of access trails, which made it impossible to hike the footpath in segments. As a result we found just about the last consecutive four-day time slot we had available and tried to find a shuttle. Help arrived in the form of Larry Adair, who picked us up in Fundy National Park and drove us the long way to the visitor interpretation centre near the trailhead of the Footpath. We said our goodbyes and set out on our respective adventures. Things went well, considering that this is certainly the toughest trail in New Brunswick and one of the more demanding backpacking trips in Canada. The few hours on the first day went well, but as we know, this was deceptive. The second day was tough, but not a problem. We camped near a beach and life was good. The third morning, just as we made our sacrifices to the god of hygiene, it started to rain. A drizzle at first, and then a steady rain, one that farmers delight in, at least if it's in the growing season. For us, delight was not the word. We retreated into the tent at first, trying to sit/lie it out, but this proved to be impossible. It rained all day. In the afternoon, the rain appeared to let up somewhat, so we packed up and left, only to run into a shower, which alternated with the steady rain. After a couple of hours we were completely wet and made camp next to a waterfall, which we assumed would promote sleep through its soothing sounds. Well, it did not. Neither of us was able to sleep with this infernal noise, especially since we had no fermented grape juice at hand to counteract the problem. The next day was quite terrible. The narrow path was soaked and slippery, and we had to pay even more attention to stay on the trail. Inevitably, this is when it happened. H.A., who had gone ahead, heard a faint yelling. Having been married for an extended period of time, he knows that this is not to be ignored. Returning a short distance, the problem became clear. Marianne had slipped, fallen down, and begun to roll down the hill. Fortunately, a tree had stopped her, as below the tree was more hill, ending in cliffs and rocks. Not a good circumstance. It took a while for H.A. to secure himself and pull his wife back up onto the trail. Fortunately, other than being a bit wobbly on her feet, Marianne had not sustained any injuries. And on we went for another couple of hours. And there it was again, the faint cry. H.A. turned around, and this time he found his wife sprawled right on the trail. This was an opportunity too good to be missed. Since there was no immediate danger, he first took a couple of pictures before assisting in the rescue. Indeed, there was a third fall, but Marianne shared this with her husband only after they were back home.

What are trails without animals? Sure, animals belong in the wild. Wild animals, that is. During the research for this edition, we were assaulted by dogs no less than five times, to which we have to add getting harassed by one of the owners. This is in contravention of Section 191 of the Municipalities Act of New Brunswick, according to which dogs have to be on a leash. What is most disturbing is that this has never happened before. No doubt, there are places for your pooch running off leash, but New Brunswick's wild isn't one of them. However, while walking the trails, we were treated to all kinds of wildlife. Although we saw lots of the ubiquitous deer, we also saw animals that are not seen as frequently. First, there are the sandpipers, which rest in the upper Bay of Fundy in preparation for their annual flight to South America. At Dorchester Cape, near the Pink Rock Trail, we were treated to a spectacle of thousands of them roosting and flying. It is a sight not to be missed. As far as unplanned encounters are concerned, there were some. Driving towards Mount Carleton, there was a moose in moult right next to the road. Similarly, when returning from a multi-day trip to hike trails along the Eastern Coast, we drove through Kouchibouguac at nighttime. The night was dark, actually black, when we noticed a movement alongside the road. The shadow became a shape, which eventually turned out to be a black bear. Thanks to all of these animals for being sufficiently patient to allow me to take their photograph. At this point we had captured visuals of all important animals except one: Canada's first engineer, the beaver. We had passed by many beaver ponds, but we had never seen signs of action in any one of them. Then came the last two hikes on an early fall day, and we returned to Fundy National Park one more time for a very short trail that we had never before considered for inclusion in our book. However, since it was there, we considered it our duty to do so. MacLaren Pond in Fundy National Park was the very last walk we had to do. We took all the measurements, and there they were: the beavers. Not one of them, not even two, but four or five of them, completely undisturbed by us and one other couple observing them. Our gratitude goes out to them.

Marianne & H.A. Eiselt

Introduction

About This Edition

For the fourth edition of *Hiking Trails of New Brunswick* we rehiked all the trails included in the third edition plus, of course, all twenty-nine new trails. The descriptions and maps represent an accurate account of the trails at this time. However, trails—particularly those outside parks—may change course or become obscured because they are subject to alterations due to logging, one of New Brunswick's key industries. When lumber workers move their trucks and other heavy equipment into an area, trails and other distinctive features are invariably destroyed. On the other hand, once the forest in a logged-over area recovers over the years, old logging roads may become new hiking trails. Beaver dams, forest fires, and other natural causes alter the landscape over time.

In addition to logging and road construction (e.g., in the area of the Fundy Trail Parkway) or rerouting of trails, as presently done in Fundy National Park, trail features and conditions change frequently. The climate and soil conditions of the Atlantic Northeast generate vigorous growth, such that trails can become quickly overgrown and impassable if not properly maintained. Part of the maintenance is actually done by the hiking public: using a trail keeps down the growth. The saying "use it or lose it" applies. In this book, we have not included trails that have deteriorated below a certain level, where the hiker will have arduous climbs over massive deadfalls or will need rubber boots to cross swampy areas.

Walking and hiking are popular outdoor activities as witnessed by the growth of new hiking clubs, full parking lots at trailheads in national and provincial parks, and the increasing number of trails and hikers in the province. Some trails are designed for and used by tough and rugged types, who push farther and farther into the wild on their long-distance hikes, their backpacks loaded with tents and freeze-dried food. Others are thrill-seekers who choose especially challenging hikes for their adrenaline-fuelled adventures. And then there is the majority of walkers, who want to get out for a few hours, experience some physical activity away from their office, and immerse themselves into nature for a few hours.

One reason for the popularity of hiking is that, in its simplest form, it does not require any special equipment. **Walking trails** (less than two hours, easy going) can be attempted by all, including kids, while **hiking trails** (up to a full day) are for reasonably fit individuals. Multi-day **backpacking** trails (two to seven days) attract physically fit nature lovers, and **long-distance backpacking** trails are for those who seriously want to get away from it all. Clearly, multi-day hikes, particularly those over difficult terrain, do require special and sometimes costly gear. In this book, we describe trails that run the gamut from easy hikes to medium and challenging day hikes to multi-day hikes. There is a trail here for everyone.

Hiking is not about arriving at a destination; it is about the experience of getting there. Hiking is almost always combined with other pursuits such as birdwatching, photography, or the plain enjoyment of the outdoors. Fresh air and fitness are extra bonuses. As a matter of fact, several studies have demonstrated the physiological, so-cial/emotional, and cognitive benefits of recreation time spent in the great outdoors. In a recent Stanford study, brain scans actually showed that walking in nature reduces activity in the subgenual prefrontal cortex that is associated with mental rumination in mood disorders. (Bratman et al. 2015; James et al. 2016; Oh et al. 2017)

In this book, we address questions such as:

- Where can I hike in the province of New Brunswick?
- What is the condition of the trail, how long will it take me to hike the trail, and is it strenuous or easy?
- What are its features?

In order to get a feel for what can be expected on the hiking trails in this province, it is useful to know some basic facts about its geography. New Brunswick's surface is about 73,000 km^2 (28,185 sq mi), 85% of which is wooded; and the elevation ranges from sea level to 820 m (2,700 ft). Even though most of the province's geologic struc-ture was formed in the Palaeozoic era about 248-590 million years ago, the surface is astonishingly diverse: it ranges from wide, sandy beaches and rocky shores to high-lands to fertile river valleys.

In this fourth edition of *Hiking Trails of New Brunswick*, we have divided the province into six geographical regions where hiking trails can be found.

The Regions

The first region is Eastern Canada's scenic **Saint John River Valley**, a fertile area where the Saint John River runs down some 640 km (400 mi) from the Madawaska region in the northwest corner of the province through Grand Falls, Woodstock, Fredericton, Grand Bay-Westfield, and Saint John to the Bay of Fundy. The Fundy Coast is the region in which most of the hiking trails are located, so we have decided to subdivide it into three separate chapters. The entire Fundy Coast is dominated by tides that can rise up to 16.3 m (53.5 ft), which is higher than a three-storey building. The tides are the highest in the world and owe their height to the funnel-like shape of the Bay of Fundy. The weather and the tides have formed a dramatic shoreline of jagged cliffs and rocky beaches, and the forest often ends abruptly at the steep cliffs. Forestry, fishing, and tourism are the main industries along the Fundy Coast. Life on the quaint Fundy Isles along **Fundy Coast – West** has a slower pace than it does on the mainland. Charming fishing communities, the Franklin D. Roosevelt cottage on Campobello Island, and whale-watching, hiking, and ocean kayaking on Grand Manan attract local and foreign tourists. **Fundy National Park**, near the charming village of Alma, encompasses a diverse landscape: the Bay of Fundy with its giant tides and softwood-clad cliffs, and in the uplands, roaring waterfalls and large stands of maple, birch, and beech. The park is a haven for hikers and naturalists. Species such as white-tailed deer, moose, black bears, beavers, martens, pileated woodpeckers, and peregrine falcons inhabit the park. **Fundy Coast – East** is a zone of transition. While its westernmost reaches around Saint John and the coast between St. Martins and Fundy National Park are still dominated by the rugged Fundy coastline, the geography changes markedly to the north and east of Fundy National Park. Wide stretches of marshes alternate with steep cliffs until they eventually vanish and the coastline becomes gentle. This is the **Acadian Coast**, which is characterized by fishing villages, lighthouses, marshes, peat bogs, and miles of sandy beaches. The dikes and sea walls in the southeast are splendid examples of how the early Acadian settlers controlled the tremendous tides. The Acadian Coast along the Northumberland Strait boasts miles of sandy beaches with the warmest salt water north of Virginia. The hinterland, however, changes gradually: it is fertile in the south and increasingly barren in the north. Bogs become more and more prevalent in and north of Kouchibouguac National Park, which features sandy beaches, salt marshes, and lagoons. Farther north, the Acadian Coast melts into Chaleur Bay, where commercial fishing is the mainstay for many Acadian residents. In New Brunswick's centre, the Miramichi River and its many tributaries rule the landscape as they flow through the heavily wooded basin. Going northwest, the land slowly rises towards the **Appalachian Highlands,** the New Brunswick portion of the mountain range that extends from the southeastern United States to Newfoundland. The rounded shape of the heavily wooded highlands was 400 million years in the making. The major feature of this region is Mount Carleton, with a height of 820 m (2,690 ft). It is the highest peak in the Maritimes and the centrepiece of Mount Carleton Provincial Park.

What's New?

Much has happened since the previous edition of this book was published twelve years ago. The number of new hiking trails has increased tremendously, mostly in the Saint John River Valley and along Fundy Coast - West. This is the result of the conservation effort by the Nature Conservancy of Canada; the Nature Trust; corporations such as Irving, Ganong, UPM Miramichi, and Twin Rivers Paper; Canoe Kayak New Brunswick; and the Meduxnekeag River Association; private land donors; along with other non-profit organizations and municipalities. In the Saint John River Valley region we added fifteen new hiking trails, and Fundy Coast - West had eleven new trails. Very few trails in these regions were not maintained and allowed to fall into disrepair, and thus are no longer featured in this guide. There were some changes in Fundy Coast-East due to the road extension of the Fundy Trail Parkway, where, for example, the scenic Big Salmon River Trail to the Hearst Lodge has not been maintained, as funds were spent on building the new road. The trails to Long Beach Brook Falls and the Walton Glen Gorge Trail, however, are now part of the Parkway Trail system. Overall we made the observation that, while keeping the vigorous growth on the trails in check is a daunting task, most trails are well groomed by maintenance crews and their (mostly volunteer) workers. A big "thank you" is due to them.

As in the previous editions, for trails to be included in this book, they had to be designed as hiking trails boasting beautiful vistas, and scenic and important natural features, such as waterfalls, lakes, beaches, tidal salt marshes, bogs, and other ecosystems. We also included short nature trails that educate the public about the flora and fauna in a hands-on approach. Most hiking trails chosen in this guide also have some historical and cultural significance not only for our province but also for Canada and our close neighbour, the United States.

How to Use This Book

Distances in the *Hiking Trails of New Brunswick* have been obtained from various sources, including a pedometer as well as signs put up by the trail builders or those who maintain the trails. In cases where our own measurements differed from those posted on signs, we chose the distances on the signs in order to avoid confusion. Hiking times are, of course, highly personal. Our times are based on a somewhat relaxed pace with a few short breaks. We know that many trails could be "done" in considerably less time, but after all, this book is about hiking, not running. Once, when we remarked to a fellow hiker about someone who had hiked through the Grand Canyon from the North to the South Rim in a single day (it took us four, plus two for side trips), he replied, "So what? The mountains don't care." This pretty much reflects our attitude. We suggest that new hikers try out some of the shorter trails first, keeping track of their own times. They can then modify the times we have given for longer trips by recalculating using the appropriate multiplier.

The description of each trail in this book starts with a heading with some short-hand information about the trail. The **hiking time** and the maps have already been discussed. Sometimes, other useful maps exist (especially in parks); in such cases we have indicated this.[1] We generally distinguish between **two types of trails**: linear and loop trails. In the case of a linear trail, hikers must retrace their steps (or find some other way out); loops end at the trailhead. The **lengths** of the trails are always the distances back to the trailhead; for linear trails, they are twice the one-way distance. This way, hikers can quickly determine whether a trail is suitable for them. Measuring the **ascent** of a trail is difficult: ideally, hikers would like to know the total ascent they have to climb. Here, however, we can only provide the vertical distance between the lowest and the highest elevations of a trail. The **difficulty** of a trail is measured on a scale from easy (E), to moderate (M), to strenuous (S) (and, in one case only, very strenuous [VS]), with intermediate degrees easy-to-moderate (E-M) and moderate-to-strenuous (M-S). Like hiking time, the difficulty of a trail is personal, so we recommend that you check your own ability and rating against ours. Information concerning the **trail condition** points out some of the obstacles found along the trail, such as wet spots or rough sections. Again, trail conditions change with the seasons: water levels tend to be higher in spring, and deadfall is likely to

---

1 There are several online resources that also provide maps of trails based on GPS data. These maps sometimes diverge from the information presented in this book or on other maps. They may show alternative routes or simply misrepresent where a trail runs if the person collecting the GPS data left the trail.

be gone from park trails by mid-season. We have also indicated whether **cell-phone** reception exists along a trail. This information should be used with a grain of salt, though, as coverage changes over time. Cellphone coverage is indicated with a Y for Yes, N for No, and P for Partial Coverage. Finally, additional trail information that will be interesting and potentially useful is offered in the sidebars.

Land ownership varies considerably depending on the trail. Some trails are clearly found within national and provincial parks, a number of trails are part of the Nature Trust of New Brunswick or the Nature Conservancy of Canada, some are on crown land, and some are community based. However, some trails may also lead across private land, at least in part. Our view is that, in the absence of No Trespassing signs, we can assume that permission to use the trail has been granted. Regardless of the issue of ownership, we encourage all hikers to exercise the utmost respect and consideration while enjoying the splendour of New Brunswick's hiking trails.

Getting Started

The tourist season in New Brunswick is concentrated between mid-June and early September as many attractions and provincial campsites open in mid-to-late June and close around Labour Day. The hiking season is, however, considerably longer. Personally, we prefer spring and fall for hiking, to avoid crowds as well as heat, humidity, and biting insects. In particular, the cool days of April to mid-May and September to the end of October (and sometimes even into November) make for excellent hiking. Mid-May is usually the time when bugs start to appear in large numbers. This onslaught lasts for some four to six weeks but does not totally vanish until the first frost in September, depending on the region. Along the Fundy Coast and in the northern part of the province, the fly season can start a few weeks later. Fortunately, blackflies and horseflies do not carry diseases, whereas mosquitoes may carry the dreaded West Nile virus. Cases of ticks carrying Lyme disease in New Brunswick are rare but not unheard of. As a precaution, we suggest you use a bug repellent and/or wear protective clothing such as long sleeves and long pants, and if you are bitten by a tick, see a doctor. In the fall, Indian summer is a particularly beautiful time to hike. This period usually lasts for about two weeks in early October. But remember: the popular deer-hunting season in the province starts about mid-October and lasts for roughly a month. If you decide to hike outside provincial and national parks during that time, wear bright clothing (preferably hunter orange) to alert hunters who may mistake you for deer, moose, or other game.

Kelci MacDonald

135. Mount Carleton Trail

56. Lighthouse Trail

Safety and Other Considerations

Gear and Supplies

Many books have been written about hiking equipment, and this is not the place to repeat their valued advice. Some good references are found in the bibliography section. Here, we list only a few items that we consider a must on any but the shortest hike.

Fly dope. Muskol and Off! have an excellent reputation. Be careful, though: their active ingredient, DEET, is said to soften the brain, and it surely dissolves plastics. Keep it away from your eyes!

First aid kit. Knowing some basics about first aid is always handy, and a first aid kit is more useful if you know what that funny-looking stuff is for.

Map. A topographical map, usually 1:50,000. Sometimes specialized hikers' maps are available, and they may be preferable as long as they show contour lines — a seemingly short distance can be very strenuous if it leads up and down steep hills! Google maps are generally okay, but they do not have sufficient contour lines and more often than not do not show the trails.

Compass. Get a trustworthy one and learn how to use it. Good brand names are Brunton, Silva, and Suunto.

Canteen with water. The 1 litre (1 quart) size is the best all-around bottle. For longer trips, you can take two bottles, or rely on a Platypus or CamelBak bladder-type system that is easy to carry and very useful, as long as it is not punctured. If you use this type of hydration system, make sure that you frequently clean and disinfect the system, as otherwise mould can develop, causing health problems.

Longer trips will require that hikers purify water found in the wilderness. To do so, one could bring the suspect water (all water taken from streams or lakes is suspect) to a boil, let it cool, and then drink it. This is not a good method, as it takes a

above: Black bear

long time to do and requires a lot of fuel. Another system relied on by many backpackers involves water filters such as Katadyn, MSR, First Need, or similar products. As long as the intake and output hoses are kept separate, so that contamination cannot occur, they are good. Another nice product is the SteriPEN, which uses ultraviolet light to purify water. It is a great system. (We have used it in Nepal on local water sources that tend to make people violently sick. Treating it with a SteriPEN did the job within a minute.) The system needs (fresh) batteries, though! A quick and relatively inexpensive method is purification tablets. Some use iodine, such as Potable Aqua; be sure to use the Potable Aqua Plus, as it includes a second bottle whose use eliminates the rather awful taste of the iodine-based chemical. Other tablets, such as Aquatabs, are chlorine based and have little aftertaste, but they are not effective against cryptosporidium. Note that none of these pills is meant for long-term use.

Sunglasses. Glasses with UV blockers are useful everywhere but are essential in higher elevations.

Sunscreen. Lotion with a factor of at least SPF 15 is recommended.

Extra clothing. Socks and rain gear along with plastic bags and freezer bags to protect items, such as cameras, IDs, etc., that should not get wet.

Extra food. High calorie snacks such as trail mix or trail bars are best.

Pocket knife. A sturdy folding knife, such as the Swiss Army knife, or mini-tools, such as Leatherman or Gerber.

Waterproof matches. Better yet a transparent Bic lighter (so you always know how much fuel is left).

Day pack or belly bag. Even though these went out of fashion some time ago, they are useful as lightweight packs for the other items listed here. Some of the more elaborate bags incorporate bottle holders.

Headlamp. You may want to invest in a very practical headlamp, whose LCDs (at least three, better five) are bright and provide light for many hours on a set of batteries. Check them out before a multi-day trip, as some of the cheaper headlamps may not be particularly bright.

Dog spray. This item may be handy as a last resort in cases of unavoidable confrontations.

Some hikers find **telescopic walking poles** useful. They provide additional stability and, especially on steep descents, take some of the load off the knees. When fording a brook is required (see also the sidebar Crossing a River, p. 227), hiking poles or wooden sticks found along the trail may provide extra balance.

Before setting out on a longer trip, it is a very good idea to test out all pieces of equipment. Nothing is worse than being in the middle of nowhere and finding out that part of the equipment does not function as anticipated. Also, all batteries should be fresh.

Safety Tips

As with any other activity, safety is crucial. Although hiking poses relatively few hazards, it pays to know about them and take appropriate precautions. Usually, "trail safety" brings to mind hazards such as falling from a cliff or the remote risk of being mauled by a bear. Either hazard is possible, but unlikely. Another problem may exist even though it has so far not crossed the line from nuisance to hazard. While easy access to trails is generally a good thing, it also provides everybody with an opportunity to reach just about any point in the woods with relative ease. While this has fortunately resulted "only" in illegal and unsightly dump sites in the woods so far, one should be cautious about possible bad encounters. For those and other reasons such as accidents, we suggest that you do not hike alone. Theft on the trail is not a problem, but it does not hurt to be careful. Vandalism at the trailhead, particularly directed against vehicles that are parked overnight, does, however, exist. Whenever possible, a well-lighted area should be chosen for parking (maybe even coupled with a short ride in a cab to the trailhead), even though that may not always be possible.

Worries about four-legged animals are not really an issue. Wild animals generally avoid humans. However, if a hiker enters an animal's fear circle, its response may be flight (the animal runs away) or fight (the animal attacks). Don't try to find out which response an animal will choose! As a general rule, signal your presence by talking or by making any other noise. If you see an animal, give it a wide berth. These rules are particularly important in the spring, when mother bears nurse and guard their January-born young, and in the rutting season of deer and moose in the fall.

One way to avoid uninvited visitors at night is to avoid carrying smelly food or other items that could cause the olfactory senses of opportunist omnivores to tingle with joy. Consider freeze-dried foods and use freezer bags to seal in smelly leftovers. Many authors suggest hanging bags of food or even entire backpacks in trees, but we have found such suggestions impractical if the campsite does not provide a scaffold (such as the one in Headwaters wilderness campground on the Mount Carleton Trail). Interesting smells will cause squirrels, raccoons, mice, rats, and other animals to chew holes in tents and packs to get at the delicacies inside.

If you must bring your dog into the wilderness, have it on a leash all the time. Dogs, when not on a leash, may (and often do) remember their half-buried hunting instincts and go after deer and squirrels. Moreover, dogs may actually sometimes attract bears, who attack them or their companions – you.

One of the most feared dangers is getting lost in the woods. The worst enemy in such a situation is panic. There are reports of hunters who have got lost, panicked, and shot themselves in their confusion. In New Brunswick, you can always reach some outpost of civilization within a couple of days and usually much sooner – provided, of course, that you are able to use map and compass. It is not smart to undertake a multi-day trip without some basic training in their use, and such training could even come in handy on long day hikes. All good compasses (other kinds are worthless at best and at worst outright dangerous) come with reasonably detailed instructions. Most books on hiking cover this subject (see the bibliography). Make no mistake, though: getting lost or temporarily disoriented can occur anywhere, not just in the middle of deep woods days from civilization. We have become disoriented at short distances from the trail, sometimes in as little as one minute. If you leave the trail, make sure that you stay alert and register where you are going and, more importantly, where you are coming from. Looking back frequently to orient yourself is always a good idea, especially if you need to go off trail.

All maps in the *Hiking Trails of New Brunswick* include an arrow pointing to **true north**. There is roughly a 22-degree difference (declination) between true north and **magnetic north**, to which every compass needle points. Failure to observe this declination results in considerable error: for every three miles hiked, you will deviate from the true course by more than one mile! In addition, hikers are advised to carry a topographical (or "topo") map of areas where trails are less groomed. Topographical maps of Canada are available free online. Maps that are newer but incomplete can be accessed at http://ftp.geogratis.gc.ca/pub/nrcan_rncan/raster/cantopo/50k_tif/. Maps that are older but complete can be accessed at http://ftp.geogratis.gc.ca/pub/nrcan_rncan/raster/canmatrix2/50k_tif. However, at times we find special maps, e.g., those offered in and for national parks or those found in books about specific trails, such as the Fundy Footpath, more useful, as they are written specifically with hikers in mind, while general topographic maps may not show the trails at all and are certainly not updated very often.

Global Positioning Systems (GPS) are widely available and can be used to pinpoint your present location – provided they function properly, have been programmed with the appropriate map datum, and are fed with reasonably fresh batteries. Do not rely on them. While it is possible to program a GPS with waypoints, this playing with electronics interferes with the true wilderness experience. Another electronic tool that has become a fixture in some people's packs is the cellphone. While it may sound appealing having such a tool ready for emergencies, its uses are very limited. Examining the coverage maps provided by the three cellphone providers – BellAliant, Rogers, and Telus – you will discover that most backcountry areas are not covered. In that sense, a cellphone may actually provide you with a misplaced sense of security.

Other hazards exist, among them unstable cliffs along Fundy coastlines and at some summits in Mount Carleton Provincial Park. Also hazardous are the high tides along the Fundy Coast. There are places where hikers may get trapped between an unscalable cliff and the rising water. None of these places are included in this book. However, for some hikes along the coast, you should carry tide tables, available on the internet at http://www.waterlevels.gc.ca/eng/find/region/5. From this site, you can navigate to the region and zone that you need.

Another problem should be mentioned here, even though it is not so much a hazard as a nuisance. In the spring, there may be a significant amount of deadfall even on maintained trails. Typically, this is the result of storms the previous fall, and it usually takes a while for the clean-up crews to finish their work. For safety's sake, follow the old-time lumberman's rule: don't step on anything you can step over and don't step on anything you can step around.

Campfires must be put out before you leave your campsite. That doesn't mean they should die down to just a few embers or a little smouldering. It means OUT COLD. The danger of forest fires in many parts of New Brunswick is amplified by the extensive planting of softwood monoculture forests. Actually, on day hikes fires are not needed at all, and on longer backpacking trips, lightweight white gas/naphtha or butane stoves are vastly superior to campfires as they cook much quicker and cleaner. We strongly recommend them.

Trail Etiquette

We've all heard the slogans "Take only pictures, leave only footprints" and "If you pack it in, pack it out." They basically say it all. Even "small" items such as candy wrappers and cigarette butts are eyesores and will soon give your fellow hikers the feeling of hiking on a dump. Following the "broken window theory," some garbage on the trail will invite others to add their own junk to it. Another problem is human waste, which may not only be a disgusting sight but may also pose a health risk. When you have to go, get away from any body of water, at least 30 m (100 ft) but preferably much farther. Otherwise, you may contaminate the water and spread diseases such as giardia. With a knife or trowel, dig a "cat hole," a small hole 10-20 cm (4-8 in) deep (any deeper and the waste will not decompose quickly). When you're finished, cover the hole and its contents, including the paper, with soil. (Some authors suggest carrying the paper out, but we cannot bring ourselves to do it.) We saw one of the worst violations of this simple process at a small campsite at a river next to a nice stand of trees. Nice it was, but closer inspection revealed that it had been used as an extensive on-ground outdoor facility. Camping nearby must have felt like sleeping and eating next to a sewer.

We sincerely hope that our readers will have as much fun hiking New Brunswick's trails as we had when writing this book. There's a lot to discover, and we wish you "Happy Trails" as you explore this diverse, beautiful province with the *Hiking Trails of New Brunswick* in hand.

Trails at a Glance

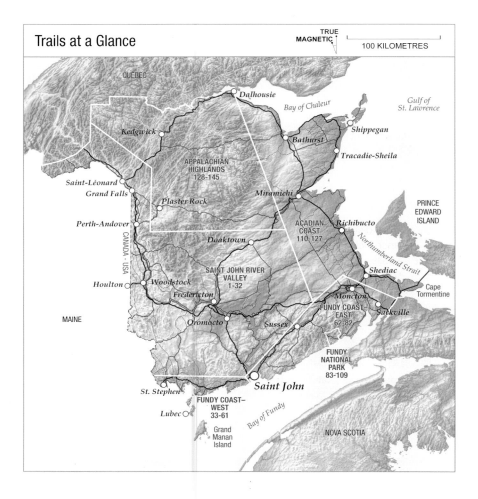

TRUE
MAGNETIC

100 KILOMETRES

QUEBEC

Dalhousie

Bay of Chaleur

Gulf of
St. Lawrence

Kedgwick

Shippegan

Bathurst

Tracadie-Sheila

APPALACHIAN
HIGHLANDS
128-145

Saint-Léonard
Grand Falls

Plaster Rock

Miramichi

PRINCE
EDWARD
ISLAND

Perth-Andover

ACADIAN
COAST
110-127

Richibucto

Northumberland Strait

Doaktown

Shediac

CANADA - USA

SAINT JOHN RIVER
VALLEY
1-32

Cape
Tormentine

Houlton

Woodstock

Fredericton

Moncton

MAINE

Oromocto

Sussex

FUNDY COAST
EAST
62-82

Sackville

FUNDY
NATIONAL
PARK
83-109

Saint John

St. Stephen

FUNDY COAST-
WEST
33-61

Lubec

Bay of Fundy

Grand
Manan
Island

NOVA SCOTIA

Trails at a Glance

For most of the trails, return distances and hiking times are shown in the table below. However, in some instances we deviate from that rule. For instance, whenever we need a trail as an access to another trail, or in case of multi-day trails, the one-way measure appears more appropriate. In particular, we use the following symbols:

* One-way distance
† Distance includes extensions or side trails
‡ Trail requires an access hike, which is not included in the distance

Key to Difficulty:
E = easy, **E-M** = easy-moderate, **M** = moderate, **M-S** = moderate-strenuous, **S** = strenuous, **VS** = very strenuous

Trail Name	Difficulty	Km (mi)	Hiking time (rtn or loop)
SAINT JOHN RIVER VALLEY			
Meduxnekeag Valley Nature Preserve (1-4)			
1. Black and Purple Trails	M	7.5 (4.7)	1 hr 45 min
2. Orange Trail	E-M	3.5 (2.2)	45 min
3. Yellow-Red-Blue Trail	E	6.5 (4)	1 hr 15 min
4. Green Trail	M-S	2.9 (1.2)	45 min
5. Maliseet Trail (Hays Falls)	E-M	3.4 (2.1)	1 hr
Big Pokiok Nature Park (6-7)			
6. Lookout–Partridge Nature Trail	E	2.1 (1.3)	40 min
7. Hiker's Dream Nature Trail	E	3.4 (2.1)	1 hr
8. Nackawic Nature Trail	E	4 (2.5)	1 hr 15 min
9. Boulderwalk Trail	E-M	3.5 (2.2)	1 hr 15 min
10. City Camp Nature Trail	E	2.8 (1.7)	45 min
11. Harvey Lakesite Nature Trail	E	1 (0.6)	20 min
Mactacquac Provincial Park (12-18)			
12. Beaver Pond Trail	E	1.3 (0.8)	30 min
13. Little Mactaquac Nature Trail	E-M	2.4 (1.5)	40 min

Trail Name	Difficulty	Km (mi)	Hiking time (rtn or loop)
14. Alex Creek Trail	E	2.2 (1.4)	45 min
15. Maple Sugar Trail	E	1.8 (1.1)	20 min
16. Murch Field Trail & Connector	E-M	2.4 (1.5)	1 hr
17. Eagle Trail*	E	2.5 (1.6)	45 min
18. Scotch Lake Road Trail	E	2.4 (1.5)	40 min
19. Killarney Lake Trail	E	1.8 (1.1)	25 min
20. Dunbar Falls Trail	E-M	1 (0.6)	30 min
21. Fall Brook Falls Trail†	E-M	6.6 (4.1)	2 hrs 45 min
22. Internment Camp Historical Trail	E	0.3 (0.2)	15 min
23. White Rapids Trail	E	0.6 (0.4)	15 min
24. Bald Hill Adventure Trail	M	1.9 (1.2)	1 hr
25. Mount Douglas Bald Trail	M	2.5 (1.6)	1 hr
26. Welsford Brook Falls	E-M	1 (0.6)	20 min
27. Cochrane Cliffs	E-M	2.5 (1.6)	1 hr
28. Turtle Mountain Trail	M	16.8 (10.4)	5 hrs 15 min
29. Hammond River Nature Trail	E-M	1.7 (1.1)	45 min
30. Moss Glen Nature Trail	E	2.3 (1.4)	45 min
31. Sea Dog Cove Nature Preserve Trail†	E	2.4 (1.5)	40 min
32. Boar's Head Nature Preserve Trail	E-M	1.5 (0.9)	1 hr
FUNDY COAST – WEST			
33. Ganong Nature Park Loop	M	3.8 (2.4)	1 hr 45 min
34. Simpson Hill Loop Trail	M-S	2.8 (1.7)	1 hr 15 min
Caughey-Taylor Nature Preserve (35-37)			
35. Sam Orr's Pond Nature Trail	M	5.6 (3.5)	2 hrs 15 min
36. Taggarts Brook Trail	E	1.6 (1)	30 min
37. Chickahominy Mountain	S	3.8 (2.4)	1 hr 50 min
38. Chamcook Mountain Trail†	M	3 (1.9)	1 hr
39. Two Meadows Nature Trail	E	0.8 (0.5)	15 min
Ministers Island (40-42)			
40. Ministers Island Perimeter Trail	E	7 (4.3)	1 hr 45 min
41. Central Trail on Ministers Island	E	3.1 (1.9)	1 hr 20 min

Trail Name	Difficulty	Km (mi)	Hiking time (rtn or loop)
42. Covenhoven Loop Trail	E	1.6 (1)	40 min
43. Clark-Gregory Loop	E-M	1.5 (0.9)	40 min
Campobello Island: Herring Cove Provincial Park and Roosevelt Campobello International Park (44-49)			
44. Herring Cove Loop Trail†	E-M	6.6 (4.1)	2 hrs 30 min
45. Meadow Brook Cove Trail	E	1 (0.6)	15 min
46. Eagle Hill Nature Trail	E	1 (0.6)	20 min
47. Friars Head Trail	E-M	3 (1.9)	1 hr
48. Upper Duck Pond Trail	E	4.8 (3)	2 hrs
49. Lower Duck Pond Trail†	E-M	6 (3.7)	2 hrs 30 min
50. Pea Point Trail (Connors Bros. Nature Preserve)	E-M	1.4 (0.9)	45 min
Grand Manan Island (51-58)			
51. Net Point Trail	E	1.4 (0.9)	30 min
52. Long Pond Trail	E	0.6 (0.4)	20 min
53. Bagley Trail	E	0.8 (0.5)	20 min
54. Red Point Trail	E	3.5 (2.2)	1 hr
55. Flock of Sheep Trail	M	6 (3.7)	2 hrs 30 min
56. Lighthouse Trail*	M-S	37.9 (23.6)	3 days
57. Money Cove Connector*	M	5.1 (3.2)	1 hr 30 min
58. White Head Island Heritage Trail	E-M	6.6 (4.1)	2 hrs 30 min
59. New River Beach Trail	E	5 (3.1)	1 hr 40 min
60. Five Fathom Hole Trail†	M	10.2 (6.3)	4 hrs
61. Black Beach Trail	E-M	4.2 (2.6)	1 hr 40 min
FUNDY COAST – EAST			
62. Taylor Island Perimeter Trail	E	7 (4.3)	2 hrs 15 min
63. Sheldon Point Trail	E-M	8 (4.9)	1 hr 20 min
Fundy Trail Parkway and Fundy Footpath (64-68)			
64. Flowerpot Rock Footpath	E	3 (1.9)	1 hr
65. Bradshaw Scenic Footpath	M	2 (1.2)	50 min
66. Big Salmon River Cemetery Trail	E-M	0.7 (0.4)	25 min
67. Long Beach Brook Falls	E-M	1.4 (0.9)	40 min
68. Fundy Footpath*‡	VS	41.4 (25.7)	4 days

Trail Name	Difficulty	Km (mi)	Hiking time (rtn or loop)
68. Fundy Footpath*‡	VS	41.4 (25.7)	4 days
69. Adair's Walton Lake Trail	E	6.1 (3.8)	2 hrs
70. Catamount Trail: Ida's Garden	E	2.4 (1.5)	1 hr
71. Walton Glen Gorge: The Grand Canyon of NB	S	4 (2.5)	3 hrs
72. Wallace Falls	E-M	0.5 (0.3)	30 min
73. Sussex Bluff Trail	E-M	5 (3.1)	1 hr 30 min
74. Friars Nose	M	0.6 (0.4)	30 min
75. Marys Point Peninsula	M-S	6.5 (4)	2 hrs 30 min
76. Crooked Creek Trail	M	3.2 (2)	1 hr
77. Hillsborough Wetland Trail	E	5 (3.1)	1 hr 15 min
78. Dobson Trail*	M-S	58.9 (36.6)	3 days
79. Irishtown Nature Park	E	3.9 (2.4)	1 hr 15 min
80. Pink Rock Trail	E	5 (3.1)	1 hr 30 min
81. Sackville Waterfowl Park	E	3.5 (2.2)	1 hr
82. Westcock Marsh	E	5.3 (3.3)	1 hr 30 min
FUNDY NATIONAL PARK			
83. East Branch	E	5.6 (3.5)	1 hr 30 min
84. Tracey Lake Trail (from Bennett Lake)	E-M	8.4 (5.2)	2 hrs 30 min
85. Tracey Lake Trail (from Laverty Lake)	E-M	5.6 (3.5)	2 hrs
86. Bennett Brook Trail	M	15.4 (9.6)	4 hrs 45 min
87. Caribou Plain Trail	E	3.4 (2.1)	45 min
88. Third Vault Falls Trail	M	7.4 (4.6)	2 hrs 15 min
89. The Forks Trail	M	6.8 (4.2)	2 hrs 30 min
90. Moosehorn Trail*‡	M	4.8 (3)	1 hr 45 min
91. Laverty Falls Trail	E-M	5 (3.1)	2 hrs
92. Dobson Link	E-M	5 (3.1)	1 hr 30 min
93. Black Horse Trail	E	4.4 (2.7)	1 hr
94. Kinnie Brook Trail	E-M	2.8 (1.7)	1 hr
95. Whitetail Trail	E	6.4 (4)	2 hrs 30 min
96. Tippen Lot (North)	E-M	4.6 (2.9)	1 hr 30 min
97. Upper Salmon River Trail*‡	S	8.8 (5.5)	3 hrs 30 min

Trail Name	Difficulty	Km (mi)	Hiking time (rtn or loop)
98. MacLaren Pond Trail	E	0.5 (0.3)	20 min
99. Coastal Trail*	M	10.1 (6.3)	3 hrs 15 min
100. Dickson Falls	E	1 (0.6)	30 min
101. Tippen Lot (South)*	M	1.9 (1.2)	1 hr
102. Matthews Head	E-M	4.5 (2.8)	1 hr 30 min
103. Herring Cove Beach Trail	E	1 (0.6)	20 min
104. Foster Brook Trail*	M-S	4.4 (2.7)	1 hr 45 min
105. Shiphaven Trail	E	1 (0.6)	25 min
106. Point Wolfe Beach	E	0.8 (0.5)	30 min
107. Goose River Trail	M	15.8 (9.8)	4 hrs 30 min
108. Marven Lake Trail	E-M	16 (9.9)	4 hrs 15 min
109. Black Hole Trail	E-M	11 (6.8)	2 hrs 30 min
ACADIAN COAST			
110. Red-winged Blackbird Trail	E	2 (1.2)	30 min
Cape Jourimain National Wildlife Area (111-113)			
111. Gunning Trail	E	2.5 (1.6)	45 min
112. Lighthouse Trail	E	2 (1.2)	30 min
113. Trenholm Trail	E	5.5 (3.4)	1 hr 30 min
114. Bouctouche Sandbar	E-M	22.6 (14)	5 hrs 15 min
Kouchibouguac National Park (115-124)			
115. Tweedie Trail	E	1.2 (0.7)	20 min
116. Osprey Trail†	E	5.1 (3.2)	1 hr 30 min
117. Claire-Fontaine Trail	E	3 (1.9)	55 min
118. Pines Trail	E	0.8 (0.5)	15 min
119. Beaver Trail	E	1.6 (1)	25 min
120. Migmag Cedars Trail	E	1.3 (0.8)	20 min
121. Salt Marsh	E	0.7 (0.4)	10 min
122. The Bog	E	1.9 (1.2)	30 min
123. La Source River Trail North	E	2 (1.2)	40 min
124. Kouchibouguac River Trail*	M	9.7 (6)	2 hrs 30 min
125. Point Escuminac Beach Trail	E	12.4 (7.7)	2 hrs 30 min

Trail Name	Difficulty	Km (mi)	Hiking time (rtn or loop)
126. French Fort Cove Trail	M	8 (5)	3 hrs
127. Daly Point Reserve Nature Trail	E	5 (3.1)	1 hr 30 min
APPALACHIAN HIGHLANDS			
128. Little Sheephouse Falls Nature Trail	E	0.8 (0.5)	30 min
129. Big Bald Mountain Trail	M	3.2 (2)	1 hr
130. Maggie's Falls	E	1.6 (1)	35 min
131. Sadlers Nature Trail	E	2.8 (1.7)	1 hr 10 min
Mount Carleton Provincial Park (132-142)			
132. Mount Bailey Summit Trail	M	7.4 (4.6)	2 hrs 30 min
133. Bald Mountain Brook Trail – West†	M	6.6 (4.1)	4 hrs
134. Bald Mountain Brook Trail – East*	M	3.4 (2.1)	2 hrs
135. Mount Carleton Trail	M-S	9.5 (5.9)	4 hrs
136. Mount Sagamook Trail†	S	7.4 (4.6)	3 hrs 45 min
137. Mount Head Trail*†‡	M	6.4 (4)	2 hrs
138. Caribou Brook Trail	E-M	10.4 (6.5)	4 hrs 30 min
139. Big Brook – Dry Brook Loop	S	19 (11.8)	6 hrs 30 min
140. Pine Point Trail	E	2 (1.2)	45 min
141. Portage Trail	E	8.4 (5.2)	2 hrs 30 min
142. Williams Falls	E	0.6 (0.4)	20 min
Sugarloaf Provincial Park (143-145)			
143. Sugarloaf Summit Trail	M-S	5.1 (3.2)	1 hr 45 min
144. Prichard Lake Trail	E-M	6.4 (4)	2 hrs 15 min
145. White Pine Trail	E-M	3.8 (2.4)	1 hr

54. Red Point Trail

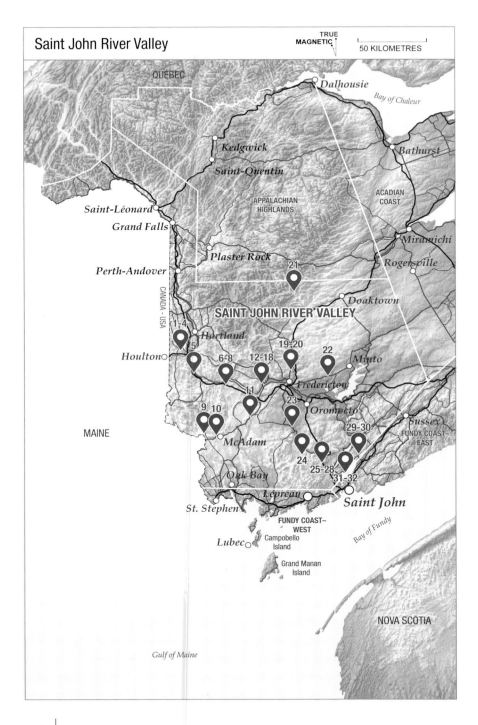

Saint John River Valley

TRUE
MAGNETIC
50 KILOMETRES

QUÉBEC

Dalhousie

Bay of Chaleur

Kedgwick

Saint-Quentin

Bathurst

ACADIAN
COAST

APPALACHIAN
HIGHLANDS

Saint-Léonard

Grand Falls

Miramichi

Plaster Rock

Rogersville

Perth-Andover

21

CANADA - USA

SAINT JOHN RIVER VALLEY

Doaktown

1-4

Hartland

5

Houlton

6-8   12-18

19-20

22

Minto

Fredericton

11

23

Oromocto

9 10

MAINE

24

29-30

Sussex

FUNDY COAST-
EAST

McAdam

25-28

31-32

Oak Bay

Lepreau

Saint John

St. Stephen

FUNDY COAST-
WEST

Bay of Fundy

Lubec

Campobello
Island

Grand Manan
Island

NOVA SCOTIA

Gulf of Maine

SAINT JOHN RIVER VALLEY

The major feature of this region is, of course, the Saint John River. Originating in northern Maine and about 724 km (450 mi) long, the river drains large areas in western New Brunswick. Although its course has changed a few times over the millennia, the river served as the first highway to diverse populations, including the Maliseet (Wolastoqiyik) people; Acadian; British Loyalists; Scottish; Irish; and Danish settlers; and many other early residents.

The river valley is very fertile and much of it is prime agricultural land. Its use changes from north to south: from the northern maple groves of the sugar-shack farmers to apple orchards and extensive potato farms, and large fields with Holsteins or grain crops in the southern valley. At the town of Grand Falls, the Saint John River drops down 23 m (75 ft) abruptly and produces the largest waterfall in New Brunswick, resulting in a narrow gorge just below the falls with rock walls over 70 m (230 ft) tall. Farther south of Grand Falls, the riverbed widens, the woods retreat, and rolling hills dominate.

Farther south at Mactaquac, a large dam was built in the 1960s to satisfy the need for electrical power. One by-product was a large lake, the Mactaquac headpond, which is nowadays used for recreational purposes. Farther downstream, the river reaches Fredericton, the province's charming and historic capital. The river continues southwards, past green meadows and numerous lakes and islands, and is joined by many rivers before passing through the city of Saint John and emptying into the Bay of Fundy.

1-4. Meduxnekeag Valley Nature Preserve

The Meduxnekeag Nature Preserve is located northwest of Woodstock and lies within the Meduxnekeag River watershed. Established in 1998 as a result of the determination of the Meduxnekeag River Association, the natural preserve now consists of fourteen private properties with a combined area of 350 hectares (865 acres). In 2015, this fragile land and watershed became a conservation area under the New Brunswick Protected Natural Areas Act Logging and construction are prohibited in order to preserve the natural area for future generations, but hiking is allowed. The trail system leads hikers to Wilson Mountain, the Vandine Falls, and the Bell and Jim Goltz Forests. The bank of the river is pretty with trilliums, blue cohosh, and wild ginger, whereas in the higher regions hardy basswood, ironwood, butternut, and white ash grow in this Appalachian Hardwood Forest – the only example of such a forest found in Atlantic Canada.

1-4. Meduxnekeag Trails

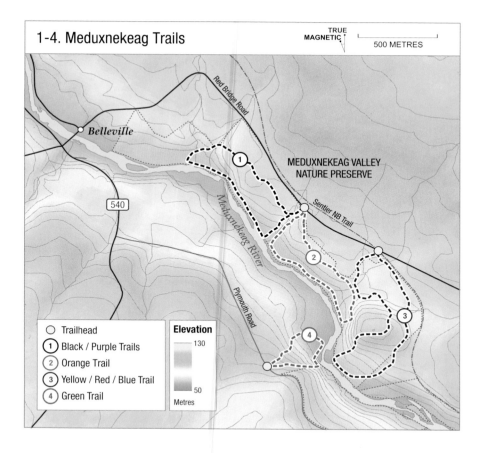

TRUE
MAGNETIC

500 METRES

Belleville

Red Bridge Road

MEDUXNEKEAG VALLEY
NATURE PRESERVE

Sentier NB Trail

540

Meduxnekeag River

Plymouth Road

○ Trailhead
① Black / Purple Trails
② Orange Trail
③ Yellow / Red / Blue Trail
④ Green Trail

Elevation

130

50

Metres

1. Black and Purple Trails

Distance: 7.5 km (4.7 mi)
Type: loop
Difficulty: moderate
Ascent: 45 m (150 ft)
Hiking time: 1 hr 45 min

Map: 21 J/4 Woodstock
Trail condition: mostly dry, some steep ascents
Cellphone coverage: P

Finding the trailhead: From Highway 2 north of Woodstock, take exit 185. At the T-junction, turn onto NB 550 towards Bloomfield and follow this road for 3.3 km (2.1 mi). Turn left onto Red Bridge Road and follow it for 2.8 km (1.7 mi) to civic number 200. There is a grassy parking lot on the left side of the road for about five vehicles. The trail starts at the far right of the lot. The two trails are marked by wooden posts with black and purple bands, respectively. The short side trail to the Vandine Falls is marked by wooden posts with red bands.

Trailhead: 46°11'43" N, 67°40'49" W

The hike: From the trailhead, the black trail enters the woods and descends. At some point, there is a deep gulch to the right with some ropes to aid hikers in the steeper sections. The path eventually reaches the river and a fork. Turn right onto the purple trail, which follows the Meduxnekeag River on the left. Just after the trail crosses a wooden bridge, remain on the purple loop, which begins to the left. The trail continues to follow the river; just before it reaches a shack, it turns to the right and ascends. It continues through the woods until it reaches a junction at a brook. At this point, a red-blazed spur continues on the other side of the brook to Vandine Falls. The main trail turns right and follows the brook back to the bridge, finishing the loop. Cross the bridge and continue to the junction of the purple trail with the black trail. Continue on the black trail and follow it above the river. Eventually, the trail reaches a T-junction, at which point you turn left onto the trail blazed in black, purple, and orange, and return the short distance to the parking lot. The main features of the trail are proximity and access to the Meduxnekeag River and the Vandine Falls.

2. Orange Trail

Distance: 3.5 km (2.2 mi)
Type: loop
Difficulty: easy to moderate
Ascent: 35 m (115 ft)

Hiking time: 45 min
Map: 21 J/4 Woodstock
Trail condition: mostly dry
Cellphone coverage: P

Finding the trailhead: From Highway 2 north of Woodstock, take exit 185. At the T-junction, turn onto NB 550 towards Bloomfield and follow this road for 3.3 km (2.1 mi). Turn left onto Red Bridge Road and follow it for 2.8 km (1.7 mi) to civic number 200. There is a grassy parking lot on the left side of the road for about five vehicles. The trail starts at the left side of the lot. The trail is marked by wooden posts with orange bands.

Trailhead: 46°11'43" N, 67°40'49" W

The hike: The trail descends gently into the valley. At some point, it joins the yellow trail and follows it for a very short distance. It continues straight as the yellow trail departs to the left. The trail continues in a big loop until it reaches a gully. It can be crossed on a large log with the help of ropes that have been installed here. (The crossing may be easier a short distance below.) At this point, hikers can either

continue to follow the trail through the woods close to the Meduxnekeag River or follow the gully to the river and then parallel the river closely for some time. Soon, the trail turns right away from the river and starts to ascend. After some time it is joined by the Black and Purple Trails, a short distance before it reaches the parking lot. This pleasant trail provides direct access to the Meduxnekeag River. Red trillium, wild ginger, fiddleheads, and blue cohosh grow here in season.

3. Yellow-Red-Blue Trail

Distance: 6.5 km (4 mi)
Type: loop
Difficulty: easy
Ascent: 20 m (65 ft)
Hiking time: 1 hr 15 min

Map: 21 J/4 Woodstock
Trail condition: mostly dry, ropes to assist steep ascents and descents
Cellphone coverage: P

Finding the trailhead: From Highway 2 north of Woodstock, take exit 185. At the T-junction, turn onto NB 550 towards Bloomfield and follow this road for 3.3 km (2.1 mi). Turn left onto Red Bridge Road and follow it for 2.1 km (1.3 mi) to civic number 260. At this point, a gravel road joins Red Bridge Road. Parking is possible along the gravel road. The trail starts on the right side of the gravel road some 100 m/yd from the paved road. The trail is marked by wooden posts with yellow, then red, then blue, and finally red bands.

Trailhead: 46°11'33" N, 67°40'22" W

The hike: As the yellow trail leaves the gravel road, it enters the woods. After some distance, it follows a brook, which it crosses on a wooden bridge. The trail continues its descent, crosses another bridge, then joins the orange trail. After a very short distance, the yellow trail turns off to the left. Follow it until you reach a turnoff to the right marked in red. Turn right at this point and follow the red trail as it ascends. Continue on the blue trail as it bends slightly to the right. It passes by a vista point with a bench and roughly stays on the contour line. Turn left at a sign pointing to the parking lot. After a short distance, turn left onto the red trail. It descends and continues for a distance, until it reaches the gravel road. Turn left and return to the parking lot. This is a pleasant walk through open hardwoods, white spruce, white pine, and eastern hemlock forest.

4. Green Trail

Distance: 2 km (1.2 mi)
Type: loop
Difficulty: moderate to strenuous
Ascent: 50 m (165 ft)

Hiking time: 45 min
Map: 21 J/4 Woodstock
Trail condition: very steep
Cellphone coverage: P

Finding the trailhead: From Highway 2 north of Woodstock, take exit 185. At the T-junction, turn onto NB 550 towards Bloomfield and follow this road for 3.3 km (2.1 mi). Turn left onto Red Bridge Road and follow it for 4.8 km (3 mi) to a junction just beyond a bridge across the Meduxnekeag River. Turn left onto NB 540 towards Richmond Corner and follow this road for 0.7 km (0.4 mi). Turn left onto Plymouth Road, a wide gravel road in good condition. Follow this road for 1.8 km (1.1 mi). At this point, the signs Jim Goltz Forest and Green Trail are visible on the left side of the road, indicating the trailhead of the green trail. Parking is alongside the road. The trail is marked by wooden posts with green bands.

Trailhead: 46°10'58" N, 67°40'43" W

The hike: The trail leads into the open woods and turns left at a junction (it will later return on the right fork). It soon starts to descend steeply. Just before it reaches the Meduxnekeag River, there is a large eastern hemlock, where bald eagles like to perch. The trail turns to the right and parallels the river, staying above it. At times, huge boulders with glacial striations can be seen. After some distance, the trail turns to the right, away from the river, and ascends to the fork. From here, it continues the short distance to the road. This trail, named after naturalist Dr. Jim Goltz, provides access to the Meduxnekeag River and passes through mixed forest, reclaimed from former farmland.

5. **Maliseet Trail** (Hays Falls)

Distance: 3.4 km (2.1 mi) rtn
Type: linear
Difficulty: easy to moderate
Ascent: 50 m (165 ft)

Hiking time: 1 hr rtn
Map: 21 J/4 Woodstock
Trail condition: dry, woodchips, rooty
Cellphone coverage: P

Finding the trailhead: From Highway 2, take exit 200 to Dugan Road and Debec. At the T-junction, turn onto Dugan Road and follow it for 400 m/yd to another T-junction. Turn right onto Route 165 and follow it for 1.8 km (1.1 mi). The trailhead is located on the right side of the highway. There are quite a few parking places. The trail is occasionally marked by blue metal blazes, some with a white diagonal bar, but it cannot be missed anyway.

Trailhead: 46°01'45" N, 67°32'35" W

The hike: This well-maintained trail gently ascends through open softwoods onto a beautiful hardwood ridge, where it levels off and swings to the left. At about 1.5 km (0.9 mi) you come to a fork. Turn right at this point to continue to the falls. As the rocky trail descends, you reach another fork. Keeping to the right leads to the bottom of the 27 m (90 ft) cascading Hays Falls. The left fork continues a short distance to a rocky cliff at the head of the falls with a picnic table. This is the end of the marked trail. The waterfalls are the major attraction of this trail. The traditional portage route, also known as the Maliseet Trail, was located in this area.

5. Maliseet Trail (Hays Falls)

Tappan Adney

Tappan Adney was born in Athens, Ohio, in 1868 and was the son of a professor at Ohio University. He was home-schooled by his father, and he gained admission to the University of North Carolina at Chapel Hill at age thirteen. He attended school for two years. After that, the family moved to New York, where Tappan developed an interest in ornithology. He studied at the Art Students League of New York in Manhattan, from which he graduated at age eighteen. From New York, he moved to Upper Woodstock in New Brunswick, where he planned to spend a month to prepare for an entrance exam. Here, he met and befriended members of the Maliseet tribe, who showed him how to build a canoe. He later built about hundred birchbark canoes based on that information. Together with Dr. Peter Paul, he put together a dictionary of the Maliseet language, which he spoke fluently. Tappan Adney is probably best known for his reports and photographs of the Klondike Gold Rush in 1897-1898. He died in 1950 and is buried in the Upper Woodstock Rural Cemetery.

6-7. Big Pokiok Nature Park

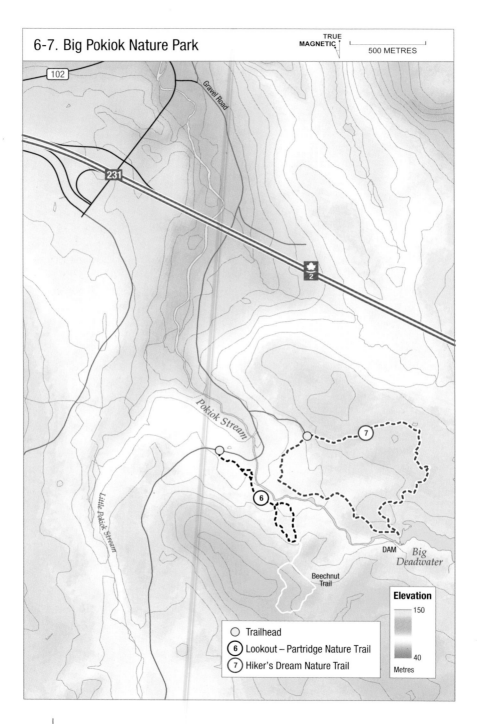

TRUE
MAGNETIC

500 METRES

102

231

2

Gravel Road

Pokiok Stream

Little Pokiok Stream

7

6

DAM *Big Deadwater*

Beechnut Trail

Elevation

150

40

Metres

○ Trailhead

⑥ Lookout – Partridge Nature Trail

⑦ Hiker's Dream Nature Trail

6-7. Big Pokiok Nature Park

The 200 hectare (500 acre) park is a natural gem not far from noisy Highway 2. AV Group NB owns the Nackawic and Atholville pulp mills and the Big Pokiok nature trails. They were developed by the former St. Anne paper mill, and the new company continues to maintain some of the trails for the enjoyment of the general public. The contact number for the condition of the trails is 506-575-3200.

The word *pokiok* derives from the Maliseet word "narrow gorge place," which aptly explains the geography of the lower Big Pokiok Stream in the park. The stream originates at Lake George, and the water flowing through it can vary from an impressive 17,000 litres (4,500 gallons) per second in the spring to 1,100 litres (300 gallons) per second in August. Another geographical feature is the many boulders. About twelve thousand years ago, the Wisconsin glaciation covered the land with ice, and two thousand years later, when the ice receded, boulders and sand deposits were left behind. That is why you encounter these boulders here and why the ground is quite rocky in most parts of the park.

6. Lookout – Partridge Nature Trail

Distance: 0.6 + 1.5 = 2.1 km (0.4 + 0.9 = 1.3 mi)
Type: loop
Difficulty: easy
Ascent: 10 m (33 ft)

Hiking time: 40 min
Map: 21 G/14 Canterbury
Trail condition: crushed rock at first, rooty later
Cellphone coverage: Y

Finding the trailhead: From Fredericton, take Highway 2 in a westerly direction. Take exit 231 towards Nackawic. Turn towards Nackawic and follow the road for 0.7 km (0.4 mi); just before Route 102, turn right onto an unnamed road. The road is paved for the first 100 m/yd, after which it continues as a gravel road. After 1.1 km (0.7 mi), the road passes underneath Highway 2. Continue for another 1.5 km (0.9 mi). Keep straight at a fork and continue for another 0.6 km (0.4 mi), crossing Big Pokiok Stream. A short distance beyond the single-lane wooden bridge, there is a parking area to the left with a shelter, two pit toilets, and space for about ten vehicles. The trailhead is located on the left side of the parking lot, indicated by some marking tape. The Lookout Nature Trail is marked with red plastic blazes, and the Partridge Nature Trail is marked with yellow plastic blazes. There are plenty of blazes, but watch out for them, as the trail sometimes swings unexpectedly.

Trailhead: 45°56'00" N, 67°14'25" W

The hike: After a short distance, the Lookout Nature Trail reaches a fork. Take the left fork and soon the Big Pokiok Stream becomes visible. The trail follows it for a short distance before reaching a picnic site directly next to the stream. Turn right, then immediately turn onto a narrow path to the left; here the yellow-blazed Partridge Nature Trail begins. For some distance it parallels the river, keeping it to its left far below. The trail then swings to the right, ascends, and continues through the woods. Watch for the blazes, as the routing of the trail is not obvious everywhere. Eventually, the trail returns to the red-blazed Lookout Trail and then to the parking lot.

7. Hiker's Dream Nature Trail

Distance: 3.4 km (2.1 mi)
Type: loop
Difficulty: easy
Ascent: negligible

Hiking time: 1 hr
Map: 21 G/14 Canterbury
Trail condition: rooty in parts
Cellphone coverage: Y

Finding the trailhead: From Fredericton, take Highway 2. Take exit 231 towards Nackawic. Turn right at the stop sign and follow the road for 0.7 km (0.4 mi). Then, just before Route 102, turn right onto an unnamed road. The road is paved for the first 100 m/yd, after which it continues as a gravel road. After 1.1 km (0.7 mi), the road passes underneath Highway 2. Continue for another 1.5 km (0.9 mi). Turn left onto a single-lane woods road next to a sign and follow it for some 400 m/yd to a large parking lot with two pit toilets in the far left corner of the lot. The trailhead is located on the right side of the lot. The trail is marked by blue blazes.

Trailhead: 45°56'04"N, 67°13'59"W

The hike: The narrow path first descends and crosses some corduroy sections before it ends at a T-junction with an old woods road. Turn left onto that wide trail. After a while, this old road reaches the wild Pokiok Stream and follows it for a short distance. It then leaves the stream and continues to the Ducks Unlimited dam and its scenic headpond. At this point, the trail turns sharply to the left into the woods and immediately turns left again. (Continuing straight for a short distance leads to a vista point overlooking the headpond.) The trail passes a number of large boulders, leads through a pretty stand of birch trees, and eventually returns to the parking lot. The trail allows access to the Pokiok Stream, a dam, and its peaceful headpond. It also features very nice stands of hardwoods, particularly birches.

Fiddleheads

One of the best-known delicacies of New Brunswick is the fiddlehead fern (Matteuccia struthiopteris), also referred to as the ostrich fern. Green fronds sprout from an upright clumpy rootstock in a graceful, arching fashion. The stalks, with their widest fronds near the top and tapering to tip and base, can grow up to 1.5 m (5 ft) tall, but they are most valued when they just begin to grow, before their fronds even unfold. The young, coiled shoots, the fiddleheads, are gathered in May along the rich soils of riverbanks and floodplains. Poached in butter and served with trout or salmon, or prepared as a cream soup, this fern is a favourite local delicacy.

8. Nackawic Nature Trail

Distance: 4 km (2.5 mi) rtn
Type: linear
Difficulty: easy
Ascent: negligible

Hiking time: 1 hr 15 min
Map: 21 G/14 Canterbury
Trail condition: dry
Cellphone coverage: Y

Finding the trailhead: From Fredericton, take Highway 2 west. Follow the highway for about 58 km (36 mi). Take exit 231 towards Nackawic and Millville. From the T-junction, turn right onto Route 102. Continue straight across the bridge (Route 102 turns off to the right) and follow the road for 1.8 km (1.1 mi), then turn right onto Otis Drive. Follow the road for 1.8 km (1.1 mi), passing Otis Cemetery on the left of the road, to a large parking lot next to the river. A map at the trailhead shows details of the route. There are no trail markings, but the trail portion along the river described here is well groomed and easy to follow.

Trailhead: 45°58'47"N, 67°14'28"W

The hike: The wide trail follows the Saint John River. On the left, there are remnants of two potato houses and the so-called Nackawic Kissing Rock. The trail closely follows the river, leads on a raised boardwalk section, and passes by some houses on its left. Walk towards the river and continue to a ballpark. A short distance beyond is the "World's Largest Axe." The main attractions of this trail are the many fine views across the scenic Saint John River and a number of historic sites. Picnic sites and benches are plentiful, and in July blackeyed Susans blossom along the trail.

9. Boulderwalk Trail

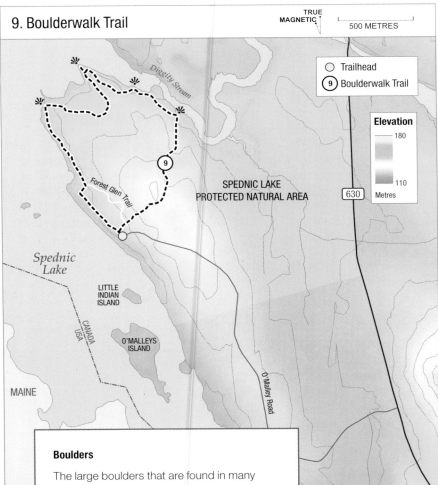

○ Trailhead

⑨ Boulderwalk Trail

Elevation

180

110

Metres

630

SPEDNIC LAKE
PROTECTED NATURAL AREA

Diggity Stream

Forest Glen Trail

⑨

Spednic Lake

LITTLE
INDIAN
ISLAND

CANADA
USA

O'MALLEYS
ISLAND

MAINE

O'Malley Road

Boulders

The large boulders that are found in many places in the southwestern part of the province were deposited by glaciers some 14,000 years ago during the last (Wisconsin) glaciation. As the glaciers retreated, they moved rocks, boulders, and other debris. The effect of the movement was similar to that made by sandpaper, scratching the earth's crust in the direction of the retreat. A glance at a map of New Brunswick reveals the effects: many of the lakes are directed southeast-to-northwest, carved out by retreating glaciers.

9. Boulderwalk Trail

Distance: 3.5 km (2.2 mi)
Type: loop
Difficulty: easy to moderate
Ascent: negligible

Hiking time: 1 hr 15 min
Map: 21 G/11 McAdam
Trail condition: dry, very rocky, and rooty
Cellphone coverage: N

Finding the trailhead: From the town of McAdam, drive on Highway 4 for 6.9 km (4.3 mi) towards the U.S. border, measured from the historic railway station. Turn right onto NB 630 north towards Canterbury, and follow this first paved, then graded, dirt road for 3 km (1.9 mi). Turn left onto O'Malley Road, which leads to Spednic Lake Protected Natural Area. After 2.9 km (1.8 mi) you reach a T-junction near the lake. The clearly marked trailhead is located a very short distance to the right on the road that leads to the campsites. For parking, turn left at the T-junction. The trail is marked by 2" × 2" blue metal blazes with a white diagonal bar, as well as yellow metal blazes of various sizes. It is prudent to pay close attention to the blazes, as the trail is obscured at times and may easily be missed.

Trailhead: 45°36'23" N, 67°26'46" W

The hike: The narrow but well-defined path traverses a nice hardwood ridge. After a short distance, keep to the right when the Forest Glen Trail turns off to the left. The main trail then passes through mixed forest before reaching an observation deck at 1.3 km (0.8 mi). Retrace your steps and turn right to follow the loop trail. Vista points along the trail allow views at the Diggity archaeological site across the Diggity Stream. The path then makes a sharp left turn near the tip of the peninsula. Here, a short spur leads to a lookout across the St. Croix River and the meandering Diggity Stream. Enjoy the view, which features several islands and a number of larger boulders deposited by glaciation. The trail continues to another lookout, then bypasses a particularly big boulder in the woods. It continues on a number of boardwalk sections before it passes a junction with the Forest Glen Trail, and soon reaches a wide dirt road at the campground. Turn left, pass several pit toilets, and return to the trailhead. This trail leads through parts of the St. Croix Heritage River system. Spednic Lake's remarkable glacial boulders and the cool breeze off its waters are additional attractions.

10. City Camp Nature Trail

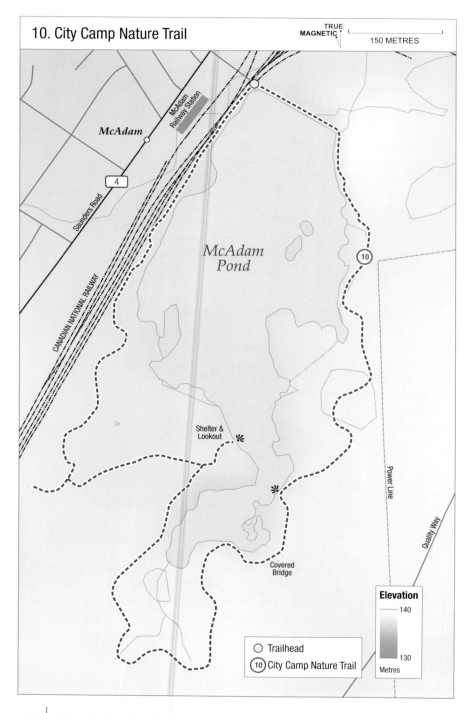

TRUE

MAGNETIC

150 METRES

McAdam Railway Station

McAdam

4

Saunders Road

CANADIAN NATIONAL RAILWAY

McAdam Pond

10

Shelter & Lookout

Covered Bridge

Power Line

Quality Way

Elevation

140

130

Metres

○ Trailhead

⑩ City Camp Nature Trail

10. City Camp Nature Trail

Distance: 2.8 km (1.7 mi)
Type: loop
Difficulty: easy
Ascent: negligible

Hiking time: 45 min
Map: 21 G/11 McAdam
Trail condition: dry
Cellphone coverage: Y

Finding the trailhead: The trail starts on the left side of the historic railroad building in McAdam. There is plenty of parking in front of the railroad building. There are occasional orange paint blazes on trees, but the trail is well groomed and easy to follow.

Trailhead: 45°35'26"N, 67°19'38"W

The hike: Cross the tracks and keep McAdam Pond to the right. At the end of the pond, a small path turns off to the right. It skirts the pond through woods with benches and picnic tables for nature observation. The path continues across a small, traditionally constructed covered bridge across Alder Creek and continues along the pond. Continuing straight at a fork leads on a short spur to the Long View Shelter and lookout. The main trail keeps to the left and keeps right at the next fork. This part of the walk takes you past tall cattails. Turn right at the railroad tracks and follow them back to the railroad station. A large number of typical New Brunswick trees are featured in this typical marsh. You will also find New Brunswick's tallest cattails, trees hit by lightning, and a small covered bridge.

McAdam Railway Station

As soon as you reach the small village of McAdam, its railroad past becomes apparent: even the signs of the street names feature an image of a railroad. The centre of the village, and its raison d'être, is the remarkable chateau-style railway station, which was built from 1900 to 1911 by the Canadian Pacific Railway (CPR) as a classic station hotel. The building was featured on a postage stamp in the 1990s, and it was designated a Provincial Historical Site in 2004. The line was built in the late nineteenth century to access the ice-free port of Saint John, as the port of Montreal could not be reached. At the turn of the century, many immigrant trains bound for Ontario and the Canadian Prairies passed through McAdam on their way west. Passenger rail service ceased in 1994, but to this day it is an active railroad yard for freight. The railway station is open to visitors during the summer months and occasionally offers "railroad pie" in its vintage 1960s diner.

11. Harvey Lakeside Nature Trail

Distance: 1 km (0.6 mi)
Type: loop
Difficulty: easy
Ascent: 10 m (33 ft)

Hiking time: 20 min
Map: 21 G/11 McAdam
Trail condition: dry
Cellphone coverage: Y

Finding the trailhead: On Highway 2, take exit 258 and turn onto Highway 3 south towards Harvey. Follow this road for 18.5 km (11.5 mi) to Harvey. Just beyond the railroad tracks and before the post office, there is a large parking lot on the right side. The trail starts on the south side of the lot. There are no trail markings, but the trail is obvious. Keep right at all times, even if the path narrows.

Trailhead: 45°43'49" N, 67°00'30" W

The hike: The trail skirts a picnic area before turning to the right and following railroad tracks for some distance. The path then reaches a viewing platform with some vistas across Harvey Cove. From here, the trail ascends through the woods of Cherry Mountain before reaching the picnic site again. The nature trail features interpretive plaques and a view across a part of Harvey Lake. Catharine Pendrel, the winner of a bronze medal in the 2016 Olympics, grew up in Harvey Station and is commemorated by the addition of her name to the trail.

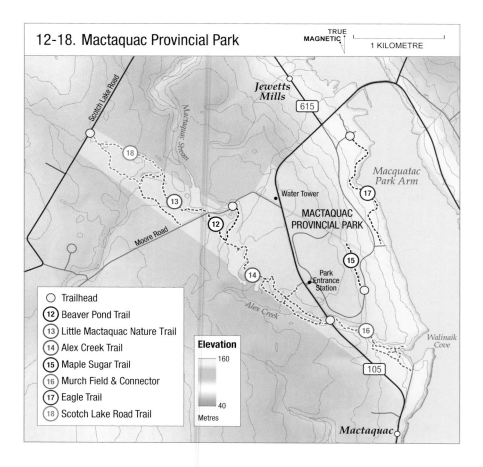

12-18. Mactaquac Provincial Park

TRUE
MAGNETIC
1 KILOMETRE

Scotch Lake Road

Mactaquac Stream

Jewetts Mills

615

18

Water Tower

Macquatac Park Arm

17

13

MACTAQUAC PROVINCIAL PARK

12

Moore Road

15

14

Park Entrance Station

Alex Creek

16

Walinaik Cove

○ Trailhead
(12) Beaver Pond Trail
(13) Little Mactaquac Nature Trail
(14) Alex Creek Trail
(15) Maple Sugar Trail
(16) Murch Field & Connector
(17) Eagle Trail
(18) Scotch Lake Road Trail

Elevation

160

40

Metres

105

Mactaquac

12-18. Mactaquac Provincial Park

Mactaquac Provincial Park was established in the 1960s. The park comprises 525 hectares (1,300 acres), and its dominant feature is the Mactaquac headpond. The headpond features two supervised beaches as well as marinas for sail and power boats, and fishing and waterskiing are permitted. A freshwater beach, supervised from July to Labour Day, invites swimming and sunbathing. In addition, the park offers a campground with three hundred sites, a picnic area, an eighteen-hole championship golf course, several hiking trails, and the Mactaquac TreeGO facility. For more information, check out the website at http://www.tourismnewbrunswick.ca/Products/Parks/MactaquacProvincialPark.aspx or call 1-800-561-0123.

For the purpose of this book, we have decided to describe the trails in the park individually, rather than putting them together. This was done so as to permit hikers to customize their itineraries. Those who desire a longer hike can very easily chain the trails and make a long loop out of the individual hikes.

You can reach the park from Fredericton by taking Route 102 in a westerly direction towards Mactaquac. At the exit to Mactaquac and Keswick Ridge, turn onto Route 105, which first crosses the Mactaquac Dam and later a causeway. The trailheads for the trails described in this book are shown in the individual descriptions.

12. Beaver Pond Trail

Distance: 1.3 km (0.8 mi) [+ 1.4 km (0.9 mi) rtn from the gate, if closed]
Type: loop
Difficulty: easy
Ascent: negligible
Hiking time: 30 min

Map: 21 G/15 Fredericton. A map of the park is sometimes available at the trailhead.
Trail condition: dry, in part gravel, and boardwalk
Cellphone coverage: Y

Finding the trailhead: On Route 102 west of Fredericton, take the exit towards Keswick Ridge and Mactaquac. Follow Mactaquac Road/Route 105 across the Mactaquac Dam and a causeway for 6.2 km (3.9 mi) to the gravel Moore Road just beyond a water tower. If the gate is open, continue for another 0.7 km (0.4 mi) to a pavilion. There is ample space for parking. If the gate is closed, park on the large lot in front of the gate and walk to the pavilion. The trail begins on the gravel road next to the pavilion. The trails are marked by 3" square orange metal blazes with black or white diagonal stripes.

Trailhead (next to a pavilion): 45°57'45" N, 66°54'34" W; alternatively, near the highway at the water tower in case the gate is locked: 45°57'49" N, 66°54'10" W

The hike: The Beaver Pond Trail first follows the gravel road, crossing a small bridge that separates two parts of a beaver pond, and then turns off to the left. The path follows the western end of the beaver pond until it reaches a long boardwalk/bridge section. From here, there are good views across the beaver pond. At the end of the bridge, short sections follow the edge of the beaver pond to the right and to the left; continue straight on the main trail. At a junction, the Beaver Pond Trail turns left and continues to the gravel road a short distance from the pavilion. Keeping straight at the junction is the red-blazed connector to the Alex Creek Trail. This connector is quite scenic and allows excellent views across a beaver pond. The trail provides good opportunities to watch the work of the beaver. There are also many signs of porcupine, deer, and moose. Different types of birds and frogs may be seen at the pond.

13. Little Mactaquac Nature Trail
(with Porcupine Path Trail)

Distance: 2.4 km (1.5 mi) [+ 1.4 km (0.9 mi) rtn from and to the gate, if closed]
Type: loop
Difficulty: easy to moderate
Ascent: 20 m (65 ft)
Hiking time: 40 min

Map: 21 G/15 Fredericton. A map of the park is sometimes available at the trailhead.
Trail condition: woodchips, gravel, dirt road
Cellphone coverage: Y

Finding the trailhead: On Route 102 west of Fredericton, take the exit towards Keswick Ridge and Mactaquac. Follow Mactaquac Road/Route 105 across the Mactaquac Dam and a causeway for 6.2 km (3.9 mi) to a gravel road just beyond a water tower. This is the Moore Road. If the gate is open, continue for another 0.7 km (0.4 mi) to a pavilion. There is ample space for parking. If the gate is closed, park on the large lot in front of the gate and walk to the pavilion. The trail begins on the gravel road next to the pavilion. The trails are marked by 3" square yellow metal blazes with black or white diagonal stripes.

Trailhead: (next to a pavilion) 45°57'45" N, 66°54'34" W; alternatively, near the highway at the water tower in case the gate is locked: 45°57'49" N, 66°54'10" W

The hike: The Little Mactaquac Trail first follows the gravel road, crossing a small bridge that separates two parts of a beaver pond, and then turns off to the right. The trail follows the edge of the beaver pond with boardwalks across some wet spots. At a junction, the Porcupine Path Trail departs to the right. It is a short, rocky, and rooty spur of 0.6 km (0.4 mi) return. At the end of the spur, you will reach the northern part of the beaver pond. Return to the main trail and turn right. The trail continues through woods until it reaches a fork; keep to the right. The left fork ascends mildly while the right fork leads down to the bridge across the Little Mactaquac Stream. The two trails will eventually rejoin.

The trail descends to the Little Mactaquac Stream and crosses a bridge, passes a BBQ pit, and continues straight for a short distance. At a fork, keep left. This scenic narrow path follows the Little Mactaquac Stream closely. After some distance, it crosses a bridge, and just beyond, the brook must be forded. Across the brook, the trail ascends and joins a wide path. The trail then leads through open woods for some distance, until it reaches an old woods/dirt road. Turn left and return to the trailhead.

14. Alex Creek Trail

Distance: 2.2 km (1.4 mi)
Type: loop
Difficulty: easy
Ascent: 10 m (33 ft)
Hiking time: 45 min

Map: 21 G/15 Fredericton. A map of the park is sometimes also available at the trailhead.
Trail condition: dry
Cellphone coverage: Y

Finding the trailhead: On Route 102 west of Fredericton, take the exit towards Keswick Ridge and Mactaquac. Follow Mactaquac Road/Route 105 across the Mactaquac Dam and a causeway for 7 km (4.3 mi). The administration building of the provincial park is located on the right side of the road just before the general entrance to the park on the opposite side of the road. Parking and the trailhead are at the back of the building. The trails are marked by 3" square blue metal blazes with black or white diagonal stripes. Connectors to the Beaver Pond Trail and Murch Field Trail are both marked by red metal blazes.

Trailhead: 45°57'17"N, 66°53'57"W

The hike: Cross the field at the far end of the parking lot to the sign for Alex Creek Trail, which is visible from the parking lot. The trail passes through old cedars and then leads into the woods. At a T-junction, the trail turns to the right. The trail leads through softwoods until it reaches a T-junction; keep to the left. Continuing to the right will connect you to the Beaver Pond Trail (the connector itself is a scenic trail marked by red blazes), while turning to the left continues the Alex Creek Trail. The trail stays close to the beaver pond. At some point, a short spur leads to a platform overlooking the beaver pond. Just before a T-junction, turn off to the right onto a narrow path. It descends to a kitchen shelter, continues directly behind it, and soon rejoins the wide road. At a junction, turn to the right and cross Alex Creek on a bridge. Turn left at a junction (the right trail is a connector to the Murch Field Trail, whose trailhead is located a short distance away on the other side of Route 105) and cross Alex Creek again on another bridge. From here on, stay on the main trail; if in doubt, keep to the right. Finally, at a bench, a spur departs to the right, which leads back to the parking lot. The woods trail follows a creek through mainly hardwoods, among them mature yellow birches. It also passes a beaver pond. Woodpeckers and porcupines can occasionally be seen.

Maple Sugar Magic

In springtime, when the nights dip below freezing and the days are warm, maple farmers in New Brunswick begin collecting the sap of mature red and sugar maple trees. The season usually runs from mid-March to the end of April. There are as many as four hundred maple syrup producers in New Brunswick. The highly regulated maple sugar industry ensures a pure, good-quality syrup, resulting in high demand on the world market. New Brunswick is the world's third-largest maple syrup producer after Quebec and Vermont.

Sap is collected either by way of an intricate system of pipes or the traditional way with buckets on trees. The sap is then put into an evaporator, which concentrates the sap. It takes about 40 litres/quarts of sap to produce only 1 litre/quart of syrup. Some of the producers offer a maple sugar–based meal in season. It typically comprises bacon, ham, beans, eggs, and pancakes covered with the thick and tasty syrup. Bon appétit!

15. Maple Sugar Trail

Distance: 1.8 km (1.1 mi)
Type: loop
Difficulty: easy
Ascent: negligible
Hiking time: 20 min

Map: 21 G/15 Fredericton. A map of the park is sometimes also available at the trailhead.
Trail condition: dry
Cellphone coverage: Y

Finding the trailhead: On Route 102 west of Fredericton, take the exit towards Keswick Ridge and Mactaquac. Follow Mactaquac Road/Route 105 across the Mactaquac Dam and a causeway for 7.2 km (4.5 mi) to the main entrance of the park on the left side of the road. Enter the park through the main gate and immediately turn right onto Mactacaddy Road. Follow the paved road for 0.9 km (0.6 mi) to where the road to the campground turns off to the right. The trailhead is located just opposite on the left of the main road. To reach the parking lot, turn right towards the campground. There is ample parking on the left side just before you enter the campground. The trail is marked by 3″ red-brown metal blazes with diagonal white stripes.

Trailhead: 45°57'16"N, 66°53'21"W

The hike: The path ascends gently through a mature mixed forest and keeps right at a fork. The trail continues through the woods and arrives at an open field. At this point, you have a good view to the right of the Mactaquac headpond and the dam. Turn right onto a small grassy road that follows the edge of the woods. After some 250 m/yd, the path ends at a gate and the trail turns right onto a blacktop road. Follow this road for 0.5 km (0.3 mi) back to the trailhead near the parking lot. The main feature of this nature trail is the large variety of trees that make up the surrounding mature forest. Sugar maples abound. These trees have been a source of sugar for Indigenous peoples for hundreds of years, and their sap is used to produce maple syrup. There are good views across the headpond.

16. Murch Field Trail & Connector

Distance: 2.4 km (1.5 mi)
Type: loop
Difficulty: easy to moderate
Ascent: 30 m (98 ft)

Hiking time: 1 hr
Map: 21 G/15 Fredericton.
Trail condition: dry
Cellphone coverage: Y

Finding the trailhead: On Route 102 west of Fredericton, take the exit towards Keswick Ridge and Mactaquac. Follow Mactaquac Road/Route 105 across the Mactaquac Dam and a causeway for 7.7 km (4.8 mi), 500 m/yd beyond the main entrance to the park, to the trailhead of the Alex Creek Connector on the left side of the road. Parking is available on the opposite side of the road. The trail is marked by white squares with black diagonals.

Trailhead: 45°57'05"N, 66°53'38"W

The hike: From Route 105, follow the red-blazed Alex Creek Connector. The trail descends steeply, crosses Alex Creek, and ascends again until it reaches the edge of campsite #4. The trail parallels the edge of the campground with Alex Creek deep below on the right. As the trail reaches a large wooden gate on the left next to camp-site #6, it descends on a narrower path. It crosses the creek and keeps it to its left. The trail then crosses a bridge and follows the creek. After some distance, it crosses the creek again across a larger bridge. Once across, keep left and continue on the level trail. Cross the creek on another bridge at Walinaik Cove, ascend, and soon you will reach a shelter with fine views. (From here, retrace your steps to the trailhead for a shorter hike.) Cross the bridge at the cove and follow the signs to Marina, York Park, ascend the wooden steps, and then keep to the left. The trail follows the deep ravine for some distance before turning right. It crosses a small field straight ahead and eventually reaches a road close to the marina at York Park. Turn right to Route 105 and right again to walk on the road back to the trailhead. The major features of this trail are a number of fine views across Walinaik Cove, the Mactaquac headpond, and the bubbling Alex Creek with picnic tables.

17. Eagle Trail

Distance: 2.5 km (1.6 mi) one way
Type: linear
Difficulty: easy
Ascent: 10 m (33 ft)

Hiking time: 45 min one way
Map: 21 G/15 Fredericton
Trail condition: muddy spots, deadfall
Cellphone coverage: Y

Finding the trailhead: On Route 102 west of Fredericton, take the exit towards Keswick Ridge and Mactaquac. Follow Mactaquac Road/Route 105 across the Mactaquac Dam and a causeway for 7.2 km (4.5 mi) to the main entrance of the park on the left side of the road. Enter the park through the main gate and immediately turn right onto Mactacaddy Road. Follow the paved road for 2.8 km (1.7 mi) to a fork. Keep right and turn right at a junction to a large parking lot. The trailhead is located at the far end of the parking lot not far from the shore. The trail is marked by 3" blue metal squares with white diagonals.

Trailhead: 45°58'10" N, 66°53'24" W

The hike: The trail follows an old woods road. It continues parallel to the Saint John River and allows occasional glimpses of it. After some time, turn right at a fork, follow the path inland, and at another fork, turn left again. Always look out for the trail markers. This section will eventually lead to the end of the trail near a small fenced pond that is quite charming.

18. Scotch Lake Road Trail

Distance: 2.4 km (1.5 mi)
Type: loop
Difficulty: easy
Ascent: 10 m (33 ft)

Hiking time: 40 min
Map: 21 G/15 Fredericton.
Trail condition: woodchips, gravel
Cellphone coverage: Y

Finding the trailhead: On Route 102 west of Fredericton, take the exit towards Keswick Ridge and Mactaquac. Follow Mactaquac Road/Route 105 across the Mactaquac Dam and a causeway for 5 km (3.1 mi) to the junction with NB 615. Turn right onto NB 615 and follow it for 2.5 km (1.6 mi). Then turn left onto Scotch Lake Road and follow it for 1.7 km (1.1 mi). The trail is located on the left side of the road opposite a house with civic number 176. Parking is alongside the road. The trail is marked by 3" green square metal blazes with black or white diagonal stripes.

Trailhead: 45°58'13" N, 66°55'43" W

The hike: The wide trail enters the woods and keeps straight at a somewhat inconspicuous junction (the trail returns here later). The trail leads through woods until it reaches a junction. In order to make a loop, turn right onto a narrow path, which is part of the yellow-blazed Little Mactaquac Nature Trail (p. 64). Follow the narrow, delightful path next to the Little Mactaquac Stream to a somewhat overgrown junction with the Scotch Lake Road Trail just before the path crosses a wooden bridge. The path continues through woods until it reaches a T-junction. Turn left and return to the road. The trail provides convenient access to the scenic Little Mactaquac Stream.

19. Killarney Lake Trail

Distance: 1.8 km (1.1 mi)
Type: loop
Difficulty: easy
Ascent: negligible

Hiking time: 25 min
Map: 21 J/2 Burtts Corner
Trail condition: dry
Cellphone coverage: Y

Finding the trailhead: From the Westmorland Street Bridge in Fredericton, take St. Mary's Street (Route 105, which later becomes Route 148) in a northerly direction and follow it for 4.6 km (2.9 mi). There is a large parking lot near the Killarney Lake Rotary Centennial Lodge. The trailhead is next to the lodge on its left side. There are no trail markings, but the trail cannot be missed.

Trailhead: 46°00'52" N, 66°37'44" W

The hike: Starting at the lodge, always keep the lake to your left. The lake is quite scenic and offers opportunities to see cormorants and red-winged blackbirds. It is also a great place for a swim on a hot summer day.

20. Dunbar Falls Trail

Distance: 1 km (0.6 mi) rtn
Type: linear
Difficulty: easy to moderate
Ascent: negligible

Hiking time: 30 min rtn
Map: 21 J/2 Burtts Corner
Trail condition: wet spots, deadfall
Cellphone coverage: P

Finding the trailhead: From the junction of Highways 8 and 10 in Fredericton north of the Saint John River, take Highway 8 towards Miramichi and follow it for 3.4 km (2.1 mi). Turn left onto Bridge Street and follow it for 1.3 km (0.8 mi), crossing the river, to the junction with Canada Street. Turn right onto Canada Street (which later joins Route 148) and follow it for 17.9 km (11.1 mi). Pass by Durham Bridge and continue straight for another 1.7 km (1.1 mi). Just before the road crosses a small bridge over the Dunbar Stream, a gravel road turns off to the left. You can park here. The trail descends a few footsteps to the river right next to the highway. There are no trail markings, but the trail cannot be missed.

Trailhead: 46°08'27" N, 66°37'03" W

The hike: Follow the narrow trail along the South Branch Dunbar Stream to the falls. The trail provides easy access to the unusually wide Dunbar Falls.

21. Fall Brook Falls Trail

Distance: 1.6 km (1 mi) rtn [+ 5 km (3.1 mi) rtn for an extension]
Type: linear
Difficulty: easy to moderate
Ascent: 100 m (330 ft)
Hiking time: 45 min rtn [+ 2 hrs rtn for the extension]
Map: 21 J/10 Hayesville

Trail condition: dry (rooty for the extension)
Cellphone coverage: N
Fee: $10 per vehicle at the gate (open from mid-May to mid-November daily from 6 a.m. to 8 p.m.). Call the McKiel gate at 506-365-0988.

Finding the trailhead: From the junction of Highways 8 and 10 in Fredericton on the north side of the Saint John River, take Highway 8 towards Miramichi and follow it for 63.1 km (39.2 mi) to Boiestown. Turn left onto Parker Ridge Road (NB 625) and follow it for 2.9 km (1.8 mi), then bear to the right. After another 1.2 km (0.7 mi), turn right onto Bloomfield Ridge Road. Continue on this road for 3 km (1.9 mi), then right again onto Holtville Road and cross the Norrad Bridge over the Miramichi River. From the junction before the bridge, drive 2.9 km (1.8 mi) to a dead-end road (paved, then gravel) that continues slightly to the left. Follow it for 3 km (1.9 mi) to McKiel gate. At this point, you have to pay a fee and continue straight on a wide gravel road for 13.3 km (8.3 mi), where a small, but marked, dirt road turns off to the left. Park the vehicle along the gravel road and continue on foot. There are no trail markings, but the trail cannot be missed. The extension is predominantly marked by yellow paint blazes and a few signs marked Trail.

Trailhead: 46°36'03" N, 66°35'11" W

The hike: The trail follows a moderately wide dirt road that descends gently, but later very steeply, as it approaches the Southwest Miramichi River. The dirt road ends near the river at the lower parking lot. From here, the narrow footpath turns off to the right. It leads directly to the waterfalls, where it ends. The extension starts at the lower parking lot and parallels the river before it ascends into the woods. It continues through the woods, then turns right onto a woods road, and turns off it to the left soon thereafter. The junctions and forks are marked by Trail signs. The trail continues above the river for some time until it ends at a woods road next to the river. Trail highlights include the river and especially the 27 m (90 ft) falls, which are the highest in New Brunswick.

21. Fall Brook Falls

Ripples Internment Camp

The internment camp on Highway 10 towards Minto was a refurbished 22 hectare (55 acre) compound that had been used during the Great Depression as a relief camp. It was one of twenty-six internment camps in Canada and the only one in the Maritimes. The camp had two distinct phases. During the first phase in 1940-1941, it housed mostly German-Jewish men between the ages of sixteen and sixty, whose loyalties to this country were suspect because of their German nationality. After a year, they would either join the military, find a sponsor to stay in Canada or the United States, or be sent to another camp. In the second phase during the years 1941-1945, the internees were prisoners of war, mostly German and Italian merchant marines, but also naturalized citizens. There were 350 guards for the 900-1,200 prisoners. The prisoners cut lumber for twenty cents per day, but there was also work in the hospital, the kitchen, or elsewhere in the fifty-two buildings. After the war, the buildings were sold, and all that remains today is part of the old water tower that you can see from the road.

22. Internment Camp Historical Trail

Distance: 0.3 km (0.2 mi)
Type: loop
Difficulty: easy
Ascent: none

Hiking time: 15 min
Map: 21 J/1 Minto
Trail condition: dry
Cellphone coverage: Y

Finding the trailhead: From the junction of Highways 8 and 10 in Fredericton on the north side of the Saint John River, take Highway 10 towards Minto and follow it for 26.3 km (16.3 mi). The trailhead is located on the left side of the road. There is parking for about twelve vehicles. There are no trail markings, but the trail is easy to follow.

Trailhead: 46°00'31"N, 66°15'44"W

The hike: Enter the woods near the water tower. Once you are in the woods, turn right and follow the signs. They offer the occasion for a self-guided tour around the compound. The interpretive plaques allow visitors a glimpse into the history of an Allied POW camp during World War II. For more information, visit the website of the New Brunswick Internment Camp Museum (http://nbinternmentcampmuseum. ca/).

above: Foundation for stove
opposite: Base of the original water tower

23. White Rapids Trail

Distance: 0.6 km (0.4 mi)
Type: loop
Difficulty: easy
Ascent: minor

Hiking time: 15 min
Map: 21 G/10 Fredericton Junction
Trail condition: dry
Cellphone coverage: Y

Finding the trailhead: From the intersection of Regent Street and Prospect Street in Fredericton, drive 37.9 km (23.5 mi) on Route 101 in a southerly direction. In Fredericton Junction, follow the road as it makes a ninety-degree turn to the right and crosses a bridge across the North Branch Oromocto River. Immediately after the bridge, turn right on Mill Pond Drive, follow it for 200 m/yd, and turn right again onto Currie Lane. After another 200 m/yd, the road ends at Currie House. The trail begins near the main entrance of the house on the right side of the road. There are no trail markings, but the trail cannot be missed.

Trailhead: 45°39'36" N, 66°36'38" W

The hike: Always keep to the right. This interpretive trail is a delightful combination of pieces of art, provincial history, and nature. The latter includes the Gaspereau Falls and White Rapids.

Fredericton Junction and Hobos

Fredericton Junction has been an important place for the railroads. The first half of the twentieth century saw lots of railroad traffic and with it came the hobos, who hopped on trains to get to the next place. The origin of the term "hobo" is in dispute; it may derive from "hoe boys" (i.e., farm boys), the greeting "Ho, boy!" or the words "homeless boys." What is not in dispute, though, is the difference between hobos and tramps. Strictly speaking, hobos are migrant workers, while tramps are individuals who work only if absolutely necessary. Both types feared the railroad police who were eager to get rid of non-paying passengers. One older hobo who passed multiple times through Fredericton Junction was an individual with an uncanny resemblance to Lord Beaverbrook, a.k.a. newspaper magnate Max Aitken from Newcastle, NB. He cultivated that image by dressing like his titled doppelgänger. It is doubtful that the two ever met. A statue of the hobo can be found at the old railway station in Fredericton Junction.

24. Bald Hill Adventure Trail

24. Bald Hill Adventure Trail

Distance: 1.9 km (1.2 mi)
Type: loop
Difficulty: easy to moderate (to peak), moderate for loop
Ascent: 100 m (330 ft)

Hiking time: 1 hr
Map: 21 G/8 Saint John
Trail condition: groomed to the top, very rocky and rooty for the loop
Cellphone coverage: N

Finding the trailhead: From Fredericton or Saint John, take Highway 7. Take exit 63 (Welsford and Fredericton Junction). At the T-junction, turn right onto Route 101 and follow it for 1.4 km (0.9 mi) to an Irving gas station. Turn right at the station and follow Route 101 towards Fredericton Junction Road for 10 km (6.2 mi). Turn left onto Ogden Road and follow it for 4 km (2.5 mi).[2] Then turn right at a ninety-degree angle and follow an unnamed rough dirt road (high clearance vehicles are recommended) for 0.7 km (0.4 mi) past waste ponds to a junction. Keep to the left. Continue for another 1.3 km (0.8 mi) just past a dirt road to the right. The trailhead is located on the right side of the road at a signpost. There is parking for about six vehicles. There are a few very faint yellow paint blazes and some orange marking tape. The signpost also shows points A, B, C, and D on the upper and lower paths.

Trailhead: 45°28'02"N, 66°30'16"W

The hike: From the trailhead, follow the path through conifers. The trail ascends gradually through a stand of maple and birch trees, then more steeply until it reaches a junction. Continue straight on the upper trail (point D) to the summit; you will return from the left on the lower trail later. After a short distance, the bald peak is reached (point A). It affords good views in a westerly direction. From this point, you can retrace your steps or hike the loop. At the far left of the rocky top, the lower trail (C) continues. It descends steeply; fortunately, there is a rope. Once the trail is below the cliffs, it continues to the left in a southerly direction. It follows the high and very impressive cliffs directly next to the trail. At the end of the cliff wall, the trail turns to the left and ascends very steeply to the junction encountered earlier. From here, the trail turns right and returns to the trailhead. The main features of this trail are the fine views from the top of the hill and the long and impressive rock wall.

---

2   The trailhead of Sand Brook Falls is located 6.6 km (4.1 mi) farther up Ogden Road on the left side of the road. A 5-minute walk leads to picturesque Sand Brook Falls.

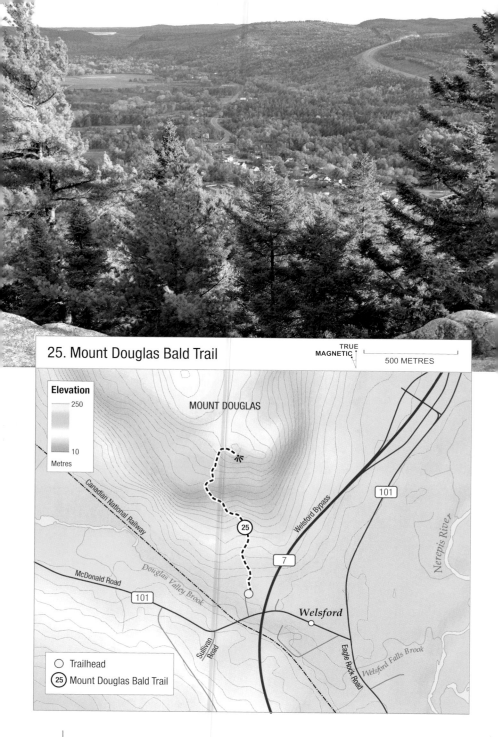

25. Mount Douglas Bald Trail

TRUE
MAGNETIC
500 METRES

Elevation

250

10

Metres

MOUNT DOUGLAS

Canadian National Railway

101

Welsford Bypass

Nerepis River

7

25

Douglas Valley Brook

McDonald Road

101

Welsford

Sullivan Road

Eagle Rock Road

Welsford Falls Brook

○ Trailhead
㉕ Mount Douglas Bald Trail

25. Mount Douglas Bald Trail

Distance: 2.5 km (1.6 mi) rtn
Type: linear
Difficulty: moderate
Ascent: 190 m (623 ft)

Hiking time: 1 hr rtn
Map: 21 G/8 Saint John
Trail condition: dry, rocky
Cellphone coverage: Y

Finding the trailhead: From Fredericton or Saint John, take Highway 7. Take exit 63 (Welsford and Fredericton Junction). At the T-junction, turn right onto Route 101 and follow it for 1.4 km (0.9 mi) to an Irving gas station. Turn right at the station and follow Route 101 towards Fredericton Junction for 500 m/yd, where — just behind a bridge on Highway 7 and before a level train crossing — a dirt road turns off to the right. (On Google maps, this dirt road is incorrectly labeled as Burton Lane.) Follow this road to its end, where there is plenty of space to park. The trailhead is located straight ahead behind the sandy incline. There are no signs, but the trail is easy to find without them.

Trailhead: 45°27'31" N, 66°20'56" W

The hike: From the trailhead, the trail continues straight and immediately ascends through lovely hardwoods. In the spring, bunchberries and lady's slippers are in bloom. The trail climbs continuously, and the last section is quite steep. From the top, you are rewarded with a great view of the town of Welsford, the wooded hills around it, and Grand Bay in the distance. Many woodland wildflowers are found along this rocky trail. Its major feature, however, is the magnificent view from the top, which makes the short and steep trail worthwhile.

26. Welsford Brook Falls

Distance: 1 km (0.6 mi) rtn
Type: linear
Difficulty: easy to moderate
Ascent: 40 m (130 ft)

Hiking time: 20 min rtn
Map: 21 G/8 Saint John
Trail condition: rocky and steep
Cellphone coverage: Y

Finding the trailhead: From Fredericton or Saint John, take Highway 7. Take exit 63 (Welsford and Fredericton Junction). At the T-junction, turn right onto Route 101 and follow it for 1.4 km (0.9 mi) to an Irving gas station. Turn right at the station and follow the road for 1 km (0.6 mi), then turn left onto an unnamed paved road. Follow this road for 1.3 km (0.8 mi). The trailhead is on the left side of the road in front of a guard rail on the left with Mud Lake on the right side of the road. Parking is alongside the road. There are no trail markings, but the trail is easy to find and follow.

Trailhead: 45°26'47" N, 66°20'55" W

The hike: The trail enters the woods and, after a very short section, reaches a clearing and power lines. It turns right, then swings to the left as it reaches the top of the cliffs high above Welsford Brook. The path follows the brook past a dilapidated house. At the end, a rope aids hikers in a short, but very steep, descent to the brook. It is possible to walk a few steps to the right (upstream) for the best view of the falls. The waterfall is particularly impressive in the spring.

27. Cochrane Cliffs

Distance: 2.5 km (1.6 mi) rtn
Type: linear
Difficulty: easy to moderate
Ascent: 10 m (33 ft)

Hiking time: 1 hr rtn
Map: 21 G/8 Saint John
Trail condition: rocky
Cellphone coverage: Y

Finding the trailhead: On Highway 7, take exit 71 to Welsford. At the T-junction, take Route 177 to Eagle Rock. Follow this road for 4.9 km (3 mi) to Cochrane Lane. Turn right onto Cochrane Lane and follow this road for 2.3 km (1.4 mi). Just before you reach a farm, there is a gate on the left side of the road. This is the trailhead. Stay on the defined trails; this is DND land and exploring is not permitted. There are no trail markings, but the trail is easy to find and follow.

Trailhead: 45°26'22" N, W66°18'25" W

The hike: Beyond the gate, the trail follows the edge of the woods. The trail then enters the woods and begins to climb, first gently, but soon steeply on steps. After some distance, the path reaches a signpost with a register and a first aid kit. (If you want to get to Gollum's Cave, continue straight on a strenuous climb over boulders to the base of the cliffs. It may be difficult to find your way back to the signpost.) Turn right towards the Waterfalls Wall and L-Shape. There are some boardwalk sections in this area. Pass by the Waterfalls Wall and continue to Pyramid on the left, a triangular climbing wall. Opposite on the right is a nice observation point that allows some views across the woods far below. From here, hikers may continue for a short distance to the L-Shape and a minor observation point opposite. The trail returns from here to the trailhead. The trail features interesting rock formations and some vista points.

28. Turtle Mountain Trail

TRUE
MAGNETIC

2 KILOMETRES

Capple Lake

Sagwa

177

7

Power Line

Gate

Robin Hood Lake

Access Road

Negro Lake

Parking

Power Line

MAWHANE MOUNTAIN

Little John Lake

Elevation

260

0

Metres

TURTLE MOUNTAIN

Ogden Lake

Duck Lake

Turtle Lake

○ Trailhead

28 Turtle Mountain Trail

West Lake

28. Turtle Mountain Trail

Distance: 16.8 km (10.4 mi) rtn
Type: linear
Difficulty: moderate
Ascent: 180 m (590 ft)
Hiking time: 5 hrs 15 min rtn

Map: 21 G/8 Saint John
Trail condition: rocky and rooty, a few mud holes
Cellphone coverage: Y

Finding the trailhead: On Highway 7, take exit 80 (Grand Bay-Westfield). Turn onto Route 102, follow it for 1.2 km (0.7 mi) then turn left onto Route 177. Follow this road for 2.9 km (1.8 mi) to civic number 513 on the left side of the road. Turn left onto a dirt road, which forks after a short distance. Keep right and follow the very rough dirt road for 1.8 km (1.1 mi). Just beyond the Highway 7 underpass, turn left and then right again. There is a gate, but it is often open. If not, this will add 3.2 km (2 mi) to your walk each way. Drive past the gate down this rocky road to its end at an ATV bridge across a narrow channel that connects Robin Hood Lake (on the right) and Little John Lake (on the left). There are a few parking spots. The trailhead is at the bridge. There are no trail markings, but the trail is generally easy to find. There are, however, a number of spurs that may be confusing. When in doubt, take the wider and more frequently used trail. There is some orange marking tape hanging from trees and white tape wrapped around trees.

Trailhead: 45°21'03" N, 66°18'34" W

Blueberries

The hike: Cross the bridge and then ascend on the rocky trail. At times, there are forks, which eventually lead back together with the main trail. After some time, the trail reaches a small, rocky plateau. The trail continues on its left side. After a while, you will reach another plateau. At this point, cross the plateau on the right first, and after descending a bit, continue on the left. The trail soon forks again, but both forks will eventually meet again. From here on, there are a number of alternative paths at forks, but they always merge again. Eventually, the trail reaches a grassy spot, where it turns sharply to the left. At this point, the trail starts to climb and eventually reaches the Turtle Mountain plateau. Continue on the ATV trail to another plateau to the right and reach the rounded granite top of Turtle Mountain. There is a sheltered area just below the summit that can serve as a campsite for those who plan to spend the night on Turtle Mountain. Hikers are richly rewarded by the beautiful panoramic views from the top of the mountain. Turtle Lake, with its small, boggy peninsula, lies just below to the southwest, with Labrador Lake, Sherwood Lake, and Hasty Lake in the distance. Big Indian Lake can be seen in a west-northwesterly direction. On a clear day you can see the Saint John smokestacks in a southeasterly direction, as well as the twin smokestacks of the Coleson Cove power generating station. In season, the blueberries along the trail and on top are delicious. Black bear, moose, and deer might also be in the vicinity.

right: Turtle Lake from the summit

29. Hammond River Nature Trail (Hammond River Park)

Distance: 1.7 km (1.1 mi)
Type: loop
Difficulty: easy to moderate
Ascent: 70 m (230 ft)
Hiking time: 45 min

Map: 21 H/5 Loch Lomond, trail map at log cabin (in season)
Trail condition: rocky and rooty, some wet spots
Cellphone coverage: Y

Finding the trailhead: From Saint John, take Highway 1 east. Take exit 142 in Quispamsis just past a trailer park and follow the road, which turns into Route 100, towards Hampton for 4.1 km (2.5 mi). With the country market on the right and Anglican church on the left, turn left onto Hammond River Road. Follow it for 3.4 km (2.1 mi), crossing the railway tracks on the way. At a stop sign, take the right fork onto Neck Road and follow it for 0.6 km (0.4 mi). Turn right onto Reynar Drive. After 300 m/yd the entrance to the park is on the right side of the street. The short access road ends at a parking lot next to a log cabin. The trailhead is located to its right. All trails in the park have names and round metal blazes of a silver hiker on a coloured background. Unfortunately, the names of the partial trails do not appear on the map next to the log cabin.

Trailhead: 45°29'14" N, 65°54'44" W

The hike: There is a dizzying array of trails in the park, such as Birch Lane, Green Ash Lane, Silviculture Lane, Lower Ironwood Trail, Ironwood Trail, and Cedar Grove Lane. Rather than offering a point-by-point description, it is easiest to simply follow the perimeter of the park, keeping to the right whenever possible. Follow the Hammond River for a while, then turn left onto "North" and climb for some distance (a silver hiker on a red background). Continue on "North" to a gravel road to reach the log cabin. The nature trail passes a number of interesting sights, ranging from old apple orchards to nurse logs and a kame (a glacial feature). There are picnic tables at the park entrance and on the balcony of the log cabin.

30. Moss Glen Nature Trail

Distance: 2.3 km (1.4 mi)
Type: loop
Difficulty: easy
Ascent: 45 m (150 ft)
Hiking time: 45 min
Maps: 21 G/8 Saint John and

https://sites.google.com/site/
kingstonpeninsulaheritage/home/
resources
Trail condition: mostly dry
Cellphone coverage: P

Finding the trailhead: Access from Quispamsis: On Highway 1 between Moncton and Saint John, take exit 141 and follow Route 119 for 5.7 km (3.5 mi) to Gondola Point. Take the ferry to the Kingston Peninsula. Drive up to the stop sign and turn left onto NB 845. Follow this road for 5 km (3.1 mi), then turn right onto Williams Road. Follow this road for 0.8 km (0.5 mi). The trailhead is located on the left side of the road, indicated by a green Moss Glen Nature Trail sign. The trail is marked by white paint blazes on trees.

Trailhead: 45°26'12" N, 66°02'40" W

The hike: Enter the woods at the sign and cross a small brook on a wooden bridge. The path immediately turns left alongside the brook and soon continues away from it. The trail ascends and after a while reaches a large boulder just before an interpretive plaque on the last ice age. At this point, the trail continues straight (passing the plaque), where it will return later via the trail on the right. The trail continues through pleasant woods, passing more interpretive plaques. It returns via the boulder to the trailhead. This trail is notable for the number and range of interpretive plaques regarding subjects such as pileated woodpeckers, which are occasionally seen in the area, glaciation, and forest management.

31. Sea Dog Cove Nature Preserve Trail

Distance: 2 + 0.4 km (1.2 + 0.3 mi) rtn
Type: linear
Difficulty: easy
Ascent: negligible

Hiking time: 40 min
Map: 21 G/8 Saint John
Trail condition: dry
Cellphone coverage: Y

Finding the trailhead: Access from Quispamsis: On Highway 1 between Moncton and Saint John, take exit 141 and follow Route 119 for 5.7 km (3.5 mi) to Gondola Point. Take the ferry to the Kingston Peninsula. Drive up to the stop sign and turn left onto NB 845. Follow this road for 16.8 km (10.4 mi). Rather than follow NB 845 to the right, continue straight on Summerville Road for 0.8 km (0.5 mi), where you can see an explanatory plaque on the left. This is the trailhead of the Sea Dog Cove Nature Preserve Trail. Parking is on the side of the road. There are no markings, but the trail is easy to follow.

Trailhead: 45°20'22" N, 66°06'16" W

The hike: The trail enters the woods at the sign. After a short distance, it reaches a T-junction, where it turns right. From here it continues to its end not far from the cliffs near Kennebecasis Bay. A narrow footpath leads a short distance down, from where an unobstructed view of north Saint John can be enjoyed. Back at the road, the short trail across from the sign leads to Sea Dog Cove with access to the water.

32. Boars Head Nature Preserve Trail

Distance: 1.5 km (0.9 mi) rtn
Type: linear
Difficulty: easy to moderate
Ascent: 50 m (165 ft)
Hiking time: 1 hr rtn

Map: 21 G/8 Saint John, also www.
naturetrust.nb.ca/wp/wp-content/
uploads/2012/08/Boars_head.pdf
Trail condition: rooty
Cellphone coverage: Y

Finding the trailhead: Approaching Saint John from the west on Highway 1, take exit 121 onto Route 100 (Chesley Drive). Turn right onto Chesley Drive, followed by a left turn onto Main Street. After 250 m/yd, turn right onto Adelaide Street. Follow this road for 600 m/yd, then turn left onto Millidge Avenue. Continue for 1.8 km (1.1 mi), then turn left onto Boars Head Road. After 1.5 km (0.9 mi), continue straight at the junction with Woodward Avenue onto Ragged Point Road. Follow this road for 200 m/yd to the Centre scolaire Samuel-de-Champlain on the left side of the road. Behind the adjacent parking lot is a soccer field. The trailhead is located at the far right of the soccer field at a small wooden bridge. The trail is marked by 3″ × 3″ reflective yellow blazes on trees and rectangular white paint blazes as well as pink-and-black striped marking tape. It is essential to look out for blazes at all times.

Trailhead: 45°17'44" N, 66°07'07" W

The hike: The trail parallels the Ragged Point Road (which cannot be seen) until it reaches Ragged Point Cove on a side trail, marked by double yellow blazes. The cove is near the confluence of the Kennebecasis and Saint John Rivers. The trail loops around and returns in a counter-clockwise manner. The main feature of the trail is the access to Ragged Point Cove, one of the few undeveloped coastline areas protected and preserved in this rapidly developing part of town.

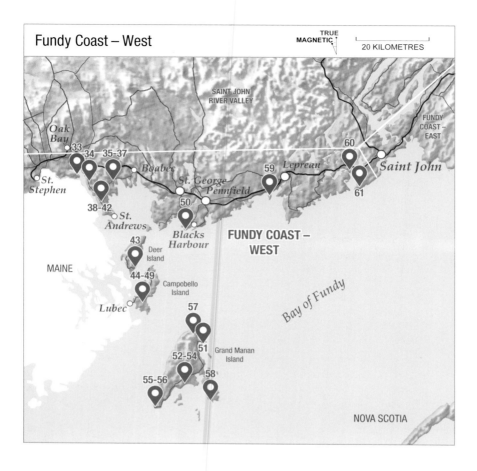

Fundy Coast – West

TRUE
MAGNETIC

20 KILOMETRES

SAINT JOHN
RIVER VALLEY

FUNDY
COAST –
EAST

Oak
Bay

33
34   35-37
Boabec

St.
Stephen

59   Lepreau

60

Saint John

St. George
Pennfield

61

38-42   St.
Andrews

50

MAINE

43   Blacks
Harbour

FUNDY COAST –
WEST

Deer
Island

44-49   Campobello
Island

Bay of Fundy

Lubec

57

51

52-54   Grand Manan
Island

55-56   58

NOVA SCOTIA

FUNDY COAST - WEST

The Passamaquoddy people plied the waters of the western Fundy Coast for millennia. In 1604, Samuel de Champlain founded a settlement on St. Croix Island, now a historic site near Saint Andrews. It was abandoned in 1605 in favour of Port Royal in what is now the Annapolis Valley, Nova Scotia.

The history of the area is dominated by the United Empire Loyalists, who, following the American Revolution, fled to New Brunswick (then a part of Nova Scotia) and settled along the Fundy Coast. They founded Saint Andrews, one of the oldest towns in the province, in 1783. Two years later, the towns of Parrtown and Carleton were incorporated in 1785 as Saint John, the first city to do so in what is now Canada. With the construction of the railway in the 1800s, the beautiful town of St. Andrews-by-the-Sea (as Saint Andrews is popularly known today) developed as a quaint summer resort. One of its citizens was William Cornelius Van Horne, the driving force behind the CPR. His family's summer estate lies just offshore on Ministers Island.

In addition to a rich history, the western coast also has a lot to offer naturalists, including the Fundy Isles: Deer Island, Campobello Island, and Grand Manan. Whale-watching and birding are favourite pastimes. The isles contain parks with beaches, rugged coastline, and trails through woods, along the coast, and across bogs. Fishing, dulse collecting, and tourism are the mainstays of the local economy.

50. Pea Point Trail

33. Ganong Nature Park Loop

33. Ganong Nature Park Loop

Distance: 3.8 km (2.4 mi)
Type: loop
Difficulty: moderate
Ascent: 60 m (200 ft)
Hiking time: 1 hr 45 min
Map: 21 G/3 St. Stephen or check a dedicated map at http://ganongnaturepark.com/hiking/

Trail condition: somewhat rooty, but generally good. The parts along the edge of a field are grassy, which makes for excellent hiking.
Cellphone coverage: Y

Finding the trailhead: On Highway 1, take exit 13 (Oak Bay) towards Oak Bay. After 3 km (1.9 mi), turn left onto Route 170 towards Waweig. After 0.9 km (0.6 mi), turn right onto Benson Road, and after another 0.6 km (0.4 mi), turn right onto Oak Haven Road. Pass by the Oak Bay Hatchery, and after 5.7 km (3.5 mi), turn left onto Todds Point Road. The road forks almost immediately; keep to the right towards the Ganong Nature Park and drive another 3 km (1.9 mi) to the gate of the park. (The gate closes at 5 p.m.) Ahead is the Quoddy Learning Centre, where additional information can be obtained. The loop described here is a combination of trails marked in various colours in this order: yellow (orange as an alternative), green, red (and purple, if desired). Directions are visible on wooden signs along the trail.

Trailhead: 45°10'22" N, 67°09'54" W

The hike: At the Quoddy Learning Centre, turn to the left on the yellow-blazed Lookout Trail. Keep right at a T-junction with a woods road and, after some distance, take the right fork, following the signs. Pass the ruins of the old John Smith farm and continue straight at a fork. The trail ascends to the Lookout. Continue at the far right end of the Lookout on the orange-blazed trail, which narrows as it descends. It eventually ends at the green-blazed Forest Pond Trail, where it turns to the left. The trail descends and, after some time, reaches a fork with a short spur to Back Beach, overlooking Pagans Cove. Beyond the fork, the trail ascends, levels off, and reaches the edge of the woods at an open field. Turn left on the red-blazed Auk Hill Trail and keep to the left at all times, except where the left fork leads down to the beach. The path passes the Ganong Cottage, a pavilion, and a huge pine tree before it returns to the parking lot.

33. Ganong Nature Park Loop

St. Croix River

The St. Croix River has a long and diverse history. The Passamaquoddy people had long established seasonal settlements along its shores, and the French began to colonize the North American continent here as early as 1604. Pierre Dugua de Mons, with Samuel de Champlain, founded a colony on St. Croix Island, where more than half of the settlers died during their first winter. The next year they moved to another location on the Fundy Coast, and later Champlain founded Quebec City. Subsequently, British Loyalists settled along the river, which constitutes the boundary between the state of Maine and the southern part of the province of New Brunswick.

34. Simpson Hill Loop Trail

Distance: 2.8 km (1.7 mi)
Type: loop
Difficulty: moderate to strenuous
Ascent: 125 m (410 ft)
Hiking time: 1 hr 15 min

Map: 21 G/3 St. Stephen
Trail condition: rocky and rooty, grassy woods road in part
Cellphone coverage: Y

Finding the trailhead: On Highway 1, take exit 25 and follow Route 127 towards Saint Andrews for 5.2 km (3.2 mi). There is a wooden cut-out of a hiker on the left side of the road. Parking is on the shoulder on either side of the road. A large number of signs are used to identify the names of short segments of trails, which can be confusing.

Trailhead: 45°09'46"N, 67°07'59"W

The hike: Enter the woods and, after a short distance, turn left onto the Old Ridge North Trail. The path leads through woods, then climbs over large boulders and, farther, steeply up to a power line. Here, it turns left and follows the line for some distance before it turns to the right into the woods. This spot is fairly inconspicuous, so it pays to watch out. The trail soon reaches a sign, Switchbacks to Old Shmo's Trail and Tabletop. Continue and at a T-junction turn left onto Valley Trail. Then continue left onto Mamie's Trail, and subsequently continue right onto Karen's Lung Lichen Trail. Pass the rope to climb up the mountain, and soon you will reach the table top. There are good views from here across Oak Bay and onto Todds Point east of St. Stephen. Behind the table top, follow the sign indicating Upper Loop to Southside Trail – Two Towers Trail – Gravel Road. After a short distance, watch carefully for the Two Towers Trail sign on a tree as it is easy to miss. If you reach the sign for Mary's Trail, you've gone too far! The Two Towers Trail leads down gently and after some distance reaches two water towers and a house. From here, walk on the grassy (gravel) road. A short distance before a dilapidated building, turn right onto an inconspicuous path that leads into the woods. This path is marked by some marking tape. This is the MacAlister Trail, which follows a small stream. It eventually leads to a junction near the trailhead. The main features of this trail are the spectacular views from the table top across Oak Bay and Todds Point.

35-37. Caughey-Taylor Nature Preserve

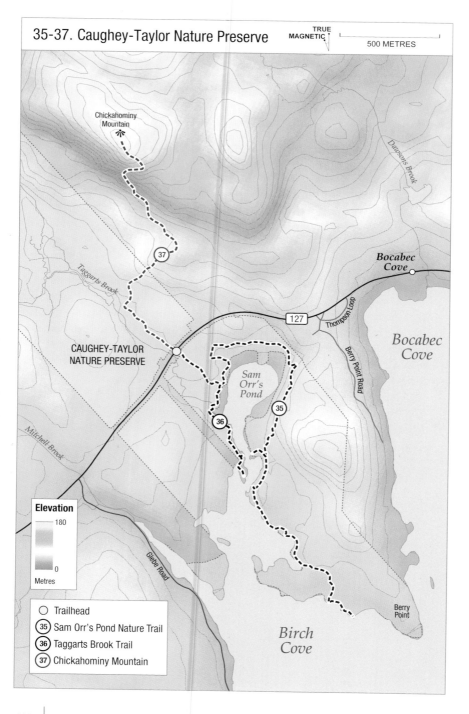

TRUE
MAGNETIC

500 METRES

Chickahominy
Mountain

37

Taggarts Brook

Dawsons Brook

Bocabec
Cove

127

Thompson Loop

Bocabec
Cove

CAUGHEY-TAYLOR
NATURE PRESERVE

Sam
Orr's
Pond

Berry Point Road

36

35

Mitchell Brook

Elevation
180

0
Metres

Glebe Road

Birch
Cove

Berry
Point

○ Trailhead
35 Sam Orr's Pond Nature Trail
36 Taggarts Brook Trail
37 Chickahominy Mountain

35-37. Caughey-Taylor Nature Preserve

In 1999, the New Brunswick Nature Trust opened its first New Brunswick land preserve, the Caughey-Taylor Nature Preserve, near Bocabec, just off Route 127 to Saint
Andrews. The Caughey-Taylor Nature Preserve set aside 120 hectares (300 acres)
of salt marsh and tidal estuary, under the trust's mandate to protect private lands
of ecological significance throughout the province. For more information, check
out the website at http://www.naturetrust.nb.ca/wp/blog/caughey-taylor-nature-
preserve/.

View of Taggarts Brook

35. Sam Orr's Pond Nature Trail

Distance: 5.6 km (3.5 mi) rtn
Type: linear
Difficulty: moderate
Ascent: 75 m (250 ft)
Hiking time: 2 hrs 15 min rtn

Map: 21 G/3 St. Stephen
Trail condition: mostly dry, some
stretches are along marshes close to
the flood line, rocky, and rooty
Cellphone coverage: P

Finding the trailhead: From Highway 1, take exit 39 and follow Route 127 towards
Saint Andrews for 7 km (4.3 mi). The trailhead is located near Bocabec on the left
side of the road between civic numbers 5185 and 5149. Parking is on the wide
gravel shoulder of the road. There is a sign of the Caughey-Taylor Nature Preserve
at Sam Orr Pond at the beginning of the trail. The trail is marked by circular white
paint blazes on trees.

Trailhead: 45°09'54" N, 67°02'51" W

The hike: The trail enters the woods and reaches a T-junction after some time. The
Sam Orr Pond Nature Trail continues to the left. The trail continues through softwoods until it reaches large rocks straight ahead. It ascends and continues to the
right, keeping the rock formation to its left. After some distance, the trail reaches
a beautiful vista. The trail continues through lush Irish moss high above Sam Orr
Pond. It then leads down to a junction. The right spur descends to the mouth of
the pond and its rock sill. You may return here on the Taggarts Trail by making the
crossing via some rocks, but only during low tide! The main trail continues along the
pond through wooded areas and across salt marshes. At the very end, the trail enters
the woods via some flags that may be missed, ending a short distance later near
Berry Point at Birch Cove on Passamaquoddy Bay. This magnificent trail offers fine
views of a quiet pond and access to Passamaquoddy Bay with its vibrant population
of shorebirds.

36. Taggarts Brook Trail

Distance: 1.6 km (1 mi) rtn
Type: linear
Difficulty: easy
Ascent: negligible

Hiking time: 30 min rtn
Map: 21 G/3 St. Stephen
Trail condition: dry, rooty
Cellphone coverage: P

Finding the trailhead: From Highway 1, take exit 39 and follow Route 127 towards Saint Andrews for 7 km (4.3 mi). The trailhead is located near Bocabec on the left side of the road between civic numbers 5185 and 5149. Parking is on the wide gravel shoulder of the road. There is a sign of the Caughey-Taylor Nature Preserve at Sam Orr Pond at the beginning of the trail. Trail markings are white painted discs on trees.

Trailhead: 45°09'54"N, 67°02'51"W

The hike: The trail enters the woods and reaches a T-junction after some time. The Taggarts Brook Trail continues to the right. It soon crosses Taggarts Brook on a wooden bridge. After that, the trail leads through a jumble of roots. The trail ends at Sam Orr Pond with a small seasonal island close by where shorebirds typically congregate. It then returns the same way. This trail makes for a nice walk through the woods with access to a quiet and scenic pond. The trail may be used in conjunction with the Sam Orr Pond Trail. However, the crossing via the rock sill is only accessible at low tide, and less so after heavy rains.

37. Chickahominy Mountain

Distance: 3.8 km (2.4 mi) rtn
Type: linear
Difficulty: strenuous
Ascent: 150 m (500ft)
Hiking time: 1 hr 50 min rtn

Map: 21 G/3 St. Stephen
Trail condition: For most part, the trail is well defined. Once into the rocks, it requires scrambling.
Cellphone coverage: N

Finding the trailhead: From Highway 1, take exit 39 and follow Route 127 towards Saint Andrews for 7 km (4.3 mi). The trailhead is located near Bocabec on the left side of the road between civic numbers 5185 and 5149. Parking is on the wide gravel shoulder of the road on either side. There is a sign for the Caughey-Taylor Nature Preserve at Sam Orr's Pond at the beginning of the trail. Trail markings are few in the first part, but the trail is well defined. Later, once into the rocks, the trail follows marking tape of various colours.

Trailhead: 45°09'55" N, 67°02'52" W

The hike: The entrance of the trail is marked by a sign indicating Caughey-Taylor Nature Preserve: Taggarts Brook. The unmarked trail is well defined. Keep right at a fork. Once the trail reaches the power lines, it turns right and ascends, following the lines for some distance and crossing them three times. The trail then turns to the left into the woods (it is joined from the right by an overgrown woods road) and starts to climb gently. After some distance, it reaches some huge boulders on the right. The trail continues between the boulders. From this point onwards, it gets narrow and faint, and very steep. Once the trail reaches a scree slope, continue to the right just below the slope. The path climbs, following the marking tape. The trail eventually reaches a sign marking End of Trail just below the summit of Chickahominy Mountain. The trail makes for a pleasant walk through young and mature woods at first, before it becomes a strenuous uphill climb. From the top, there are some views of the surrounding area across Chamcook Lake, Chamcook Mountain, and Passamaquoddy Bay.

38. Chamcook Mountain Trail

Distance: 2.5 km (1.6 mi) rtn [+ 0.5 km /0.3 mi loop]
Type: linear
Difficulty: moderate
Ascent: 125 m (410 ft)

Hiking time: 1 hr rtn
Map: 21 G/3 St. Stephen
Trail condition: wide old wagon road
Cellphone coverage: Y

Finding the trailhead: On Highway 1, take exit 39 and turn onto Route 127 west towards Bocabec and Saint Andrews. Follow this road for 12.7 km (7.9 mi) to the Rossmount Inn opposite civic number 4598. The driveway approaches the inn and turns left to the parking lot, while the right lane leads to the trailhead. Park in the parking lot and follow the driveway directly left of the inn, a short distance upwards. There are no trail markings, but the wide trail cannot be missed.

Trailhead: 45°07'15" N, 67°04'40" W

The hike: Behind the Rossmount Inn, continue straight up an old wagon road, which makes a sharp turn to the right as it reaches the carriage house. Opposite the carriage house, the trail turns onto a small path that soon reaches the road again. Turn left and follow the sign to Chamcook Mountain. After a steady climb and some switchbacks, wooden steps lead up to the top of the hill. We strongly suggest that hikers continue for a short distance in a southwesterly direction, as this leads to an open area that allows more fine views. Return to the trailhead following the trail in reverse. Just before reaching the trailhead, there is the possibility to engage in a leisurely stroll around a meadow. The Meadows Trail starts very close to the trailhead. It turns off the main trail, turns right after a short distance, and leads around a large meadow. The grassy trail ends at the Rossmount Inn parking lot. The main features of this trail are the fine views of Chamcook Lake and Passamaquoddy Bay. There are a number of granite explanatory plates along the trail, featuring interesting facts about this former horse-and-buggy trail and its history.

Chamcook Mountain

This mountain has seen many years of visitors. In modern times, the Townshend brothers of Chamcook, carpenters and shipbuilders, purchased the property, which was later acquired by Sarah and Henry Ross in 1902. They renamed the property Rossmount. They constructed a wide wagon road to the top of the hill, where they would have picnics with family and their prominent American friends. On the way up, there are vistas onto Passamaquoddy Bay, including Hospital Island. Among the more than ten thousand immigrants who passed through Saint Andrews in the years 1815-1860, some four hundred of them, mostly Irish, fell ill and died on Hospital Island. A Celtic cross in Saint Andrews serves as a reminder.

39. Two Meadows Nature Trail

Distance: 0.8 km (0.5 mi)
Type: loop
Difficulty: easy
Ascent: negligible

Hiking time: 15 min
Map: 21 G/3 St. Stephen
Trail condition: dry
Cellphone coverage: Y

Finding the trailhead: From Highway 1 take exit 25 to Saint Andrews. Pass the Saint Croix Island International Historic Site and continue along Route 127 for 15.7 km (9.8 mi). Keep to the right towards downtown Saint Andrews. After 0.5 km (0.3 mi) from this junction, turn right onto Harriet Street, and after 0.3 km (0.2 mi) at a T-junction, turn right onto Joes Point Road. Beyond Charles Street, continue for some 300 m/yd to a red hydrant and a wooden trail sign on the right side of the street. There is parking for three vehicles. The narrow nature path is clearly marked throughout. There are twenty explanatory plaques along the trail.

Trailhead: 45°04'40"N, 67°04'01"W

The hike: After a short distance, there is a fork in the trail. Keep left and follow the numbered plaques. At a junction, turn left. The trail soon returns to the parking lot. This trail is particularly beautiful in the spring when the apple and cherry trees are in full bloom. It is maintained by the Sunbury Shores Arts and Nature Centre.

40-42. Ministers Island

Ministers Island has a rich history. Its human settlement began more than two thousand years ago, when the Passamaquoddy people settled here. In 1777 United Empire Loyalists migrated to Chamcook, as the island was called back then. In 1790 the Reverend Samuel Andrews purchased the island for 250 pounds, hence its name. The railway icon William Cornelius Van Horne purchased part of the island in 1890 for his summer resort. He built a windmill, a large barn, and the estate he named Covenhoven, a fifty-room summer cottage. After his death, the property stayed in the hands of the Van Horne family, but it fell into ruin, and in the 1960s it was sold to developers. In 1977 the island became a protected area, and starting in 1983 the first visitors were allowed on the island. In 1996 the island was designated a National Historic Site, and visitors are welcome to drive across a natural causeway at low tide and explore the island.

For access to all trails on Ministers Island: Take exit 25 on Highway 1 and follow Route 127 south towards Saint Andrews for 11.6 km (7.2 mi), then turn left towards Ministers Island onto Ghost Road. Follow this road for 0.9 km (0.6 mi), then turn right at a T-junction (also Route 127) towards Saint Andrews. Follow this road for 2.7 km (1.7 mi), then turn left onto Bar Road and follow it for 1.3 km (0.8 mi). This road leads directly to the bar that allows you to cross over to Ministers Island at low tide. Tide tables are found at http://www.ministersisland.net/tide-schedule.htm. At the booth you will pay for access to the island. There may also be a separate trail fee. Access to individual trails is described from here. A good map of the trails on the island can be found at http://www.ministersisland.net/PDF/Carriage-Trails-Brochure-English.pdf.

The bathhouse at Covenhoven

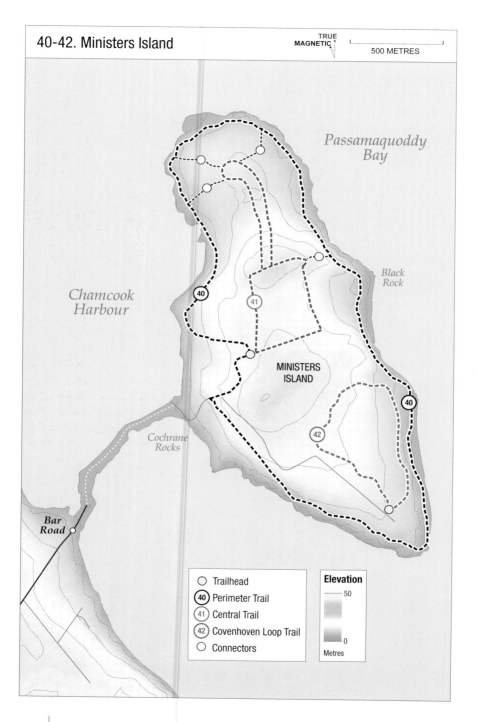

40-42. Ministers Island

TRUE
MAGNETIC

500 METRES

Passamaquoddy Bay

Chamcook Harbour

Black Rock

40

41

MINISTERS ISLAND

40

Cochrane Rocks

42

Bar Road

○ Trailhead
④ Perimeter Trail
④ Central Trail
④ Covenhoven Loop Trail
○ Connectors

Elevation
— 50

0
Metres

40. Ministers Island Perimeter Trail

Distance: 7 km (4.3 mi)
Type: loop
Difficulty: easy
Ascent: negligible
Hiking time: 1 hr 45 min
Map: 21 G/3 St. Stephen; better is the trail brochure at http://www.ministersisland.net/PDF/Carriage-Trails-Brochure-English.pdf. The brochure also includes tide tables, which are mandatory for the ocean crossing.
Trail condition: well-groomed trail, wide and grassy in the open, cleared in the woods
Cellphone coverage: Y

Finding the trailhead: From the booth at the entrance to the island, drive up the gravel road for 500 m/yd to parking lot C, next to a large barn. Follow the gravel road in front of the barn for a short distance. Just as the road makes a right turn, the trail departs from it, leading straight across a field. There are multiple markers at critical junctions with numbers that refer to the trail map. They are numbered from P1 to P16. In addition, if there is a fork without a marker, keep to the left, close to the coast.

Trailhead: 45°06'23" N, 67°02'42" W

The hike: Follow the grassy path for a short distance until you reach a T-junction at marker P1. Turn left towards the next marker, P2. From here on, the directions are shown by similar markers, numbered P2, P3, P4, etc. At P16, turn left, following the sign to the barn. Once on the gravel road, turn right and return to the parking lot. The trail features a number of fine views across Chamcook Harbour and Passamaquoddy Bay. There are also pleasant open areas with fields where wildlife may be observed. Noteworthy, of course, is the Van Horne estate, including the circular bathhouse that is located at marker P12, right next to the trail.

41. Central Trail on Ministers Island

Distance: 3.1 km (1.9 mi)
Type: loop
Difficulty: easy
Ascent: negligible
Hiking time: 1 hr 20 min
Map: 21 G/3 St. Stephen; better is the trail brochure at http://www.

ministersisland.net/PDF/Carriage-Trails-Brochure-English.pdf. The brochure also includes tide tables, which are mandatory for the ocean crossing.
Trail condition: good
Cellphone coverage: Y

Finding the trailhead: From the booth at the entrance to the island, drive up the gravel road for 500 m/yd to parking lot C, next to a large barn. Follow the gravel road in front of the barn for a short distance. Just as the road makes a right turn, the trail departs from it, leading straight across a field. There are multiple markers at critical junctions with numbers that refer to the trail map.

Trailhead: 45°06'23" N, 67°02'42" W

The hike: Follow the grassy path for a short distance until you reach a T-junction at marker P1/C1. Turn right and continue to marker C1.5, at which point turn left on to a wide gravel road that skirts a field and eventually reaches C2. Continue through the woods to a roundabout with connectors to the perimeter trail, and at C3, depart from the main trail to the coast at P3. Here you continue to P4 and P5, at which point you return inland to C5. At C6, cross through the picnic site and walk straight down the grassy path through the fields to C7, and finally the parking lot. There are fine stands of hemlock and maple and beautiful fields of wildflowers. The trail also provides access to the coast.

42. Covenhoven Loop Trail

Distance: 1.6 km (1 mi)
Type: loop
Difficulty: easy
Ascent: negligible
Hiking time: 40 min
Map: 21 G/3 St. Stephen; better is the trail brochure at http://www.ministersisland.net/PDF/Carriage-Trails-Brochure-English.pdf. The brochure also includes tide tables, which are mandatory for ocean crossings.
Trail condition: wide trail that has some less pleasant parts of rough gravel; otherwise the trail is dry and partially grassy.
Cellphone coverage: Y

Finding the trailhead: From the access booth on the island, drive up the gravel road for 300 m/yd, then turn right following the sign marked House. Park at parking lot D, in front of the house. The trailhead is located close to the windmill at the edge of the woods. There are signposts marked C9 (the trailhead), C10, C11, P9.5, P10, P11, C8, and back to C9.

Trailhead: 45°05'57" N, 67°02'05" W

The hike: This short trail is easy to walk and to navigate. It provides a condensed version of what the island has to offer, including fields, coast, views, wildlife, windmill, and the summer home of the Van Horne family.

The barn at Covenhoven

43. Clark-Gregory Loop

Distance: 1.5 km (0.9 mi)
Type: loop
Difficulty: easy to moderate
Ascent: 10 m (33 ft)
Hiking time: 40 min

Map: 21 B/15 Campobello Island
Trail condition: generally dry, rooty
Cellphone coverage: N

Finding the trailhead: On Highway 1, take exit 56 and turn onto Route 172 towards St. George and Deer Island. Continue on this road for 16.3 km (10.1 mi) to the ferry at Letete. For the ferry schedule, see http://grandmanan.coastaltransport.ca/. On the island, follow NB 772 west for 6.8 km (4.2 mi), then turn left and continue on that unnamed road for another 4.7 km (2.9 mi). At civic numbers 1500 and 1502, turn left onto a gravel road and follow it for 200 m/yd. The trailhead is located on the left side of the gravel road at a sign that reads "Walk-ins welcome, no vehicles please." Trail markings consist of yellow blazes, and there are also signs at forks and junctions.

Trailhead: 44°57'01"N, 66°58'17"W

The hike: Walk on the wide, grassy trail. At a junction, turn right. This leads to a large shelter or blind that allows wildlife observation. From here, the trail continues on the side of the building along the coastal wooded area. It is marked by yellow signs on trees. Turn right at a T-junction to a lookout. Continue and turn right at another junction, after which the trail soon reaches the road. Turn left and after another 150 m/yd, you reach the gravel road. Turn left again and return to the trailhead. The trail provides interesting views across the Bay of Fundy.

44-49. Campobello Island: Herring Cove Provincial Park and Roosevelt Campobello International Park

Campobello Island is located in the Bay of Fundy opposite the town of Lubec, Maine. The French were the first European settlers, but the British established settlements around 1758. In 1767 the island was granted to Captain William Owen of the Royal Navy. Owen named the island in honour of his donor, governor of Nova Scotia Lord William Campbell. Today, the island of Campobello boasts two parks. The 1,130 hectare (2,800 acre) Roosevelt Campobello International Park was established in 1964 and is jointly administered by Canada and the United States. The main feature of the park is the thirty-four-room summer cottage where Franklin Delano Roosevelt spent most summers during his first forty years. Herring Cove Provincial Park features a large campground, a golf course, hiking trails, a long beach along the bay, and a huge boulder, a souvenir of the last ice age, which formed this area. For more information about the park, call 506-752-7010 or 1-800-561-0123, or check online at www.tourismnewbrunswick.ca/Products/Parks/HerringCoveProvincialPark.aspx.

Both parks can be reached by driving from New Brunswick through the state of Maine. To do so, cross the border at St. Stephen/Calais, then follow Highway 1 (Coastal) south to the town of Whiting. Turn left onto Highway 189 and drive to Lubec. Cross the border back into Canada over the Roosevelt International Bridge. Remember to carry appropriate identification for the border crossings. Alternatively, you can first take a toll-free ferry from Letete, NB, on Route 172 to Deer Island, NB (information for provincial ferries is available at 1-888-747-7006 and at www.deerisland.nb.ca/ferries.htm), and then take the toll ferry to Campobello. The latter trip is only possible between the last week in June and mid-September, when East Coast Ferries, Ltd., operates. For information, refer to the website at https://www.visitcampobello.com/ferry-schedule or call 506-747-2159 or 1-877-747-2159.

Lubec, ME, from Campobello Island

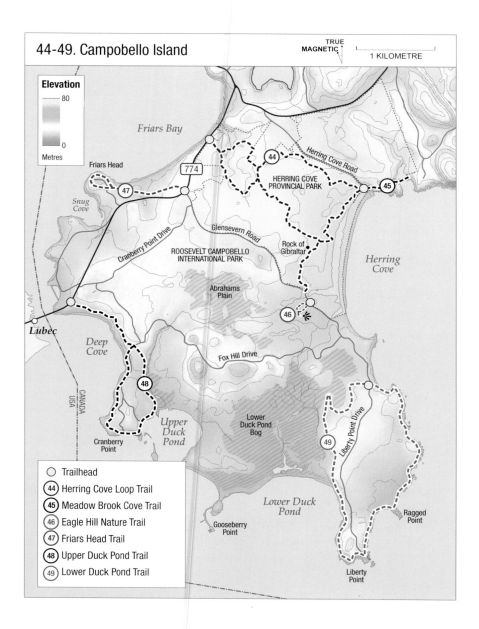

44-49. Campobello Island

TRUE
MAGNETIC
1 KILOMETRE

Elevation

80

0

Metres

Friars Bay

Friars Head

774

47

Snug Cove

44

HERRING COVE
PROVINCIAL PARK

Herring Cove Road

45

Cranberry Point Drive

Glensevern Road

ROOSEVELT CAMPOBELLO
INTERNATIONAL PARK

Rock of
Gibraltar

Herring
Cove

Abrahams
Plain

46

Lubec

Deep
Cove

Fox Hill Drive

48

CANADA
USA

Upper
Duck
Pond

Cranberry
Point

Lower
Duck Pond
Bog

Liberty Point Drive

49

Lower Duck
Pond

Gooseberry
Point

Ragged
Point

Liberty
Point

○ Trailhead

44 Herring Cove Loop Trail

45 Meadow Brook Cove Trail

46 Eagle Hill Nature Trail

47 Friars Head Trail

48 Upper Duck Pond Trail

49 Lower Duck Pond Trail

44. Herring Cove Loop Trail (with side trails to "Rock of Gibraltar," Hubbard Cottage, and Adam's Estate)

Distance: 6.6 km (4.1 mi) including side trails
Type: loop
Difficulty: easy to moderate
Ascent: negligible

Hiking time: 2 hrs 30 min
Map: 21 B/14-15 Campobello
Trail condition: dry, long boardwalk sections, few wet spots
Cellphone coverage: P

Finding the trailhead: Beyond the customs house, follow NB 774 for 3.8 km (2.4 mi). Turn right and stay on NB 774 towards Herring Cove Provincial Park. Keep right at a fork and follow Herring Cove Road to a large parking lot at the beach on Herring Cove. There are quite a few picnic sites and facilities. The trailhead is located to the right of the parking lot. Herring Cove Loop Trail as described here is a combination of a variety of differently named and blazed trails. Almost the entire loop is marked by metal 3" x 3" blazes. In particular, the markings are as follows (in the order they are hiked): the Rock of Gibraltar Trail is red, the Lake Glensevern Trail is blue, the Carriage Road Trail is yellow, the Adams Estate Promenade is orange, and the Herring Cove Trail is purple, and is also named "Beach."

Trailhead: 44°52'30"N, 66°55'45"W

The hike: As the Herring Cove Road ends at the parking lot, turn right and follow the wide, gravelly path that parallels the edge of Lake Glensevern and passes by two pit toilets, picnic sites, and a playground before it continues into the woods. This is where the red-blazed Rock of Gibraltar Trail begins. The rooty trail parallels Lake Glensevern. Cross a woods road, where a trail joins from behind. Turn right and continue on the path that is marked with red and blue blazes as it joins the Lake Glensevern Trail here. Soon the trail reaches a four-way junction. To the left, there is the spur to the "Rock of Gibraltar" formation and the Glensevern Road beyond it; the woods road straight ahead is unmarked, and the trail to the right is the blue-blazed Lake Glensevern Trail.

Spur to "Rock of Gibraltar": After a short distance, the red-blazed trail reaches the "Rock of Gibraltar," a huge rock on the right side of the trail, deposited here during the last ice age. Continue on this trail, which eventually leads to its end at Glensevern Road.

At the junction, turn right onto Lake Glensevern Trail and follow the blue blazes. The trail almost immediately swings to the left, is joined by a wide trail from the left, and leads through a stand of birch trees. At one point, there is a boardwalk around a mud hole. After that, there are a few more mud holes, which can easily be bypassed. The trail then continues through softwoods and reaches a junction. Turn

left onto the yellow-blazed Carriage Road Trail. Almost immediately, the trail leads into softwoods with a remarkable and very pretty moss cover on the ground. At a T-junction, turn left. This part of the loop is blazed in green and yellow as it joins the Friars Bay Trail. A short distance beyond, there is a yellow-blazed turnoff to the right. Ignoring the turnoff, the green-blazed Friars Bay (spur) Trail eventually leads to Hubbard Cottage.

Turn right on the yellow trail and continue on some boardwalk sections. The trail soon reaches a T-junction. The orange-blazed spur to the left is Adam's Estate Promenade with its fine views across Friars Bay, while the main trail departs to the right. It is marked by yellow and orange blazes.

Turn right and follow the yellow- and orange-blazed trail. It crosses a small bridge next to a pond and reaches another T-junction. Turn left and follow the trail, which at one point turns sharply to the right. It leads through some steep gullies and crosses a number of small bridges. After a while, the narrow path ends at a woods road that is used by ATVs. Continue straight on this road and follow the orange blazes. After a short while, the trail ends at the campground near campsite #28. Continue left at the signpost, keeping the grassy field to the right. Turn right at a T-junction (the left leads to the campground entrance), and just before you reach a fork in the gravel road, turn left onto another woods road that is prohibited for cars. This is the Herring Cove Trail, signed Beach. It ends after a short distance at the Herring Cove parking lot.

The main attractions of the trail are the glacial "Rock of Gibraltar" formation, and the vistas from the former Adam's Estate Restaurant and Terrace. The park's visitor centre, the Roosevelt Cottage, and part of the Hubbard Cottage are open to visitors during the summer months.

45. Meadow Brook Cove Trail

Distance: 1 km (0.6 mi) rtn
Type: linear
Difficulty: easy
Ascent: negligible

Hiking time: 15 min rtn
Map: 21 B/14-15 Campobello
Trail condition: dry
Cellphone coverage: N

Finding the trailhead: Beyond the customs house, follow NB 774 for 3.8 km (2.4 mi). Turn right and stay on NB 774 towards Herring Cove Provincial Park. Keep right at a fork and follow Herring Cove Road to a large parking lot at the beach on Herring Cove. There are quite a few picnic sites and facilities. The trailhead is located on the far left of the parking lot. There are no trail markings, but the trail is easy to find.

Trailhead: 44°52'31"N, 66°55'42"W

The hike: Walk up the wide gravel road to the top of a small hill. To the right of the road, there is a vista point across Herring Cove. Continue to the turnaround and the end of the road, and continue straight on a narrow path behind a No Camping sign. The trail ends at a gravel beach. To the left there is a picturesque inland lake, and to the right is Eastern Head Cove.

Beach peas

46. Eagle Hill Nature Trail

Distance: 1 km (0.6 mi)
Type: loop
Difficulty: easy
Ascent: 30 m (100 ft)

Hiking time: 20 min
Map: 21 B/14-15 Campobello
Trail condition: mostly boardwalk, steps
Cellphone coverage: N

Finding the trailhead: From the customs house, continue straight ahead on NB 774 for 2.3 km (1.4 mi). Turn right onto Glensevern Road and follow it for about 2.3 km (1.4 mi). The parking lot and trailhead are located on the right side of the road. There are no trail markings, but the trail is obvious.

Trailhead: 44°51'40" N, 66°56'17" W

The hike: Enter the boardwalk and keep left at a fork. The boardwalk trail leads through the bog. After some distance, a spur departs to the left. Take it and pass the end of the boardwalk. As the ground ascends, the trail swings to the left and climbs a number of steps, which lead to an observation platform. From here, the trail returns to the trailhead. The self-guided walk offers insights into the unique ecosystem of bogs. Furthermore, there are some good views from Eagle Hill across Herring Cove and the rocky islands known as The Wolves.

Pitcher plant

47. Friars Head Trail

Distance: 3 km (1.9 mi) rtn
Type: linear with loop
Difficulty: easy to moderate
Ascent: 20 m (65 ft)

Hiking time: 1 hr rtn
Map: 21 B/14-15 Campobello
Trail condition: dry
Cellphone coverage: N

Finding the trailhead: From the customs house, continue straight ahead on NB 774 for 2.3 km (1.4 mi). Turn left into the large parking lot at the Roosevelt Cottage. The trailhead is located at the far end of the parking lot. There are no trail markings, but the trail is easy to find.

Trailhead: 44°52'27" N, 66°57'38" W

The hike: The wide trail immediately enters the woods and crosses two gravel roads. Once the trail leads out of the woods, it enters an open field and becomes grassy. Turn right at a fork. The trail then enters the woods. At another fork, a spur to the right leads to the beach. At low tide, the solitary rock called Friars Head may be seen.

The main trail takes the left fork and ascends. Once it reaches the top there is a vista point with views across the water towards Maine. The trail continues below the lookout. The trail descends through woods and then reaches a T-junction at a gravel road. Turn right and pass a picnic site; a gravel road joins from the left. After some distance, continue on a grassy trail that departs to the left towards a trail sign. After a short distance, turn right at a T-junction and return to the trailhead. The main features of the trail are the access to the beach, the views towards Eastport, Maine, and the picturesque fields framed by mixed woods.

Fireweed

48. Upper Duck Pond Trail

Distance: 4.8 km (3 mi)
Type: loop
Difficulty: easy
Ascent: negligible

Hiking time: 2 hrs
Map: 21 B/14-15 Campobello
Trail condition: mostly dry
Cellphone coverage: Y

Finding the trailhead: Park at the NB Tourist Information Centre just beyond the FDR Memorial Bridge on the right side of the road. The trailhead is just below the centre towards the bridge and is visible from NB 774. There are no trail markings, but the trail is relatively easy to follow.

Trailhead: 44°51'45" N, 66°58'29" W

The hike: The grassy trail first parallels the road towards the bridge. Keep left; about 15 m/yd beyond an orange navigational sign, the trail turns into the woods. It switchbacks close to the coast and offers occasional views over Deep Cove. There are boardwalk sections across muddy areas. At 1.1 km (0.7 mi) you reach an open field that used to be the location of a fox farm. The trail first crosses the field, then a gravel road, and continues across the field towards the woods.

Upon entering the softwoods, the trail descends, then levels off, keeping a salt marsh to its left. The trail continues on an old woods road. Two small side trails depart to the left to the Lubec Channel at Upper Duck Pond; keep straight. Just beyond a short bridge, you reach a turnaround at the end of a gravel road at Upper Duck Pond. Continue straight on the gravel road to the next parking area and continue on a narrow path at the far left end. The trail leads down to a bench, where it ends. From here on, scramble down the rocks and turn right to walk around the cove to a clearly visible ladder. Walk up the steps to another parking area at Cranberry Point. (In case of high tide or if rock scrambling is not your thing, you can walk on the gravel road instead.) Follow the gravel road straight ahead and walk uphill for some 200 m/yd, where a trail on the left side of the road departs. It is signed Fox Farm.

The trail skirts the bay, and at one point there is a large, white naval structure to the left of the trail. The trail passes another large, orange navigational sign and continues along the bay. The path ends at a dirt road. Turn left onto the dirt road and follow it for some 500 m/yd, at which point you are back at the field where the old fox farm once stood. Return to the NB Tourist Information Centre the same way you came.

49. Lower Duck Pond Trail

Distance: 6 km (3.7 mi)
Type: loop and side trails
Difficulty: easy to moderate
Ascent: 30 m (100 ft)
Hiking time: 2 hrs 30 min

Map: 21 B/14-15 Campobello
Trail condition: rooty, boardwalk sections, some multi-use trails
Cellphone coverage: Y

Finding the trailhead: From the customs building, continue straight ahead on NB 774 for 2.3 km (1.4 mi). Turn right onto Glensevern Road and follow it for about 2.8 km (1.7 mi). Turn right onto Liberty Point Drive and follow it for 0.8 km (0.5 mi) until you reach Raccoon Beach. At this point, the road divides into two roads and you will pass picnic sites and a pit toilet along the way. The trailhead is located at the far left side of the picnic area, just before the divided roads join. Parking is available on a grassy area next to the cliffs to the left of the trailhead. There are no trail markings, but the trail is relatively easy to follow.

Trailhead: 44°51'08"N, 66°55'40"W

The hike: For a short distance, the trail is a grassy, tree-lined wagon road. As it approaches the tip of a peninsula, it narrows considerably and swings to the right with a long pebble beach below. The trail continues up and down and on many boardwalk sections along the cliffs and through softwoods high above the Grand Manan Channel. At one point, a small spur departs to the left and allows a scenic view. Some distance ahead, there is a bench, at which a spur leads to the left for some 300 m/yd to a sculpture at Ragged Point. The trail continues and arrives at 3 km (1.9 mi) at Liberty Point with its fine views.

From here, walk up the road to the right for about 200 m/yd, where a narrow path signed Lower Duck Pond departs to the left; follow it. The path leads up and down, passing a white naval marker and benches, then it reaches a gravel road at Yellow Bank with a picnic table overlooking the bay. Continue along the coast. A long pebble beach becomes visible on the left and, after some distance, the trail ends at the end of a gravel road at Lower Duck Pond. Turn right and walk up the road for a short distance. Then turn left onto a multi-use trail into the woods.

For some distance, this easy trail parallels the gravel road. It then leads into the woods, where blue paint blazes on trees mark the way. The path makes a few sharp turns, indicated by double blazes. After a while, a T-junction is reached. A spur to the left leads for some 200 m/yd to a bench overlooking a bog. Turning right at the junction, the trail ends at the gravel road near the trailhead.

50. Pea Point Trail (Connors Bros. Nature Preserve)

Distance: 1.4 km (0.9 mi) rtn
Type: linear
Difficulty: easy to moderate
Ascent: 20 m (65 ft)
Hiking time: 45 min rtn
Map: 21 G/2 St. George

Trail condition: The main trail is a wide gravel road. Access to the island, a distance of maybe 100 m/yd, may be wet and slippery with rockweed.
Cellphone coverage: Y

Finding the trailhead: Take exit 60 on Highway 1 and follow Route 176 for 9.8 km (6.1 mi) towards Blacks Harbour and Grand Manan. The trailhead is located at a parking lot on the left side of the highway a short distance before entering the large parking lot of the ferry service to Grand Manan. There are no trail markings, but the trail is easy to find.

Trailhead: 45°02'42" N, 66°48'14" W

The hike: From the parking lot, the trail enters the nature preserve through a gate and follows a wide gravel road into the woods. After some distance, it swings to the right. At this point, the top of the lighthouse becomes visible. Follow the grassy road for a while. At some point, a small trail departs to the left to Lumberyard Beach. This is an alternative that follows the beach for a while. The main trail reaches the Bay of Fundy. At low tide it is possible to cross over to Pea Point (for tide tables, refer to http://www.waterlevels.gc.ca/eng/station?type=0&date=2016%2F09%2F04&sid=42&tz=ADT&pres=1). Keep to the right to cross the ocean floor, and ascend the island on its right (northwesterly) side. Above the waterline, some large cement blocks will aid the ascent. Once the top is reached, there is a bridge that leads to the lighthouse. From here, narrow footpaths on the island facilitate further exploration. The trail allows access to a charming island with a lighthouse and marvellous vistas, especially at dawn and dusk.

56. Lighthouse Trail (Hole in the Wall)

51-58. Grand Manan Island

The beautiful island of Grand Manan is located in the Bay of Fundy only a short distance from the coast of Maine. The Passamaquoddy people, who came in summer to collect the eggs of gull, tern, and eider, called it *mun a nouk*, meaning "island in the sea." According to legend, Samuel de Champlain added the word "Grand" to *menan*, the French corruption of the local Indigenous name, for its present name. During the American Revolution, United Empire Loyalists arrived on the island, and most of the current residents are their descendants. Island residents are chiefly employed in the lobster and herring fishing industry, and a modern processing plant is located at Seal Cove. Grand Manan also boasts the dulse (edible seaweed) capital of the world in Dark Harbour. As well, the island is known for its unique geological formation: the east side is volcanic and the west side is sedimentary rock. It is also a destination for birdwatching – about 250 species have been sighted – and whale-watching.

Grand Manan is reached from mainland New Brunswick via Blacks Harbour, an important sardine-processing centre located about 80 km (50 mi) from Saint John. From Saint John, take Highway 1 in a westerly direction and follow it to exit 60, where Route 176 departs to Blacks Harbour and Grand Manan. Follow this road for 10.1 km (6.3 mi) to the ferry terminal.

From there, a 1½-hour toll ferry operates year-round from three to five times daily between Blacks Harbour on the mainland and North Head on Grand Manan. For information regarding ferry schedules, see www.coastal-transport.ca or call their ticket office on North Head at 506-662-3724. For general inquiries about Grand Manan, see the website www.grandmanannb.com or call 1-888-525-1655. A small booklet entitled *Heritage Trails and Footpaths of Grand Manan, New Brunswick, Canada* (Stone, ed.) can be obtained in local gift stores.

51. Net Point Trail (see map p. 139)

Distance: 1.4 km (0.9 mi) rtn
Type: linear
Difficulty: easy
Ascent: negligible
Hiking time: 30 min rtn

Map: 21 B/15 & 21 B/14 (combined),
Campobello Island
Trail condition: rooty, grassy
Cellphone coverage: Y

Finding the trailhead: From the ferry terminal, turn right onto Pettes Cove Road and follow this short dead-end road to the beach. Park just before the road turns to the left at a small gravel lot. There is space for a couple of vehicles. The path enters below a grey house right above the beach. The trailhead is not marked and fairly inconspicuous. The trail is marked by some red metal discs on trees.

Trailhead: 44°45'47"N, 66°44'31"W

The hike: The narrow trail skirts the cliff's edge around the small Net Point peninsula. There are beautiful views towards Swallowtail Lighthouse, Long Island, and the ferry at the terminal. The trail passes below some private houses and ends at a commercial property, which is fenced and to which access is prohibited. The end of the trail is marked by a sign. The main feature of this short trail is its beautiful views.

52. Long Pond Trail (see map p. 132)

Distance: 0.6 km (0.4 mi) rtn
Type: linear
Difficulty: easy
Ascent: negligible

Hiking time: 20 min rtn
Map: 21 B/10 Grand Manan Island
Trail condition: dry
Cellphone coverage: P

Finding the trailhead: At the T-junction just beyond the ferry terminal, turn left onto NB 776 and follow it for 15 km (9.3 mi). Turn left onto Anchorage Road towards the Anchorage Provincial Park. Bear left at a fork onto Long Pond Road (the right fork leads to the campground); 1.6 km (1 mi) after leaving NB 776, the trailhead is located on the left side of the gravel road. There is some parking next to a bench nearby; otherwise there is ample parking a short distance farther down the gravel road. There are no trail markings, but the trail is obvious.

Trailhead: 44°39'39"N, 66°48'06"W

The hike: The short trail is easy to follow. A platform and two blinds allow visitors to observe ducks and other wildlife. The blind that is at the far end of the trail probably allows the best views of the pond.

53. Bagley Trail (see map below)

Distance: 0.8 km (0.5 mi) rtn
Type: linear
Difficulty: easy
Ascent: negligible

Hiking time: 20 min rtn
Map: 21 B/10 Grand Manan Island
Trail condition: dry, grassy
Cellphone coverage: P

Finding the trailhead: At the T-junction just beyond the ferry terminal, turn left onto NB 776 and follow it for 15 km (9.3 mi). Turn left onto Anchorage Road towards the Anchorage Provincial Park. Bear left at a fork onto Long Pond Road (the right fork leads to the campground); the road reaches a large parking lot at the Long Pond Bay. Turn left and continue parallel to the bay for another 0.8 km (0.5 mi). The trailhead is located on the left side of the gravel road. There are five or six parking spaces right next to the trailhead. There are no trail markings, but the trail is obvious.

Trailhead: 44°39'38" N, 66°47'28" W

The hike: The short trail is in the shape of an hourglass and is easy to follow. The trail leads through an interesting short stretch of bog with stunted growth and some softwoods. It also provides some vistas of a salt marsh.

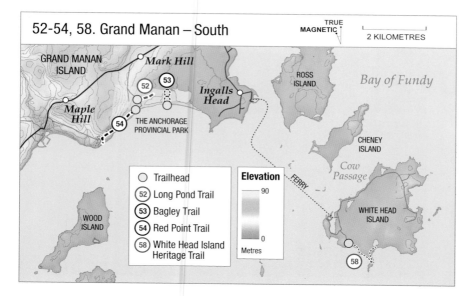

54. Red Point Trail (see map p. 132)

Distance: 3.5 km (2.2 mi) rtn (includes spur to the Red Point Fault)
Type: linear
Difficulty: easy
Ascent: negligible
Hiking time: 1 hr rtn

Map: 21 B/10 Grand Manan
Trail condition: dry, long boardwalk sections, some grassy parts, and a gravel road at the very end.
Cellphone coverage: P

Finding the trailhead: At the T-junction just beyond the ferry terminal, turn left onto NB 776 and follow it for 15 km (9.3 mi). Turn left onto Anchorage Road towards the Anchorage Provincial Park. Bear left at a fork onto Long Pond Road (the right fork leads to the campground) and drive to a T-junction. Turning right at the junction leads directly to a large parking lot. The trailhead is located at the far end of the parking lot right next to a roofed picnic table. The trail cannot be missed.

Trailhead: 44°39'33" N, 66°48'08" W

The hike: At the beginning of the trail on the left, there is a beautiful memorial honouring the sailors who were lost at sea. This nature walk with interpretive signs leads along the bay and provides some views across it. Benches provide moments of relaxation at some nice lookouts along the level path. The Red Point Trail ends at a turnaround next to a dirt road. To see the red-and-grey rock formations, continue straight to a gravel road, turn left, and continue for another 250 m/yd to the coast at a turnaround with picnic tables. To the left is the geological feature that gives the trail its name. A short, steep path provides access to the beach at this point. There are fine views towards Wood Island and across the red and grey rock formations. The key features of this trail are the fine views across the bay to Wood Island. Red Point is geologically significant, as here the boundary between the red sedimentary rocks (about 600 million years old) on the eastern side of the island and the much younger grey basalt lava rocks (about 200 million years) on the western side of the island becomes visible.

55. Flock of Sheep Trail (see map p. 135)

Distance: 6 km (3.7 mi) rtn
Type: linear
Difficulty: moderate
Ascent: 45 m (150 ft)

Hiking time: 2 hrs 30 min rtn
Map: 21 B/10 Grand Manan
Trail condition: dry
Cellphone coverage: Y

Finding the trailhead: From the ferry terminal, follow NB 776 south for about 27.7 km (17.2 mi) to its end at the Southwest Head Lighthouse. About six vehicles can park here. The trailhead is located just south of the foghorn next to the fence. The trail is marked by red metal discs.

Trailhead: 44°36'01" N, 66°54'16 W

The hike: Walk south from the parking lot and take the narrow path across the heath. Dense woods and open areas alternate. When the path reaches a dirt road, turn right onto it and follow it for a short distance. Just before you reach a house, take the trail that turns left into the woods. The trail runs parallel to the coastline and leads to the Lower Flock of Sheep, named for a number of round, whitish boulders that were deposited here during the last ice age. Fishermen likened them to a flock of sheep when seen from the sea. The trail continues along the cliffs and reaches the Upper Flock of Sheep. There are a few steep ups and downs. As the trail rounds Pats Head, you will walk on a flat rock shelf, caused by glacial movement, for a very short distance before the trail leads back into the woods. Soon the trail reaches the road. The trail end is clearly marked on the road itself. From here, you can either return on the same trail or via the paved road, a 1.9 km (1.2 mi) walk. The main features of this trail are the white, rounded granite boulders and the impressive views from the edges of the cliffs along the trail. At times the trail is very close to the edge of the cliffs. Notice the basalt columns, typical of the western part of the island.

The boulders called "Flock of Sheep"

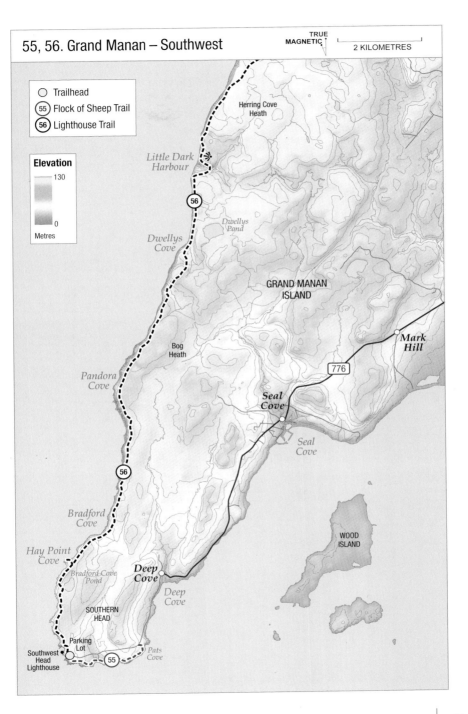

55, 56. Grand Manan – Southwest

TRUE
MAGNETIC

2 KILOMETRES

Legend
- ○ Trailhead
- (55) Flock of Sheep Trail
- (56) Lighthouse Trail

Elevation

130

0

Metres

Herring Cove
Heath

Little Dark
Harbour

(56)

Dwellys
Pond

Dwellys
Cove

GRAND MANAN
ISLAND

Bog
Heath

Mark
Hill

Pandora
Cove

776

Seal
Cove

(56)

Seal
Cove

Bradford
Cove

WOOD
ISLAND

Hay Point
Cove

Bradford Cove
Pond

Deep
Cove

Deep
Cove

SOUTHERN
HEAD

Parking
Lot

Southwest
Head
Lighthouse

(55)

Pats
Cove

56. Lighthouse Trail (in 5 sections) (see maps pp. 135, 139)

Distance: 37.9 km (23.6 mi), one way
Type: linear
Difficulty: moderate to strenuous
Ascent: several steep ascents and descents
Hiking time: 3 days

Maps: 21 B/15 Campobello and 21 B/10 Grand Manan
Trail condition: generally good, rooty and rocky in parts, a few boggy spots; dogs permitted (on leash)
Cellphone coverage: Y, except in some places along the southwest

Summary

Section 1: (Southwest Head Lighthouse via Hay Point to Little Dark Harbour) 13.5 km (8.4 mi), 7 hr 30 min

Section 2: (Little Dark Harbour to Dark Harbour) 6.4 km (4 mi), 3 hrs

Section 3: (Dark Harbour to Indian Beach Junction) 4.5 km (2.8 mi), 2 hrs 15 min; (Indian Beach Junction to The Whistle) 4.3 km (2.7 mi), 2 hrs 15 min

Section 4: (The Whistle to Whale Cove) 5.6 km (3.5 mi), 2 hrs 45 min

Section 5: (Whale Cove via Hole in the Wall to Swallowtail Lighthouse and ferry terminal) 3.6 km (2.2 mi), 2 hrs 15 min

Trailhead: 44°36'04.2" N, 66°54'19.3" W

Finding the trailhead: From the ferry terminal, follow NB 776 south for about 28.3 km (17.6 mi) to its end at the Southwest Head Lighthouse. There is space for about six vehicles. The trailhead is located just north of the foghorn. The trail ends near the Swallowtail Lighthouse. The trail is marked by red metal blazes (3¼" × 4½" rectangles, 3¼" discs, and 1½" discs) as well as orange/red marking tape. Beyond Whale Cove there are red paint blazes on trees. It is strongly advised to watch out for the red blazes and orange marking tape at all times, as there is often a confusing array of ATV trails criss-crossing the terrain. These are muddy and not fit for hiking.

We suggest you either leave your car at the hotel or inn where you spend the night before heading out, or near the ferry terminal. Leighton Spicer provides transportation to the trailhead at Southwest Head Lighthouse; call 506-662-3708 or cellphone at 506-662-4904. Please note that there are no pit toilets on this trail.

The hike:

Section 1: Southwest Head Lighthouse to Little Dark Harbour

From the lighthouse, follow the edge of the cliffs in a northerly direction. There are frequent detours around wet spots on the wide tracks, typically to the left closer to the cliffs, and many spectacular vistas across the Bay of Fundy. A narrow path parallels the muddy tracks. Just before reaching a house at a lake, a wooden sign points left to Spring Rocks and Hay Point. Keep left to Hay Point, crossing a bridge with the help of an installed rope, and later follow the sign to Spring Rock. The path leads to a picnic table, from where you have a grand view of the bay.

Turn right towards Hay Point and Bradford Cove, where the path soon joins the muddy tracks again, with Bradford Pond directly opposite. Turn left and follow the tracks for a very short distance, where another narrow path turns off to the left. (Follow the rule that whenever you see a house, turn left onto a path into the woods.) This junction is easily missed; look out for the red blazes. Keep left at a fork and follow the sign for Red Trail, Hay Point, and Bradford Cove. (The right fork leads to Deep Cove.) After some distance, a short spur to the left leads to Hay Point Overlook with its stunning vista onto Hay Point and the bay. Continuing straight and keeping right at a fork, the trail leads out of the woods onto a grassy field with low conifers. A spur to Hay Point itself keeps to the left, where the trail descends, first gently but soon steeply, to Hay Point. At this point there is a picnic table, and from here whales may be sighted in the bay.

Return to the grassy field and cross it straight to the "sign tree," a tree with numerous signs. Keep straight and follow the trail marked High Road into the woods. Just before you reach an old burn or cut, turn left. This junction is easily missed. After a while, the trail joins the path marked "Lower Road" and continues in a northerly direction. It then descends steeply to cross a brook, which it then follows back towards the coast, passing a house along the way. Continue on the trail, and just before it reaches a cabin, turn left onto a path that leads some 30 m (100 ft) to a lookout (below is Bradford Cove with a herring weir). Then keep left on a very narrow path that parallels the coast (the trail on the right leads to the other side of the island).

Pass a green hut on a clearing high above the water. Walk through a grassy area, then again straight into the woods. Pass by a grey cottage in an area with many buoys in trees, and continue straight. The trail is first wider, but it narrows later. Walking here is mostly good, aside from a few mud holes. There are occasional vistas to the left towards the Maine coastline. A short distance before reaching Big Head, there is a lookout with some rocks in the water far below where seals may be sighted. From here on, walking is good on grassy tracks. The trail is fairly level and there are many spectacular lookouts, such as the view from Big Head south to Hay Point. Eventually, the path joins a deeply rutted ATV track and passes a dilapidated grey house. Continue parallel to the coast. The trail continues for a while in this fashion. Follow the red blazes as the trails swings to the right. For some distance the trail is very muddy. Pass a turnoff to the right and later another to the left of the red Teddy Bear Trail house; the main trail continues straight.

Shortly after the house, the trail turns off the ATV tracks to the left. Don't miss it! Watch out for the red blazes in this area, and be prepared to backtrack if you have not seen them for a while. After a while, the trail reaches a brook. Follow it for a short distance, then cross it. Continue straight/left at a marked junction towards Dark Harbour and Dwellys Pond (Big Pond); the wide path to the right leads to Seal Cove on the other side of the island. The left trail continues through woods, passes a swamp, crosses a brook (which can usually be accomplished on rocks), leads down a steep hill, where some ropes have been installed to guide hikers, keeps right at a fork, and ascends. It eventually reaches grassy fields and areas with pretty ferns (camping is good in this area), crosses a wide spur to the cliffs on the left, and continues parallel to a dirt road on its right. After a short distance, there is another wide access road to the cliffs. Continue straight towards Dark Harbour (the right leads to Dwellys Pond). Finally, the trail descends and reaches a brook at Little Dark Harbour.

Section 2: Little Dark Harbour to Dark Harbour

Cross the brook, and at a T-junction with ATV tracks, keep to the left and continue through woods. Turn left at another fork. At a three-way fork with a large beech tree, keep left. The trail climbs and reaches a first lookout over Little Dark Harbour with primitive benches. Just beyond, there is another lookout over the bay near a cabin with benches high on the cliff. The trail follows the tracks directly in front of the cabin, then starts to climb and continues through woods, where it is well marked. The trail descends for a short while, then levels off. Walking is easy in this area of mature beech and birch trees, apart from some ATV mud holes.

At some point the trail makes a ninety-degree turn to the left while wide tracks continue straight; keep close to the coast. After some ups and downs, the trail reaches the upper lookout, providing the most spectacular view of Dark Harbour. The trail then descends, following a sign marked Main Road, and reaches the lower lookout. The vista is close to the cliffs; access to the rim is very steep and slippery, and extreme caution is advised. Beyond the lookout, the trail continues to descend steeply and reaches Dark Harbour Brook. This is the first reliable source of water. The brook

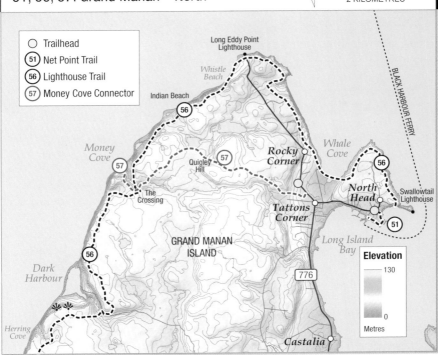

TRUE
MAGNETIC
2 KILOMETRES

○ Trailhead
51 Net Point Trail
56 Lighthouse Trail
57 Money Cove Connector

Long Eddy Point
Lighthouse

Whistle
Beach

BLACK HARBOUR FERRY

Indian Beach

56

Money
Cove

57

Quigley
Hill

57

Rocky
Corner

Whale
Cove

56

North
Head

Swallowtail
Lighthouse

The
Crossing

Tattons
Corner

51

56

GRAND MANAN
ISLAND

Long Island
Bay

776

Elevation
— 130

Dark
Harbour

0

Metres

Herring
Cove

Castalia

must be forded. At times, it may be possible to cross the brook on rocks. The trail then ascends and reaches a large parking lot at the road to Dark Harbour.

Section 3: Dark Harbour to The Whistle

The trail continues on the other side of the road some 200 m/yd to the right, well to the right of the end of the steep cliffs. There is a wooden sign mounted on a tree that reads Red Trail. The trail gains altitude quickly, then levels off with some ups and downs. After some time, a junction is reached. The trail to the left continues towards Money Cove, Indian Beach, and The Whistle, while the blue-blazed ATV trail to the right leads inland. Here, the trail is narrow and walking is excellent. The trail continues through woods along the cliffs with good views across the bay. It then passes a beaver pond, ascends, levels off, continues through ferns, and turns inland, away from the shoreline. As the trail descends, it crosses a seasonal brook, climbs for a very short distance, and keeps left at a junction. Shortly after, turn right at a fork towards North Head. The trail then turns left again, almost immediately turns right, and crosses a wooden bridge. At the time of writing, the bridge across a small stream and pond is in pretty rough shape. If it is no longer usable, it is best to cross the brook some 100 m/yd downstream (towards the left).

The trail then reaches another four-way junction at Money Cove Junction. To the left, there is access to the beach at Money Cove, while the wide trail to the right leads to the other side of the island. Continue straight towards North Head, but *immediately* turn left after some 6 m (20 ft), following a sign pointing towards The Whistle. This junction is not obvious, particularly due to a flurry of signs that are irrelevant

---

Dark Harbour Dulse

Dulse, a reddish-purple edible seaweed, has a long history. Its use dates back at least to tenth-century Ireland, where monks reportedly harvested seaweed. Three centuries later, Icelandic sagas report of sinister characters who gave dulse in milk to heroes to lull them into sleep so that they could kill them. Later, dulse was sold at the Irish Galway market as an excellent remedy for a hangover! Today, dulse is an important crop in the tiny settlement of Dark Harbour, the "dulse capital of the world." Dulse is harvested every two weeks between June and September by pickers, who clamber over slippery rocks and haul away the harvest in flat-bottom boats. On land, the crop is put through a shaker to remove shell pieces before being spread thinly on a net to let it dry. The product is then rolled into large bales and packaged for sale. Today, sun-dried dulse is eaten as a healthy snack or ground into powder as a condiment, seasoning, or medicinal or dietary supplement. It is high in vitamins A and B6, iron, fluoride, potassium, and iodine, and relatively low in sodium.

Beals Eddy Pond

for our purpose (e.g., the yellow signs pointing straight ahead to North Head). The trail first climbs before reaching a sign in the woods that reads Whistle Light via Indian Beach. The trail continues to climb through dense woods. It is fairly rocky, and it stays close to the ravine with Money Cove at its end. The narrow path is rocky and leads through ferns.

It eventually reaches an outcropping high above Money Cove with a bench. On the slope across at the south side of Money Cove, one can see a nice stand of mature maples. The trail then swings to a northeasterly direction and stays close to the cliffs high above the coast. Caution is advised, as the trail sometimes leads very close to the cliffs. Look down onto a lagoon with driftwood. This is Beals Eddy Pond. The trail then descends steeply into a rocky and muddy ravine. Once out of the dense woods, look back onto Beals Eddy Pond. The trail skirts the cliffs before it descends and turns inland away from the coast. It crosses a brook and reaches a T-junction. The trail to the left leads down to Indian Beach; continue straight/right on what is marked Coastal Trail. A short distance beyond, keep left at a clearly marked fork. The trail climbs steeply at first and then levels off, but it climbs and descends sometimes, stays at some distance from the cliffs, and reaches a lookout with a great view of The Whistle lighthouse and Northern Head. There is some spectacular camping in this area. From here, the narrow and rocky path descends. The trail reaches a narrow clearing, turns right for a very short distance, and then turns left again into the woods. After some distance, the trail crosses underneath some power lines, turns sharply to the left, and follows the lines down towards the bay to a junction. Turn right and walk up the paved road to the lighthouse.

Swallowtail Lighthouse

Section 4: The Whistle to Whale Cove

Walk up to the The Whistle lighthouse and its adjacent helicopter pad, where just in front of it the narrow path continues. This part is the Thomas B. Munro Memorial Shoreline. Ascend the cliffs and look across The Bishop formation, a lichen-covered rock in the shape of a man with a cape. The trail goes up and down and is very rocky and rooty in this area. At some point, a narrow spur to the left leads steeply down to The Bishop formation. A short distance beyond, keep right at a marked junction towards Ashburton Head; the steep trail to the left leads down to the shore. There are more steep ups and downs in the area, and one really steep descent can be managed with installed ropes. The trail then crosses the now overgrown site of an old burn. A spur to the left leads to the Ashburton Head lookout, a rocky outcrop with some views.

The trail then turns into a grassy woods road that leads away from the bay. At a T-junction, turn left onto a bigger woods road. After some distance, the trail turns off to the left onto a smaller path that leads to the Eel Brook Falls, the second re-liable source of water along the trail. This is a great place to rest and even camp. Some distance upstream, the trail crosses the brook, turns left, and leads through a former burn site at Ashburton Head. At a T-junction, turn left towards Whale Cove (the right trail with its blue blazes leads to Whistle Road). Here begins the Seven Days Work Cliff Nature Preserve. The path crosses a small grassy field and descends through alders and birches. Keep right at a fork (the left fork leads down steeply to Eel Brook Beach). The trail ascends and passes some claim lines. At one point, a very large access road allows access to the cliffs; the path continues directly across. Pass by a huge wooden cottage. In this area, there are some nice views of Ashburton Head, Seven Days Work, and North Head from a bench here. Cross two streams and a waterfall on rocks, keep to the left after the second stream, and continue along the coast. Turn right at a T-junction with a dirt road, keep straight at a marked four-way junction, and turn off to the left before reaching a house. The trail follows the coastline and reaches Whale Cove at a boat launch. Here, you will have a great opportunity to stock up on fresh water at a spout.

Section 5: Whale Cove via Hole in the Wall to Swallowtail Lighthouse

Walk along the pebble beach for some 500 m/yd to the end of Cemetery Road and the continuation of the trail towards Swallowtail Lighthouse. From here, the narrow path skirts the cove. At some point, the trail turns to the right onto a grassy woods road. The road swings left, and a clearly marked path departs to the left to the Hole in the Wall, a spectacular rock formation with a hole in the middle that protrudes into the bay. (Notice that from this point onward, the trail passes through private land and development. At the time of writing, access to the trail described here is free, walking the inland section requires a day pass.)

Continue in a northeasterly direction and keep left at a junction that descends steeply. The right fork leads to an old airfield on private property. The views from Fish Head, a rocky outcrop at the northernmost point of North Head, are spectacular. From here, the trail still hugs the coastline, passing by a multitude of private campsites in the Hole in the Wall Park & Campground. Follow the red paint blazes. At Cliff 26, a wide grassy trail leads just above Cliffs 27 to 34. At Cliff 34, leave the grassy trail and follow the red trail to campsite 34 and farther into coastal woods.

Soon the trail gets into the open at the shoreline, and Swallowtail Lighthouse becomes visible directly. At a T-junction with a grassy woods road, turn right and reach the end of the trail. Turning left leads to Swallowtail Lighthouse and its grounds, a vista not to be missed. Turning right leads to a T-junction. Turn left onto the Old Airport Road. The road ends at yet another T-junction. Turn right onto Pettes Cove Road and reach the ferry terminal after a short distance.

This coastal trail leads from the southernmost lighthouse via the northernmost lighthouse to the picturesque Swallowtail Lighthouse. It passes by such idyllic places as Hay Point, lookouts to Little Dark Harbour, Dark Harbour, Beals Eddy Pond, and Eel Brook Falls, as well as the interesting Hole in the Wall formation on the northeastern coast. The occasional bench and picnic table invite one to rest and take in a vista.

57. Money Cove Connector (see map p. 139)

Distance: 5.1 km (3.2 mi) one way
Type: linear
Difficulty: moderate
Ascent: 130 m (430 ft)

Hiking time: 1 hr 30 min one way
Map: 21 B/15 Campobello Island
Trail condition: wet spots, rocky, rooty
Cellphone coverage: P

Finding the trailhead: From the North Head ferry terminal, follow NB 776 for 1.4 km (0.9 mi), then turn right onto Whistle Road. Follow this road for 500 m/yd, then turn left into Alexandra Park, a playground and nearby baseball diamond/dog park. There is plenty of parking. The trailhead is located on the right side of the lot next to a small building. Most of the trail is marked by yellow discs on trees as well as some wooden arrows nailed to trees. Due to the multitude of trails and tracks that criss-cross the island, it is mandatory that hikers follow the trail description closely and watch for the yellow blazes.

Trailhead: 44°46'06"N, 66°46'05"W

The hike: The main function of this trail is to provide access to the Lighthouse Trail. It enables hikers who started at the Southwestern Head to exit the trail at The Crossing without walking to The Whistle, Whale Cove, and the Hole in the Wall. On the other hand, if hikers start the Lighthouse Trail at Swallowtail, they could shorten their walk and get out at The Crossing via the Money Cove Connector.

From the trailhead at the playground at Alexandria Park to The Crossing at Money Cove: The wide trail ascends gently. Ignore some smaller side trails departing to the right and follow the yellow blazes. Continue straight at a fork. After some distance, the trail is joined by a woods road from the left. Follow the wide dirt road for some distance, then turn off to the right. Keep left at a fork and turn left at an intersection. Keep right at another fork, cross straight underneath power lines, and keep right at a fork directly after. Walk straight across a woods road, and follow the sign for North Trail and Money Cove. In this area, there are wet areas and the trail is quite rocky and rooty. Keep right at a fork and walk straight across a clearing with a confusing array of trails. Soon there is a sign to the left pointing to Quigley Hill. This spur is overgrown and can be ignored.

The trail continues slightly to the right and descends. It then turns right on a wide grassy road. It follows the road for some distance, then turns left at an inconspicuous fork off the four-wheel track. There is a sign for Little Eel Lake. The actual lake can be seen to the right. Another trail joins from behind on the left. At a T-junction, turn left and follow the sign to Money Cove. At what looks like another T-junction, continue straight onto a narrow path. In this area, the trail is mossy and often wet.

There are only a few small yellow disks, but the wide trail cannot be missed. The trail crosses a wide grassy trail and reaches a junction named The Crossing just beyond a sign that points backwards towards North Head via Quigley Hill. Hikers who want to continue on the Lighthouse Trail in a northerly direction will make a sharp right turn just before reaching The Crossing, while those who want to continue in a southerly direction will walk straight through The Crossing. (Hikers can also access Money Cove by turning to the right at The Crossing. It is a 40-minute return trail. The Money Cove has its name because the pirate Captain William Kidd presumably buried treasure here.)

From The Crossing to the playground at Alexandria Park: From The Crossing, the trail ascends and keeps to the right at a fork (the left fork is the Lighthouse Trail towards The Whistle on Northern Head), following the sign towards North Head via Quigley Hill. The trail soon passes a wide grassy trail. There are few yellow metal disks in this area, but the trail is obvious here. The trail then climbs and swings to the right. It continues to a clearing and turns weakly to the right. It then leads straight across a small open area. Soon after, turn right at a clearly marked junction. Keep left at a fork, following a wooden arrow. Pass by a sign indicating Little Eel Lake, which can be seen on the left. In an open forest, keep slightly to the right. The trail then swings to the right onto a grassy woods road. After some distance, turn off the wide trail to the left. Very soon thereafter, the trail turns right. This spot is not obvious. This area is overgrown, so hikers need to pay close attention to the blazes. After some distance,

there is a sign pointing right to Quigley Hill. Continue straight and, after some distance, turn right onto a clearing. Keep right at a fork, and walk straight through a major junction. Directly after crossing underneath power lines, keep left at a fork. At some point, a wide trail joins from behind on the right. Walk straight through a junction and keep right at a fork. The trail then joins a wide woods road and continues to the left. Keep left at a fork, and immediately thereafter left again at another fork. From here, the trail continues to the playground at Alexandria Park.

The main feature of the trail is to provide access to and from the Lighthouse Trail.

Trail markers

Long Point lighthouse

58. White Head Island Heritage Trail (see map p. 132)

Distance: 6.6 km (4.1 mi) rtn
Type: linear
Difficulty: easy to moderate
Ascent: negligible
Hiking time: 2 hrs 30 min rtn
Map: 21B/10 Grand Manan
Trail condition: The first part of the beach consists of large pebbles, which make for unpleasant walking. It gets better beyond the lighthouse, where the trail above the beach is grassy. Alternatively, it is possible to walk on the beach most of the way.
Cellphone coverage: Y

Finding the trailhead: From the ferry terminal on Grand Manan, turn left onto NB 776 and follow it for 12.3 km (7.7 mi). Turn left onto Ingalls Head Road and follow it for 3.3 km (2.1 mi). This leads directly to the terminal of the toll-free ferry to White Head Island. For the ferry schedule, see http://whitehead.coastaltransport.ca/schedule.html. The capacity of the ferry is ten to fourteen vehicles, depending on size. From the ferry terminal on White Head Island, turn right onto White Head Road and follow it for 0.4 km (0.2 mi), then turn left onto Long Point Road to its end at the beach. A few parking spaces can be found here. There are a few red metal disks above the beach, but since the trail follows the beach, it cannot be missed.

Trailhead: 44°37'12"N, 66°43'05"W

The hike: At the end of the road, turn left and follow Battle Beach towards the Long Point Lighthouse, which can be seen in the distance. It may be easier to walk on the beach rather than the wide rocky road above the beach. At the lighthouse, the trail turns to the left and follows the long Sandy Cove. At its end at an outcrop, climb up a few rocks on a gently sloping beach and follow the shoreline to a bench just above the beach. This site affords beautiful views across the Bay of Fundy. The trail ends here. It is possible to continue beyond this point and there are even a few blazes, but the trail is so badly churned up by ATVs that walking is a struggle rather than a pleasure. The main features of this trail are the long sandy beaches, the chance to see the shorebirds that typically frequent the area, and the Long Point Lighthouse.

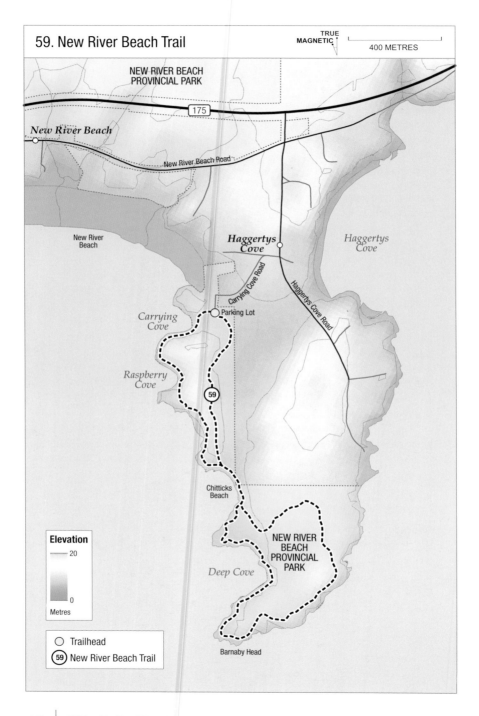

59. New River Beach Trail

TRUE
MAGNETIC

400 METRES

NEW RIVER BEACH
PROVINCIAL PARK

175

New River Beach

New River Beach Road

New River
Beach

Haggertys
Cove

Haggertys
Cove

Carrying Cove Road

Haggertys Cove Road

Carrying
Cove

Parking Lot

Raspberry
Cove

59

Chitticks
Beach

Elevation

—— 20

NEW RIVER
BEACH
PROVINCIAL
PARK

0

Metres

Deep Cove

○ Trailhead

59 New River Beach Trail

Barnaby Head

59. New River Beach Trail

Distance: 5 km (3.1 mi)
Type: loop
Difficulty: easy
Ascent: negligible
Hiking time: 1 hr 40 min
Map: 21 G/2 St. George

Trail condition: rooty, generally dry, some wet spots at tip of peninsula and bog, long boardwalk.
Cellphone coverage: Y
Fee: in season

Finding the trailhead: From the junction of Highways 1 and 7 in Saint John West, take Highway 1 west for about 26 km (16.1 mi). Take exit 86, turn left at the T-junction, and follow Route 175 west. Turn right after 0.9 km (0.6 mi), and continue on Route 175 west for 7.1 km (4.4 mi). Turn left, and after 0.6 km (0.4 mi) turn right onto Carrying Cove Road. After another 300 m/yd you will reach the parking lot. The trailhead is located at the far left of the parking lot. There are no trail markings, but the trail is obvious.

Trailhead: 45°07'50"N, 66°31'32"W

The hike: The trail first leads to a small beach on Carrying Cove. Turn left and left again onto a wide, groomed gravel trail, which continues on extensive boardwalk sections to Raspberry Cove and then to Deadmans Cove. Continue to gravelly Chitticks Beach, where the trail reaches a meadow. The trail continues to skirt the Bay of Fundy. Keep right at a fork and follow the trail along the rugged coast. (The trail will later return to the fork.)

Continue straight ahead at Deep Cove; the trail to the left is a shortcut leading to a bog. At Barnaby Head a bell buoy can be heard that warns skippers of the dangerous waters. Beyond Barnaby Head platform, the trail continues parallel to, but at a short distance away from, the coast, with some very short side trails leading to spectacular lookouts at sheer cliffs. As soon as the trail turns inland, the terrain transforms from a windswept coastal forest to a bog. Beyond the bog, the trail continues through the forest, with a spur to the left connecting it to the coast. Back at the clearing at Chitticks Beach, the trail crosses to the far right of the clearing, where it turns left again. At one point, a short but wide boardwalk to the right leads to a nice lookout overlooking another bog. Continue straight across a tiny covered bridge before it reaches the parking lot. The main features of this trail are the spectacular coastline with its shore life – barnacles, sea urchins, rock crabs, and sand dollars. The bog is notable for its dwarf conifers, insect-eating pitcher plants, sundews, and Labrador tea.

60. Five Fathom Hole Trail

Distance: 9.4 km (5.8 mi) round trip [plus 800 m/yd rtn spur to Butler Creek Beach]
Type: linear
Difficulty: moderate
Ascent: 30 m (100 ft), some steep ups and downs
Hiking time: 3 hrs 45 min + 15 min for spur to Butler Creek Beach
Map: 21 G/1 Musquash
Trail condition: Boardwalks and bridges across creeks and muddy sections. The trail is very rooty and there are some wet spots.
Cellphone coverage: Y

Finding the trailhead: From the intersection of Highways 1 and 7 in Saint John West, follow Highway 1 in a westerly direction for 10 km (6.2 mi) and take exit 103 (Prince of Wales). Turn left at the T-junction, follow the road for 0.6 km (0.4 mi), and turn left at stop sign onto Five Fathom Hole Road. Follow the road, which swings to the right at 1.5 km (0.9 mi). It reaches a parking lot on the left side of the road at 2.1 km (1.3 mi). The trailhead is located at the far end of the parking lot. The trail is well marked by 5" × 2¾" red metal blazes. There are additional yellow blazes when the trail makes a sharp turn.

Trailhead: 45°11'31"N, 66°15'18"W

The hike: The trail immediately enters softwoods and descends. It continues for about 1 km (0.6 mi) until it reaches a fork. The right fork leads for some 400 m/yd through raspberry bushes to Butler Creek Beach. From here, you can get a glimpse of the Musquash Marine Protected Area. Back at the fork, the main trail takes the left fork and continues straight. The trail leads through mixed forest and passes along a beach, and then it follows the coast with occasional spurs to vista points. There are many ups and downs in the area, some of them fairly steep. The trail then reaches another beach, follows it to its end at the opposite side, and again enters the woods. At some point, huge rocks become visible to the left of the trail. The trail then reaches a T-junction. Turn right, and after some distance, the trail reaches its end at the Musquash Estuary, overlooking the water to Musquash Island and the west side of the estuary. The trail through this 1,700 hectare (4,200 acre) protected area features typical coastal woods with views of and across the Musquash Marine Protected Area. Some further details can be found at http://www.natureconservancy.ca/en/where-we-work/new-brunswick/our-work/musquash_estuary_coastal_trails_completed.html.

61. Black Beach Trail

Distance: 4.2 km (2.6 mi)
Type: loop
Difficulty: easy to moderate
Ascent: 30 m (100 ft)
Hiking time: 1 hr 40 min

Map: 21 G/1 Musquash
Trail condition: rooty, a few wet spots, a few steep ascents and descents
Cellphone coverage: Y

Finding the trailhead: From the intersection of Highways 1 and 7 in Saint John West, follow Highway 1 in a westerly direction for 1.4 km (0.9 mi) and take exit 112 (Lorneville). Turn left at the T-junction and follow the King William Road for 8 km (5 mi). Keep right (the left fork leads to the Coleson Cove Generating Station) and follow the road for another 2.6 km (1.6 mi) to the end of the road at Black Beach. Parking is available for about eight vehicles. The trailhead is located on the far right of the parking lot. The trail is well marked by 5" × 2¾" red metal blazes. There are additional yellow blazes when the trail makes a sharp turn.

Trailhead: 45°09'17" N, 66°13'41" W

The hike: From the parking lot, the wide trail ascends for a short distance to a plateau. The actual trail starts behind a large sign at the top of metal stairs. Descend the stairs and immediately enter the woods. The trail winds through coastal forest to a vista point that overlooks Musquash Estuary. From here, the trail continues to snake through forest until it reaches another vista point

that overlooks Frenchmans Creek. The trail ascends and continues to wind through woods until it reaches a wide grassy area. Shortly beyond, it ends at a T-junction with the spur that led to the plateau. Turn left and return to the parking lot. The trail features a coastal forest with occasional vistas across the Musquash Marine Protected Area and Frenchmans Creek Estuary. Some further details can be found at http://www.natureconservancy.ca/en/where-we-work/new-brunswick/our-work/musquash_estuary_coastal_trails_completed.html.

Fundy Coast – East

TRUE
MAGNETIC
50 KILOMETRES

Northumberland Strait

SAINT JOHN
RIVER VALLEY

ACADIAN
COAST

Shediac

79

Minto

Moncton

77
78

81-82

Cape
Tortmentine

Peticodiac

**FUNDY
COAST –
EAST**

75-76

80

Sackville

Oromocto
Gagetown

73-74

69-70

64-68

Alma

NOVA SCOTIA

71-72

FUNDY
NATIONAL
PARK

62-63

FUNDY COAST
WEST

Saint John

Bay of Fundy

FUNDY COAST – EAST

The eastern Fundy Coast boasts the world's highest tides, which can vary as much as 16 m (52.5 ft), the height of a four-storey house, between high and low tide. Another amazing sight are the tens of thousands of migratory shorebirds that stop here to feed on the tidal flats around Dorchester and St. Marys Point in the summer. The scenic Fundy Coast east of the town of St. Martins features high cliffs, sandy beaches, pebble beaches, and caves. The Fundy Parkway is a stretch of coastal wilderness that has stunning vistas. From the Parkway at Big Salmon River, the rugged Fundy Footpath leads experienced backpackers over numerous mountains and streams along the coast, but mostly through woods to Fundy National Park.

The biggest city of this region is Moncton, New Brunswick's largest. It was named in honour of Colonel Robert Monckton, commander of the British forces that in 1755 captured Fort Beauséjour, which was subsequently called Fort Cumberland. Later, the French name was revived and is still in use today. Moncton is home of New Brunswick's first multi-day hiking trail, i.e., the Dobson Trail, which runs from Moncton-Riverview to Fundy National Park.

The university town of Sackville in southeastern New Brunswick is located near the centre of a marshland that has been reclaimed from the sea. In the early days, the Acadians accomplished that task by building aboiteaux, systems of dikes and dams. In Sackville's centre is the famous Waterfowl Park, a sanctuary for birds, frogs, and muskrats.

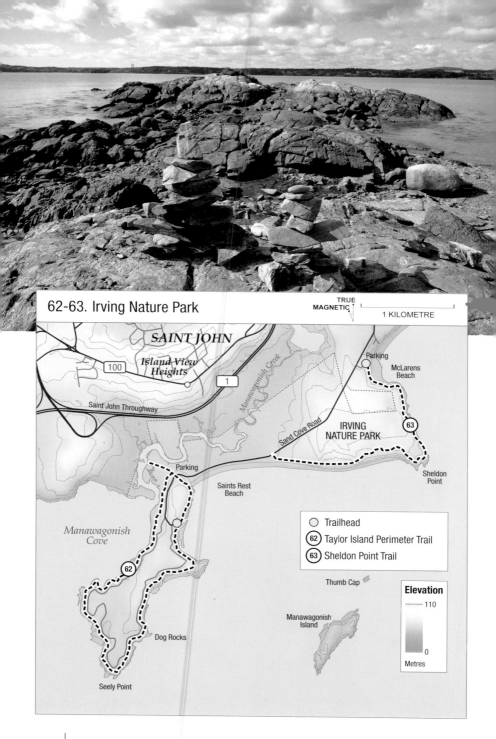

62-63. Irving Nature Park

TRUE
MAGNETIC

1 KILOMETRE

SAINT JOHN

Island View
Heights

100

1

Manawagonish Creek

Saint John Throughway

Parking

McLarens
Beach

Sand Cove Road

IRVING
NATURE
PARK

63

Parking

Saints Rest
Beach

Sheldon
Point

Manawagonish
Cove

62

○ Trailhead

62 Taylor Island Perimeter Trail

63 Sheldon Point Trail

Thumb Cap

Elevation

110

Dog Rocks

Manawagonish
Island

0

Metres

Seely Point

62. Taylor Island Perimeter Trail

Distance: 7 km (4.3 mi)
Type: loop
Difficulty: easy
Ascent: negligible
Hiking time: 2 hrs 15 min

Map: 21 G/1 Musquash (specialized leaflets available at park)
Trail condition: very well maintained
Cellphone coverage: Y

Finding the trailhead: Approaching Saint John from the west on Highway 1, take exit 119 A-B to the Reversing Falls. Turn right at the traffic light onto Bleury Street for 0.4 km (0.2 mi), and turn right again onto Sand Cove Road. Follow this road for 3.1 km (1.9 mi) until the pavement ends at a sign for the Irving Nature Park. Continue on the dirt road for another 0.8 km (0.5 mi), to where the road forks and starts to ascend; bear to the right onto a one-way road. Continue for another 0.6 km (0.4 mi) to a fork. Turn left into a parking lot just above an information pavilion. From here, walk up a few wooden steps to the upper parking lot. The trail starts on the far right, next to the cliff. There are no blazes and only occasional signs, but for the most part the trail is obvious. Be advised that the park is usually open from early May to mid-October from 8 a.m. to 8 p.m. To confirm, call 506-653-7367.

Trailhead: 45°13'09" N, 66°07'46" W

The hike: The trail, marked as Seal Trail, parallels the rocky coast of the Bay of Fundy and the gravel road; note the abandoned herring weir. At an outcrop, there are some short spur trails; keep to the right. The trail continues along the peninsula and looks out over the beach far below the cliff. At some point, the trail becomes the Heron Trail. The footpath winds along the cliffs until at 2.7 km (1.7 mi) it reaches the south-western tip of Taylor Island, where a lookout provides views of the bay.

From here, the trail rounds the peninsula, and the cliffs are no longer so steep. Keep left at a fork. When the trail reaches a road, turn left and walk along the beach. Towards the end of the beach at a Heron sign, turn to the right away from the beach (it is easy to miss). Once in the woods, make a left turn (continuing straight leads to facilities). Before the trail reaches the road again, it turns off to the left. The trail continues along the coast, passes a few beaches, and leads along mud flats, where shorebirds stop to feed during the fall migration. In case of doubt, keep to the left. One of the shortcuts, named Frog Trail, departs to the right. At 5.8 km (3.6 mi), a long boardwalk departs to the left into the Saints Rest Marsh.

Continuing straight, the path crosses a dirt road, passes a facility, and ascends. It crosses another dirt road and heads into the woods. The trail passes straight through a four-way intersection with an old woods road (the trail to the left leads down to the lower parking lot) and continues along the cliffs. After a short distance, the trail reaches the upper parking lot and completes the loop.

View of Sheldon Point

63. Sheldon Point Trail

Distance: 8 km (4.9 mi) rtn
Type: linear
Difficulty: easy to moderate
Ascent: negligible

Hiking time: 1 hr 20 min rtn
Map: 21 G/1 Musquash
Trail condition: dry
Cellphone coverage: Y

Finding the trailhead: Entering Saint John from the west on Highway 1, take exit 119 A-B to the Reversing Falls. Turn right at the stop sign onto Bleury Street for 0.4 km (0.2 mi), and turn right again onto Sand Cove Road. Follow this road for 1.7 km (1.1 mi). On the left side of the road is a sign welcoming visitors to the Irving Nature Park. In season, there is parking here for about twenty vehicles. The trailhead is located at the far end of the lot next to a big barn. The gates of the parking lot are locked in the evening. After hours, parking is alongside the road. There are occasional wooden signs with green arrows, but the trail is obvious and cannot be missed.

Trailhead: 45°14'07"N, 66°06'15"W

The hike: The wide, gravelly trail descends from the barn, turns right, and leads into the woods. The path ascends and continues high above the Fundy Coast through mixed woods. At about the halfway mark, the trail enters an open field at Sheldon Point. (At this point, you may retrace your steps and return or continue.) The trail soon reaches the end of a dirt road next to a pit toilet. It enters the woods straight ahead, then turns sharply to the right into an open area, where it ends at a dirt road. Turn left onto the dirt road, which soon leads to a large gravel pit, continues through it, and then turns left and descends to the beach. It continues along the sandy cliffs and the bay to its end at a parking lot. This part of the trail may be impassable during high tide. Should you get surprised by the incoming tide, you need to scramble up the steep cliffs and make your way through alders. From the trail end, you can either retrace your steps or turn right onto the paved road and return to the parking lot.

64. Flowerpot Rock Footpath

64-68. FUNDY TRAIL PARKWAY and FUNDY FOOTPATH

The Fundy Trail Parkway makes previously remote coastal areas of stunning natural beauty along the Bay of Fundy accessible to the general public. The Fundy Trail Parkway and adjoining Fundy Footpath encompass a 2 km (1.2 mi) wide corridor (1 km [0.6 mi] of land and 1 km [0.6 mi] into the Bay of Fundy) stretching from Fownes Beach east of St. Martins to the western boundary of Fundy National Park. Most of the ecosystem dynamics of the Bay of Fundy exist within this corridor, including salt marshes, tidal flats, and the dramatic Fundy tides. The Fundy Trail Parkway leads as far as Tufts Point, a good distance beyond the Fundy Trail Interpretive Centre at Big Salmon River, and is paralleled by a multi-use trail. This section will describe only those trails that are exclusively footpaths. The parkway also provides access to the Fundy Footpath. For more information, call 1-866-386-3987 or check out the websites at http://fundytrailparkway.com/en/the_fundy_footpath/ and http://fundyfootpath.info/trip-planning/. Typically, the Fundy Trail is open from mid-May to mid-October, but call to ensure. There is a per-person fee to enter the parkway.

Finding the trailhead: On Highway 1, take exit 137 to the Fundy Trail, St. Martins, and the airport. Turn onto Route 111 east and follow this road for 39.1 km (24.3 mi) to St. Martins. At a gas station, turn right onto Main Street, which leads through a covered bridge. Pass the sea caves and keep right at a fork to Little Beach Road. After another 4.1 km (2.5 mi), you reach the pay station at the entrance to the Fundy Trail. Distances to all trails along this trail are measured from here.

64. Flowerpot Rock Footpath

Distance: 3 km (1.9 mi) rtn
Type: linear
Difficulty: easy
Ascent: 30 m (100 ft)

Hiking time: 1 hr
Map: 21 H/6 Salmon River
Trail condition: grassy, dry
Cellphone coverage: N

Finding the trailhead: From the entrance station of the Fundy Trail, drive 0.9 km (0.6 mi) to the Fownes Head parking lot on the south side of the road. The trail starts right there and cannot be missed.

Trailhead: 45°23'11" N, 65°27'22" W

The hike: The trail first descends on wooden steps, then continues its slight descent through woods to two beautiful vistas overlooking flowerpot formations formed by the Bay of Fundy. The grassy, level path skirts the bay through wildflowers and lower brush vegetation, then enters woods lined with fern and reaches a junction with a multi-use trail at a turnaround at 1.5 km (0.9 mi). The lookout on the right offers good views over the sandy Pangburn Beach. From here, retrace your steps to Fownes Head parking lot.

65. Bradshaw Scenic Footpath and Melvin Beach

Distance: 2 km (1.2 mi) rtn
Type: linear
Difficulty: moderate
Ascent: 45 m (150 ft)

Hiking time: 50 min
Map: 21 H/6 Salmon River
Trail condition: steep, one ford
Cellphone coverage: N

Finding the trailhead: From the entrance station of the Fundy Trail, drive 2.7 km (1.7 mi) to the Bradshaw Lookout parking lot. The trail starts right there. The trail cannot be missed.

Trailhead: 45°23'55" N, 65°27'38" W

The hike: The trail first descends on wooden steps and turns left at a T-junction. (The very short spur to the right leads to a nice vista point.) The trail soon descends very steeply with the help of a wooden ladder and wire rope and continues to descend to a brook. The brook must be crossed on rocks, aided by a wire rope. The trail turns left immediately, and from this point on, a number of wooden structures help to avoid slippery sections of the trail. The trail follows the west branch of Fuller Brook until it ends at a narrow paved road. An optional extension turns left, crosses the brook on a bridge, continues for a very short distance, and then descends to the right on wooden steps to Melvin Beach. The trail provides access to a secluded beach and sea caves.

66. Big Salmon River Cemetery Trail

Distance: 0.7 km (0.4 mi) rtn
Type: linear
Difficulty: easy to moderate
Ascent: 60 m (200 ft)

Hiking time: 25 min rtn
Map: 21 H/6 Salmon River
Trail condition: steep, dry
Cellphone coverage: P

Finding the trailhead: From the entrance station of the Fundy Trail, drive 10.8 km (6.7 mi) to the Cranberry Brook Lookout. There are no trail markings, but the trail cannot be missed.

Trailhead: 45°25'34" N, 65°24'19" W

The hike: From the Cranberry Brook Lookout, descend a few stairs and turn right. The trail descends, at times steeply, to the Big Salmon River Cemetery. Attractions include scenic views across the bay and a white-fenced cemetery.

67. Long Beach Brook Falls

Distance: 1.4 km (0.9 mi) rtn
Type: linear
Difficulty: easy to moderate
Ascent: 10 m (33 ft)

Hiking time: 40 min rtn
Map: 21 H/6 Salmon River
Trail condition: rocky
Cellphone coverage: P

Finding the trailhead: From the entrance station of the Fundy Trail, drive the parkway for 17.5 km (10.9 mi), then turn right to parking lot P12. The trailhead is located on the left side of the lot. There are no trail markings, but the trail is easy to follow.

Trailhead: 45°25'39" N, 65°22'22" W

The hike: Starting at the P12 parking lot, the trail begins by climbing stairs into the woods. Signs indicate Trans Canada Trail and Sentier NB Trail. Ignore the large white paint blazes on the trees that indicate the Fundy Footpath. After a short distance, the trail swings to the left and soon emerges onto the main road. It crosses the main road at an angle, turns left, and enters the woods again some distance to the right. It soon descends with the help of a guide rope. The trail then reaches a rocky streambed, which it follows. After climbing very steeply again (conveniently, there is a guide rope), the path then dips down to Long Beach Brook and the falls. The falls are the main attraction of this trail.

View of Martin Head

68. Fundy Footpath

Distance: 41.4 km (25.7 mi) plus 7.7 km (4.8 mi) Goose River Trail one way
Type: linear
Difficulty: very strenuous
Ascent: 200 m (650 ft), 1,600 m (5,250 ft) cumulative

Hiking time: 3½-4 days one way
Maps: 21 H/6 Salmon River and 21 H/11 Waterford
Cellphone coverage: P

Trail condition: Rocky, rooty, very steep, and slippery in parts; watch tides in spots. Ladders are provided for steep ascents and descents in the first section of the trail. Goose Creek can only be crossed during low tide. Similar conditions apply to the Goose River at the boundary of Fundy National Park. However, there is a high-water detour that can be used at any time. It provides permanent access at the cost of two additional steep climbs. In spring and after heavy rainfall, the Little Salmon River, Wolfe Brook, Quiddy River, and Rapidy Brook may be impassable. Be warned not to cross or swim across dangerously overflowing waters. Tide tables are available at http://www.waterlevels.gc.ca/eng/station?sid=129 for St. Martins and at http://www.waterlevels.gc.ca/eng/station?type=0&date=2017%2F09%2F13&sid=140&tz=ADT&pres=1 for Herring Cove (in Fundy National Park).

Finding the trailhead: Hikers should enter and exit the trail from the Fundy Trail Parkway Interpretative Centre and the Point Wolfe parking lot in Fundy National Park. From the entrance station of the Fundy Trail, drive the parkway for 10 km (6.2 mi), then turn right to parking lot P8. Hikers are required to register at the Interpretive Centre above the parking lot. The Fundy Trail Parkway is typically open from mid-May to mid-October around 8 a.m. to 5 p.m.. For details, call 1-866-386-3987 or visit the website at www.fundytrailparkway.com.

Trailhead: 45°25'20" N, 65°24'24" W. The trail is described from west to east, i.e., from the Fundy Trail Parkway near St. Martins to the western boundary of Fundy National Park.

The Fundy Footpath is marked with white paint blazes. Most of the trail is marked well and confusion rarely arises. It is often possible to see one blaze in front of you and one behind. Pay close attention, though, especially to double blazes. They indicate a sudden change of direction. Blue blazes lead to campsites and lookouts while yellow paint blazes are used for access trails These yellow blazes mark ATV trails connecting the footpath with dirt roads. We suggest that hikers ignore them. These ATV trails should not be relied upon as exit points as they lead to an area with little to no habitation. Moreover, signage of the ATV roads is inconsistent and several of them will be closed due to the extension of the Fundy Parkway.

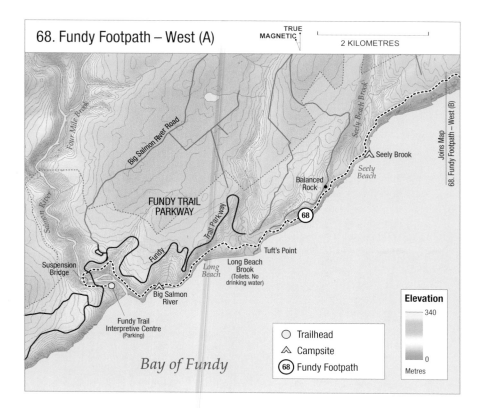

Four Mile Brook

Salmon River

Big Salmon River Road

Seely Beach Brook

Joins Map

68. Fundy Footpath – West (B)

Seely Brook

Seely Beach

Balanced Rock

FUNDY TRAIL PARKWAY

Trail Parkway

68

Fundy

Suspension Bridge

Long Beach

Tuft's Point

Long Beach Brook (Toilets. No drinking water)

Big Salmon River

Fundy Trail Interpretive Centre (Parking)

Bay of Fundy

○ Trailhead

⛺ Campsite

68 Fundy Footpath

Elevation

340

0

Metres

The hike: From the parking lot at P8 below the Interpretive Centre, follow the river a short distance upstream, then continue underneath the automobile bridge to a suspension bridge across the Big Salmon River. Cross this bridge and turn right. The trail parallels the river downstream, first underneath the automobile bridge, and then follows white blazes on rocks. After some distance, the trail ascends on long wooden steps. Once on top, the trail continues up and down to a bench, overlooking the beach down below. From here on, the trail leads back into the woods and crosses several creeks on small, wooden bridges. There are campsites A on the left of the trail and B and C to the right. The trail leads through ferns and beech and birch trees. There is a steep drop to the right of the trail. Another brook is crossed, and then the trail reaches the Long Beach parking lot at 4.4 km (2.7 mi).

Cross the parking lot straight ahead and follow the trail, marked only by signs Sentier NB Trail and Trans Canada Trail straight ahead on wooden steps. At a fork, continue straight, parallel to the road on the left of the path. A spur to the left leads to Tufts Plateau with access to the beach. (It was boarded up at the time of writing in the late summer of 2017.) After some distance, a brook is forded directly below a culvert with the new road high above. Here, the trail ascends steeply and eventually

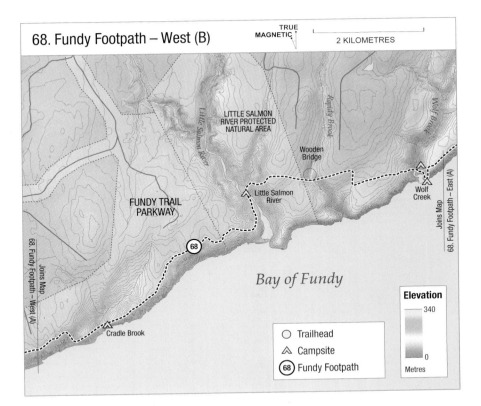

68. Fundy Footpath – West (B)

TRUE
MAGNETIC

2 KILOMETRES

Little Salmon River

LITTLE SALMON RIVER PROTECTED NATURAL AREA

Rapidy Brook

Wolf Brook

Wooden Bridge

Little Salmon River

Wolf Creek

FUNDY TRAIL PARKWAY

68. Fundy Footpath – East (A)

Joins Map

68. Fundy Footpath – West (A)

Joins Map

Bay of Fundy

Cradle Brook

Elevation

340

0

Metres

○ Trailhead
⛺ Campsite
(68) Fundy Footpath

turns away from the road. Pass the Balanced Rock formation and continue towards Seely Beach. Here, the forest consists mostly of spruce trees. There are some level spots where camping is possible.

After a short distance, the trail descends steeply to Seely Beach. Follow the beach in an easterly direction and cross a brook. Directly beyond, there are a few campsites. ATVs may also use these sites on weekends. Follow the beach some 300 m/yd to the tip of a small bay just before a rocky outcrop on the beach.

At this point, turn left into the woods and follow the trail towards Cradle Brook. The path leads first up some wooden steps with a wire guide; once the top of the steps has been reached, turn east (i.e., to the right) immediately. The trail leads up and down before ascending steeply for quite some distance. After some more ups and downs, a yellow-blazed access trail departs to the left. For some distance, there are the usual ups and downs through the woods before the trail turns left and ascends again up a long flight of wooden steps with a wire guide. Here, after a short distance, the trail starts to descend steeply. It continues to do so on wooden steps; then it leads westwards for some distance before it continues to descend on another set of steps. At the foot of the steps, turn left immediately and continue below stone

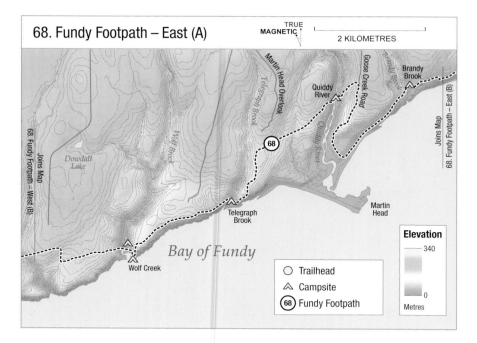

68. Fundy Footpath – East (A)

TRUE
MAGNETIC

2 KILOMETRES

Martin Head Overlook
Telegraph Brook
Goose Creek Road
Brandy Brook
Brandy Brook
Quiddy River
Joins Map 68. Fundy Footpath – East (B)
68
Wolf Brook
Joins Map 68. Fundy Footpath – West (B)
Dowdall Lake
Quiddy River
Telegraph Brook
Martin Head

Bay of Fundy

Wolf Creek

Elevation

— 340

○ Trailhead
⚊ Campsite
68 Fundy Footpath

0

Metres

cliffs. Turn left and descend on more steps. At the foot of the steps, turn right. Here, the trail continues to descend steeply on switchbacks. Pass by a sign that advertises a Million Dollar View. The trail descends through the woods, then on another long set of steps, before it finally reaches the beach.

Cross Cradle Brook, follow it a short distance upstream, and then turn away from it to the right. There are some campsites in the woods. The trail then starts to ascend steeply in switchbacks. At the top, the trail becomes fairly level and continues through the woods. At some point, there is a yellow-blazed side trail to the McCumber Brook access road. For some distance, the trail is fairly level; then it starts to descend. The descent becomes steep; the trail then crosses a brook and leads down to the western side of the Little Salmon River. At a sign, the trail turns left and leads next to the river through a riparian area passing a campsite.

As the river forks (the left fork is Little Salmon River, which leads to the Eye of the Needle, while the right fork is Dustin Brook), it needs to be forded. There is a white sign on the eastern side of the river that indicates the continuation of the Fundy Footpath. There is a large camping area here with a privy toilet. The Dustin Brook access trail starts here, not to be confused with the Fundy Footpath. Continue the ascent of the main trail. It is very steep and very long. Along the way, some red blazes indicate a short spur that leads to a vista point on top of the cliffs. Caution is advised here. The trail continues to climb before it finally reaches a mossy plateau. The trail soon starts to descend gently and crosses a small open area. There are some

muddy spots around here. Soon the trail reaches an old woods road. It turns left, follows the woods road for a short distance, and then turns off it to the right.

The trail descends to Rapidy Brook and crosses it on a wooden bridge, referred to as Mayo's Crossing. After the crossing, the trail ascends steeply, turns left, and continues its steep climb. Near the plateau, a yellow-blazed access trail departs to the left. The trail is fairly level in this area, and it leads through several muddy spots. The path then starts to descend, first gently and increasingly more steeply. The trail finally reaches Wolfe Brook and crosses it. To the left of the trail a large, shady campsite can be found. The narrow path continues a short distance downstream on Wolfe Brook with some remnants of old dams; it requires crawling over a rock before the path reaches the beach. There is a nice wilderness campsite here.

The trail continues directly behind the campsite near the beach. The narrow path ascends very steeply in switchbacks. It gradually levels off until it encounters a yellow-blazed turnoff to the left. It continues and then descends to Hunter Brook. The brook needs to be forded, which is typically possible on some rocks. It climbs for a short distance before it descends steeply to Telegraph Brook, with two campsites. Note the waterfalls at this point. The trail then ascends again, and steeply, but not for too long. It then reaches a plateau, which makes much easier walking. The trail crosses a woods road straight on, and then a yellow-blazed access road departs to

above: Telegraph Brook

the left. Continue straight and cross another woods road. As a small creek is crossed, there is a campsite to the left of the trail. Continue on more or less level terrain before another woods road is crossed straight on. The trail then descends again, first gradually, then more steeply, to Quiddy River, with a large campsite. Camping at Martin Head, however, is not recommended on weekends.

From here on, the trail again ascends steeply. As the path reaches more level ground, a wide woods road (Martin Head Road) is crossed. After that, the trail descends again, first mildly, but later steeply. The path now parallels the woods road at some distance. The path then crosses another woods road. The level trail continues straight into the woods, allowing occasional glimpses of the beach down below. Another woods road is crossed, and after some distance a large sinkhole is noticeable to the left of the trail. The narrow path starts to ascend again. It tends to be slippery, so caution is advised. As soon as the path reaches a summit, it descends again. The descent becomes very steep, until it ends at Brandy Brook. Cross the brook, ascend shortly first, then descend steeply until a large campsite at Goose Creek is reached. From the beach there are good views in a westerly direction towards Martin Head and eastward towards the impressive Centurion Head. Also note that a short distance east of the campsite, there is yellow-blazed ATV access.

At this point it is necessary to ford Goose Creek. This is best accomplished a few hours before and after low tide. Actually, there are four arms of the creek that need to be forded. Note that the water in Goose Creek, even if it flows out towards the bay, is typically brackish, as it is water that was pushed inland by the tides. The trail continues at the opposite (east) side of the river. It is marked by a large white blaze on a tree. There is a campsite where the trail re-enters the woods and starts to ascend steeply, before it flattens after some distance and crosses a brook, where hikers can refill their water bottles. In this area, the trail leads up and down before it passes by a "rock garden" and crosses another brook.

It then crosses Jim Brook, with a campsite. Pass by another yellow-blazed access trail and cross a few (usually dry) brooks. The path then descends steeply through young growth and reaches Rose Brook and Azors Beach. From this point, the coast of Nova Scotia can be seen. The path follows Rose Brook upstream for a short distance before it turns off to the right away from the brook. Pass by yellow and blue signs at the Primrose Campsite. From here, the trail follows the dry creek bed down and crosses it before reaching the end of the trail at km 0 next to Goose River.

Turn right and ford the river. There is a blue sign with a white hiker on the other side. Follow the narrow path that passes by an old dam whose remnants can be seen in Goose River on the right. Continue, and soon the path reaches a grassy field. At this point, the tides will determine how to proceed. In case of low tide, you can continue along the line of trees on the left to the delta of the Goose River until you reach the end of the Goose River Trail in Fundy National Park.

In case of high tide, at the grassy field turn left as the trail reaches the waterline Here, orange (and sometimes blue) marking tape indicates the continuation of the

68. Fundy Footpath – East (B)

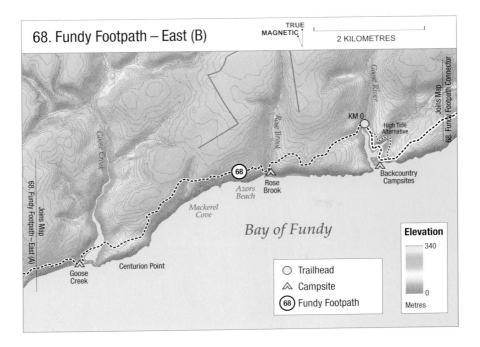

alternate trail, which leads across another two hills to the Goose River Trail. Just as the trail enters the woods, there is another blue metal sign with a white hiker. The narrow, and at times quite slippery, trail ascends very steeply next to a significant drop-off before it finally reaches Rossiter Brook. Ford the brook and continue a very short distance downstream. Again, the narrow path ascends steeply. After it levels off after some time, walking becomes more pleasant. The trail continues through softwoods until it finally reaches the Goose River Trail in Fundy National Park a short distance below campsite 4. Turn left and continue for some 7.7 km (4.8 mi) to the Point Wolfe parking lot (see the Goose River Trail description on p. 243).

This strenuous trail leads across unspoiled wilderness along the uninhabited Fundy Coast. Remnants of dams and old woods roads are reminders of logging and copper mining activities in the late 1800s. The forests, waterfalls, and streams are pristine and the cliffs dramatic, the viewpoints often obscured by mature woods. The footpath is tough because of its length, numerous ups and downs, and fast weather changes. It is especially dangerous because of its steep and narrow descents along steep cliffs.

68. Fundy Footpath Connector – Goose River Trail

TRUE
MAGNETIC

1 KILOMETRE

FUNDY
NATIONAL PARK

Point Wolfe Campground
(Parking)

Covered Bridge

First Mile Brook

68

Hastie
Hill

Point Wolfe

Bay of Fundy

Goose River

Rossiter Brook

68. Fundy Footpath East - B

Joins Map

KM 0

High Tide
Alternative

Backcountry
Campsites

Elevation

— 290

0

Metres

○ Trailhead

⚠ Campsite

68 Fundy Footpath Connector
(Goose River Trail)

69. Adair's Walton Lake Trail

Distance: 6.1 km (3.8 mi) rtn
Type: linear
Difficulty: easy
Ascent: 40 m (130 ft)

Hiking time: 2 hrs
Map: 21 H/11 Waterford
Trail condition: dry
Cellphone coverage: Y

Finding the trailhead: Take Route 121 to Sussex Corner. At the junction with Route 111, turn right towards St. Martins. At 0.5 km (0.3 mi), keep left at a fork towards Waterford onto Dutch Valley/Waterford Road. Pass by Poley Mountain 8.8 km (5.5 mi) from the junction. After another 2.7 km (1.7 mi), keep left at a fork onto Creek Road (the right fork leads to Walker Settlement) and keep right at another fork 0.3 km (0.2 mi) later. Follow this road for 9.3 km (5.8 mi) to Adair's Wilderness Lodge, which is located on the right side of the road. The public is welcome to hike the trail. The trailhead is signed and can be found straight ahead from the entrance of the lodge. The trail is marked by signs, white blazes on trees, and pink ribbons.

Trailhead: 45°35'53"N, 65°19'02"W

The hike: The trail descends and skirts the water reservoir before it turns slightly to the right into the woods. Soon the narrow path crosses a small footbridge, continues through an alder-strewn area, and then enters a beautiful stand of softwoods. From here, the trail descends gradually to Anderson Brook and a cascading waterfall. It then ascends and continues through a stand of mature maple trees. On top of the hill, keep slightly to the left and follow the pink and sometimes orange ribbons on this ridge trail, keeping the valley to the right below. At 1.5 km (0.9 mi), the footpath descends and Walton Lake becomes visible on the right. Some distance later, cross another brook on small rocks and enjoy more views of the lake. At 2.9 km (1.8 mi), take the short side trail down to the lake, from where you can see the lodge and grounds. From here, return to the main trail. For a shorter hike, turn left and retrace your steps to the lodge. For the full hike, turn right and continue for a short distance to a large pine, at which point a small path leads along the edge of the estuary to the road, then turn right and walk 2 km (1.2 mi) on the road to the lodge.

70. Catamount Trail: Ida's Garden

69-70. Adair's Trails

TRUE
MAGNETIC

1 KILOMETRE

○ Trailhead
69 Adair's Walton Lake Trail
70 Catamount Trail: Ida's Garden

McNutt Road

Walton Lake

Cardigan Lake

Creek Road

Anderson Brook

Elevation
340
210
Metres

Bear Lakes

69

70

Adair's Wilderness Lodge (Parking)

Schoales Lake

Long Settlement Road

70. Catamount Trail: Ida's Garden (see map p.175)

Distance: 2.4 km (1.5 mi) rtn
Type: linear
Difficulty: easy
Ascent: 10 m (33 ft)

Hiking time: 1 hr rtn
Map: 21 H/11 Waterford
Trail condition: mostly dry
Cellphone coverage: Y

Finding the trailhead: Take Route 121 to Sussex Corner. At the junction with Route 111, turn right towards St. Martins. At 0.5 km (0.3 mi), keep left at a fork onto Dutch Valley/Waterford Road towards Waterford. Pass by Poley Mountain 8.8 km (5.5 mi) from the junction. After another 2.7 km (1.7 mi), keep left at a fork onto Creek Road (the right fork leads to Walker Settlement) and keep right at another fork 0.3 km (0.2 mi) later. Follow this road for 9.3 km (5.8 mi) to Adair's Wilderness Lodge, which is located on the right side of the road. The trailhead is opposite the lodge on the left side of the road. It is part of the Catamount Trail. The trailhead is somewhat hidden behind some trees. Do not take the wide ATV gravel road, which is located to the right of the hiking trail. The trail markings are blue paint blazes on trees.

Trailhead: 45°35'53" N, 65°18'57" W

The hike: As the trail enters the woods, it follows a narrow overgrown woods road with soft moss. After some distance, the trail leaves the woods road, departs to the right, and climbs through softwoods. After 350 m/yd, the trail crosses two woods roads, each time entering the woods directly across the road. After some distance, it reaches a small clearing, locally referred to as the Boneyard, as rangers used to dispose of roadkill in this area. The trail continues on the other side of the clearing, enters the woods, continues through them, and reaches an open rock garden. This is Ida's Garden, a treasure trove of club mosses, Irish mosses, bunchberries, lady's slipper orchids, and other wildflowers. The narrow path continues, crosses another woods road, and then reaches Schoales Lake. At this point, retrace your steps to return to the lodge.

71. Walton Glen Gorge:
The Grand Canyon of New Brunswick

Distance: 4 km (2.5 mi) rtn
Type: linear
Difficulty: strenuous
Ascent: 140 m (460 ft)
Hiking time: 3 hrs

Map: 21 H/6 Salmon River
Trail condition: The first part is groomed. The part along the river is very rocky and rooty
Cellphone coverage: P

Finding the trailhead: From Adair's Wilderness Lodge (see trailhead directions for trail 70, p.176) continue on Creek Road for 1.5 km (0.9 mi) to the junction with the Shepody Road. Keep left on Shepody Road, pass Crawford Lake, and reach another fork at 1 km (0.6 mi). Turn right onto Little Salmon River Road. After 1.7 km (1.1 mi) from the last junction, continue right at a fork on Little Salmon River Road. After another 9 km (5.6 mi), reach an entrance station of the Fundy Parkway. From the entrance, continue for another 1 km (0.6 mi), then turn left onto a parking lot. The trail starts on the right side of the road before reaching the Interpretive Centre. The first part of the trail is marked by signs at all junctions. The trail that leads to the overlook is easy to find. At the sign indicating Hiking Trails not far from the overlook, there is (at the time of this writing) a confusing array of pink and orange flags down to the river. Once the river has been reached, stay on the right side of the brook to the gorge.

Trailhead: 45°29'25" N, 65°18'36" W

The hike: From the trailhead, walk along the wide trail. Keep straight at a couple of junctions, and follow the signs to Walton Glen Gorge. At another fork, keep to the right (the left fork returns to the Interpretive Centre). Continue for some distance and take another right fork to an observation point with a fine view of the gorge. Return to the last fork before the observation point and turn right, following the sign of a hiker and the many coloured flags that indicate the paths down to Walton Glen Brook.

Once you reach the brook, you may turn left (upstream) on a spur that leads to McLeod Falls. In order to do so, follow the river upstream for some distance, then turn left,

when the waterfall becomes visible. There are stairs next to the falls that lead out of the gorge.

Alternatively (or additionally), turn right and follow the brook downstream. The trail becomes increasingly rough. At one point, a huge rock wall becomes visible on the opposite side of the now narrow gorge. At this point, you are at the top of some minor falls. From here, the trail continues through the woods near the brook downstream. Just before the brook joins the Little Salmon River, it passes through what is called locally the Eye of the Needle, where the walls close in from both sides. Further exploration includes getting your feet wet and scrambling over rocks, and the water at the small opening may be breast high. Hikers who continue down the Little Salmon River will eventually find themselves on the Fundy Footpath.

72. Wallace Falls

Distance: 0.5 km (0.3 mi) rtn
Type: linear
Difficulty: easy to moderate
Ascent: 20 m (65 ft)
Hiking time: 30 min

Map: 21 H/11 Waterford
Trail condition: dry, ascent and descent on an old ladder
Cellphone coverage: N

Finding the trailhead: From Adair's Wilderness Lodge (see trailhead directions for trail 70, p.176) continue on Creek Road for 1.5 km (1 mi) and bear left at a junction onto Shepody Road. Pass Crawford Lake, and after 1 km (0.6 mi), keep right at a fork onto Little Salmon River Road. After another 1.7 km (1.1 mi), swing to the left onto unmarked Cross Road. After 0.5 km (0.3 mi), a small wooden bridge is crossed, and after 1.7 km (1.1 mi), a large dirt road (Dustin Brook Road) departs to the right. Continue straight on Cross Road for another 2.3 km (1.4 mi). The road is rough in parts, but passable without four-wheel-drive vehicles. Park at the Quiddy River pedestrian bridge. Trail markings feature blue and orange blazes on trees.

Trailhead: 45°34'03" N, 65°13'59" W

The hike: The wide trail enters the woods on the right-hand side of the road. Follow the blue blazes while the trail leads through mature softwoods. After some distance, the trail reaches a fork, which is marked with orange blazes. Keep left; going straight connects with the Fundy Footpath via the Quiddy River access road. The trail descends, reaches a set of stairs, then descends to the Quiddy River, the cascading Wallace Falls, and a pool – a great spot for a plunge.

73. Sussex Bluff Trail

73. Sussex Bluff Trail

Distance: 5 km (3.1 mi) rtn
Type: linear
Difficulty: easy to moderate
Ascent: 50 m (165 ft)

Hiking time: 1 hr 30 min rtn
Map: 21 H/11 Waterford
Trail condition: dry, rooty
Cellphone coverage: Y

Finding the trailhead: Follow Route 121 through Sussex to Sussex Corner. At a fork in Sussex Corner, turn left onto Route 111 and follow the road for another 1 km (0.6 mi). Turn right onto Sullivan Drive, which angles to the right onto Pugsley Street, which, in turn, makes a ninety-degree turn to the left, here named Rockridge Drive. Follow Rockridge Drive for 0.8 km (0.5 mi) to a parking lot in front of a fenced water tower. The trail is unmarked but relatively easy to follow.

Trailhead: 45°42'26" N, 65°27'41" W

The hike: Keep to the right of the fence. As the trail passes the tower, it enters the woods. Keep to the right at a fork. Soon you will be rewarded with fine views of Dutch Valley far below the cliffs you are standing on. From here on, there are numerous forks and junctions along the trail. As a general rule, keep to the right and follow the cliffs. After some time, the trail again emerges from the woods and leads along the edge of the cliff. This is the best part of the trail: the views are spectacular. The trail passes along stunted oak trees, then dips down and rises again towards the bluff above a farm with two silos. Beyond this point, the trail re-enters the woods and begins to descend steeply on switchbacks before it eventually ends at a dirt road above the farm seen earlier. Retrace the trail to the start. The main features of this trail are the great views of the pastoral landscape of Dutch Valley and the surrounding hills.

73. Sussex Bluff Trail

74. Friars Nose

Distance: 0.6 km (0.4 mi) rtn
Type: linear
Difficulty: moderate
Ascent: 80 m (260 ft)

Hiking time: 30 min rtn
Map: 21 H/11 Waterford
Trail condition: rocky, steep, rutted
Cellphone reception: N

Finding the trailhead: From the junction of Routes 121 and 111 in Sussex Corner, continue on Route 111 in a southerly direction towards St. Martins. After 0.5 km (0.3 mi), keep left on Waterford Road at a fork towards Waterford. From here, continue for 5.7 km (3.6 mi) to a junction with Parlee Brook Road. Turn right onto that road and follow it for 4.8 km (3 mi). At this point, Arnold Hollow Drive turns off to the right. Here, you can either park just beyond the turnoff on the side of the road (there are a few spaces), or, if you have a high-clearance vehicle, turn right and continue for another 1.1 km (0.7 mi) up the narrow and rocky Arnold Hollow Drive. At that point, there is a small grassy area on the right that provides space for five cars. The trailhead is directly opposite this spot. There are no trail markings, but it is easy to find.

Trailhead: 45°39'10"N, 65°25'13"W

The hike: Walk up the steep, slippery, and very rutted road, which is pretty much torn up by ATVs. At the first fork in the trail, turn left. After another short climb, the trail ends at a plateau. The views of the surrounding wooded hills are quite spectacular. This is one of those trails where the destination justifies the effort – in this case, the gorgeous view.

75. Marys Point Peninsula
(Shepody National Wildlife Area)

Distance: 5 km (3.1 mi) rtn for the beach walk, 6.5 km (4 mi) for the entire loop
Type: loop
Difficulty: moderate to strenuous for the entire loop, easy for the first part
Ascent: 50 m (165 ft)
Hiking time: 2 hrs 30 min

Map: 21 H/10 Alma
Trail condition: sandy beach, rocky, slippery; much of the trail is impassable at high tide. For tide tables, see http://www.tides.gc.ca/eng/station?sid=160
Cellphone coverage: P

Finding the trailhead: From Riverside-Albert, take NB 915 in a southerly direction for 3.3 km (2.1 mi) to Harvey. Turn left and follow Marys Point Road for 3.7 km (2.3 mi). A parking lot and the visitor centre of the Marys Point Shorebird Reserve are located on the left side of the road. The trail is unmarked, but it is not difficult to find and follow.

Trailhead: 45°43'38" N, 64°40'20" W

The hike: The narrow path starts next to the visitor centre, where information on bird migration is available. The path descends and continues to the end of the trail at an observation area next to New Horton Flats. At the beach, turn left and continue along the shoreline. Walking along the beach is usually slow and tiring. Keep the wooded section of Marys Point to the left. Eventually, the beach swings to the right and gets rocky. Starting at about 2.5 km (1.6 mi) at the southwestern tip of the peninsula, a lot of scrambling over slippery rocks, rockweed, and mud is required. Some hikers may wish to retrace their steps here.

For those who continue on, you pass by a sea stack up close before reaching the easternmost point of the peninsula. From here, you can see a lighthouse on neighbouring Grindstone Island. As the rocky shore swings to the left, the shore continues with its small marshy inlets along Marys Point Reef. After some time, you approach an open area. Turn left and walk across the high grass, keeping the woods directly to your left, until you reach the New Horton Flats. Turn right and return to the observation area and from there to the parking area. The main features of this trail are the unique plants, crustaceans, and shorebirds in the ecosystem of beach and mud flats. The views of Grindstone Island and its lighthouse are quite scenic.

From mid-July to the end of August, the trail ends here. The reason is the tens of thousands of shorebirds, mostly semipalmated sandpipers, that congregate here to feed on tiny mud shrimps and worms in preparation for their long flight south. Birdwatching is best during the first two weeks of August at low tide. Hikers cannot proceed beyond the beach during high tide. Furthermore, vehicles of any kind are not allowed on the beach.

Warning: At the rocky tip of the island, the tide comes in fast and furious, while it takes a lot longer for the mud flats to fill up. Therefore, it is best to start the trail when the tide goes out. If the tide then comes in at the tip of the peninsula, there is still sufficient time to safely finish the loop.

Grindstone Island

76. Crooked Creek Trail

Distance: 3.2 km (2 mi) rtn
Type: linear
Difficulty: moderate
Ascent: 130 m (425 ft)
Hiking time: 1 hr rtn

Map: 21 H/15 Hillsborough and 21 H/10 Alma (or get a map from the village office by calling 506-882-3022)
Trail condition: dry
Cellphone coverage: N

Finding the trailhead: From the junction of Route 114 and NB 915, drive through Riverside-Albert for 0.6 km (0.4 mi). Where the road makes a ninety-degree turn to the right, continue for another 200 m/yd. There is a small parking lot on the left-hand side of the road, just across from the village office. There are some markings at intersections, making the trail obvious.

Trailhead: 45°44'57"N, 64°44'23"W

The hike: From the trailhead, the trail passes a small old dam on the left and starts to climb. A few steps on wooden stairs then lead down to a bridge that crosses the brook. The trail continues through softwoods. At some point, a dirt road joins from the left. After some time, the trail reaches a clearing with power lines. Turn right, cross the clearing, and continue on a gravelly path until the trail reaches an observation platform. From here, there are some views across the town of Riverside-Albert and the Shepody Marsh in the distance. The trail continues to the left into the woods just behind the platform. It continues to climb through mixed open forest, crosses a wide dirt road, and reaches its end at a parking lot. Do not miss the observation platform at the edge of the parking lot that overlooks a stunning forested ravine on Caledonia Mountain. The major attractions of this trail are the exceptional views from the observation platforms, especially during the fall colours.

Lobster mushroom

Gypsum Mill in Hillsborough

Gypsum rock found in the Hillsborough area in Albert County has been used for a long time. Early settlers hauled the material to ports, from where they sold it for processing in the American Northeast. In 1854, the Tomkins family from New York moved to the area, established the Albert Manufacturing Company, and built a mill in Hillsborough, where they produced their Hammer Brand Plaster, a high-quality product. The quarry and the mill provided work for about three hundred men. The mill burned down in 1873 and again in 1911, and each time it was rebuilt as a larger and more modern plant. In 1930 the operation was sold to the United States Gypsum Company, which operated the mill until 1980, when it was finally closed for good.

77. Hillsborough Wetland Trail

Distance: 5 km (3.1 mi) rtn
Type: linear
Difficulty: easy
Ascent: negligible

Hiking time: 1 hr 15 min rtn
Map: 21 H/15 Hillsborough
Trail condition: dry
Cellphone coverage: Y

Finding the trailhead: Follow Route 114 from Moncton towards Fundy National Park or from Fundy National Park to Moncton. In the town of Hillsborough, follow the signs to the New Brunswick Railway Museum. Parking is available below the museum. The trailhead is directly opposite the parking lot at a small wooden bridge next to public toilets, a small playground, and a visitor centre. The trail is unmarked but easy to follow.

Trailhead: 45°55'21" N, 64°38'39" W

The hike: Follow Steeves Road with a pond on your right for a short distance, then turn right, keeping the pond to your right. Cross a bridge, turn left, and enter the woods. The trail soon emerges from the woods and follows the edge of a field. It turns right at a ninety-degree angle, keeping the marshes to its left, until it reaches a dirt road where it turns left. After some distance, the wide trail reaches a large pond, which it keeps to its left. This birch-lined stretch of trail is very pleasant, and the wildlife in the pond is also remarkable. The trail then swings to the left, gets out in the open, and reaches a T-junction at a sign marked Walking Trail. Turn right and immediately right again. Walk along the tailings of the old gypsum mine until you reach two gypsum silos. At this point, it is definitely worthwhile to climb up the dike that protects the farmland from the Peticodiac River. Walk on the dike until it reaches a wooded area. Retrace your steps from here.

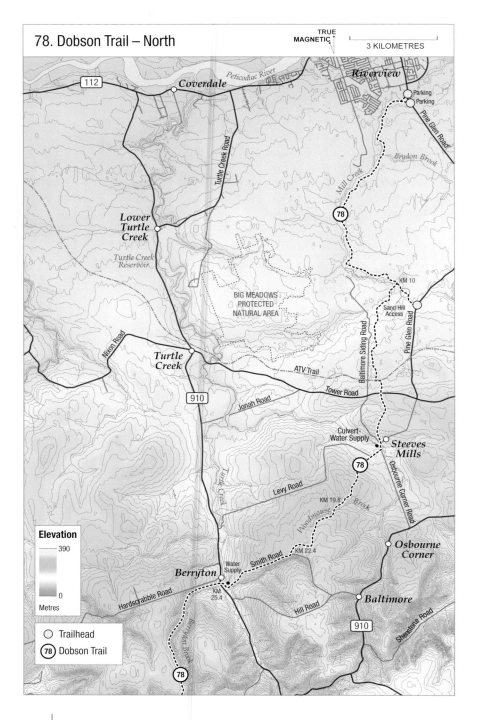

78. Dobson Trail – North

TRUE
MAGNETIC

3 KILOMETRES

112

Coverdale

Peticodiac River

Riverview

Parking
Parking

Pine Glen Road

Turtle Creek Road

Brydon Brook

Mill Creek

Lower
Turtle
Creek

78

Turtle Creek
Reservoir

KM 10

Sand Hill
Access

BIG MEADOWS
PROTECTED
NATURAL AREA

Pine Glen Road

Nixon Road

Turtle
Creek

ATV Trail

Baltimore Siding Road

910

Jonah Road

Tower Road

Culvert-
Water Supply

Steeves
Mills

78

Turtle Creek

Levy Road

Osbourne Corner Road

KM 19.8

Woodmouse   Brook

Elevation

390

KM 22.4

Osbourne
Corner

0

Berryton

Water
Supply

Smith Road

Metres

Hardscrabble Road

KM
25.4

Hill Road

Baltimore

910

Shenstone Road

○ Trailhead

Berryton Brook

78 Dobson Trail

78

78. Dobson Trail (in 7 sections)

Distance: 58.9 km (36.6 mi) one way
Type: linear
Difficulty: moderate to strenuous
Ascent: 330 m (1,100 ft)
Hiking time: 3 days one way
Maps: 21 I/2 Moncton,

21 H/15 Hillsborough, 21 H/10 Alma
and 21 H/11 Waterford
Trail condition: good, some rocky and
boggy areas
Cellphone coverage: P

Summary:
Section 1: 9.6 km (6 mi)
Section 2: 5.1 km (3.2 mi)
Section 3: 10.9 km (6.8 mi)
Section 4: 6.8 km (4.2 mi)
Section 5: 6.5 km (4 mi) [+ 1 km (0.6 mi) rtn]
Section 6: 9.4 km (5.8 mi)
Section 7: 10.6 km (6.6 mi)

Finding the trailhead: The trailhead is located south of Moncton on Pine Glen Road in Riverview. From Moncton, take the causeway across the Petitcodiac River and turn onto Route 114/Coverdale Road south. In Riverview, turn right onto Pine Glen Road just before an Ultramar station. Proceed for 3.2 km (2 mi). The trailhead is indicated by a sign on the right side of the road at a large parking space next to a large cairn. Note that just before the main trailhead there is another parking lot from which the Dobson trail can also be accessed.

The trail end can be reached by entering Fundy National Park on Route 114, at its northwest entrance near Wolfe Lake. About 1.2 km (0.7 mi) south of the park entrance, Old Shepody Road departs to the left. Follow this gravel road for 10.9 km (6.8 mi). The end of the Dobson Trail is located a short distance beyond Haley Brook at 45°41'44" N, 65°0'29.5" W. At this point, the Dobson Link (see Fundy National Park) connects with the Laverty Falls Trail on the right. A sign on the left shows the end of the Dobson Trail. Some parking spots are found on the side of the road.

The trail is marked by 6" x 2" blue plastic blazes or equivalent paint blazes. Distances (in kilometres) are shown between horizontal green bars. In general, **one blue blaze** marks the trail. **Two blue blazes**, one above the other, indicate that the trail changes its direction. **Yellow blazes** mark side trails, and **white blazes** indicate short spurs to camping sites and outhouses. Distances are indicated on trees between **double green lines**. In some areas, large numbers of **red paint blazes** mark the trees; they indicate boundaries and claim lines and can be ignored. At times, **blue marking tape** may be used. **Caution:** follow the blue blazes at all times because the Dobson Trail frequently leaves the larger trails (e.g., old woods roads) and continues on smaller footpaths!

For additional information or any questions, check the Facebook page of the Fundy Hiking Trail Association at https://www.facebook.com/pages/Fundy-Hiking-Trail-Association-Dobson-Trail-Fundy-Footpath-Catamount-Trail/359191730813070 or contact Alonzo Leger at leger@nbnet.nb.ca.

Trailhead: 46°02'28" N, 64°47'14" W
The junction of Pine Glen Road with the Sand Hill side trail is at 45°58'34" N, 64°47'09" W

The hike:

Section 1: Pine Glen Road to Beaver Pond

The trail starts on the right side of the parking lot next to a large cairn. It leads through Mill Creek Nature Park with its mature mixed woods and some bird feeders. A yellow-blazed loop trail departs to the right. It follows Mill Creek for some distance and then, at a meeting place with benches and a fire pit, it turns right onto the blue-blazed Dobson Trail. The trail soon reaches a power line at 0.9 km (0.6 mi), where it continues straight ahead. Mill Creek can sometimes be seen to the right of the trail.

At 1.6 km (1 mi) the trail reaches another clearing with power lines. It crosses a snowmobile track below the lines and then enters the woods again as a narrow footpath. Follow this small path. The following section consists mostly of softwoods. Mill Creek is still to the right of the trail, deep below. The trail continues straight until it reaches a T-junction. Turn right and cross Brydon Brook.

After some distance, the trail reaches a partially overgrown clearing with power lines. Keeping the creek to the right, cross the clearing parallel to the creek. In the process, cross a dirt road straight ahead (the dirt road crosses a bridge on the right). The trail enters the woods immediately above the creek. After a short distance, the trail joins an old woods road. From here on, the Dobson Trail meanders about this woods road, alternately on its right and on its left. These narrow trails are to be preferred over the woods road, as the latter tends to be riddled with a number of large mud holes.

At some point a meadow becomes visible to the right. At a T-junction, turn left onto a woods road and, immediately after, turn right into the woods, where the main road takes a ninety-degree left turn. The narrow path skirts a meadow. At some point, a wider road is reached. Turn right and immediately left again. There is a picnic place and campsite on the left just before the sign marked 9 km.

Section 2: Beaver Pond to Tower Road

The trail continues on the east side of the pond. Just after the trail crosses a small end section of the swamp meadow (called Mill Creek Meadows), it reaches a junction at the 10 km sign. Here the yellow-blazed 1.2 km (0.7 mi) **Sand Hill side trail** leaves to the left and connects with the paved Pine Glen Road. This access trail starts on the Pine Glen Road 12.5 km (7.8 mi) from the Ultramar station. The wide, groomed trail passes a BBQ pit with benches and a pit toilet, and then reaches a small iron bridge. Beyond the bridge, the trail narrows and soon becomes very wet. The corduroy sections do help somewhat. The twenty-minute path ends at a T-junction with the blue-blazed Dobson Trail.

The main path crosses Mill Creek and continues through mixed woods and sheep laurel in a southwesterly direction. This is quite a muddy section. At 11.9 km (7.4 mi) the footpath reaches a gravel road with the Hillsborough power lines just beyond. The trail continues on the other side of the dirt road some 15 m/yd to the right. From here on out, the walking is swampy, even though there are some logs across wet spots. Eventually the trail ascends, and at 12.6 km (7.8 mi) there is a beautiful big pine tree in the middle of the trail. Hiking through the open hardwoods is very good in this area.

Pass a seasonal pond on the right, and at 14.3 km (8.9 mi) the trail reaches the former tracks of the CN railway at Baltimore Station, now a very rough dirt road. The trail follows the dirt road to the left in an easterly direction for some 200 m/yd; then it turns right into the woods. The hiking is good until you reach the wide Tower Road at 14.8 km (9.2 mi).

Section 3: Tower Road to Berryton

Cross Tower Road, continue through woods, and reach a clearing with young growth at 15.8 km (9.8 mi). Proceed through softwoods, pass a small clear-cut, then cross an old woods road straight ahead. The trail dips down and reaches the paved Osborne Corner Road. Turn right onto that road, pass Steeves Mills Road, and proceed across the culvert across East Turtle Creek. This is a good spot to replenish your **drinking water**, which can be achieved by a short, but very steep, access trail on the far (south) side of the brook. About 50 m/yd beyond the culvert, Levy Road East leaves to the right. The trail follows this road for about 300 m/yd, and then, just as Levy Road swings right, it enters the woods to the left at a sign marked Dobson Trail just behind a four-wheel trail, which it parallels for some distance. At first, the trail leads through nice hardwoods. Hiking is good here with some possible sites for camping. This part of the trail parallels four-wheeler tracks that tend to be torn up and very muddy. After some time, the trail turns left, crosses the four-wheeler tracks, and joins a woods road soon thereafter. The road ascends, and after a short distance, the blue-blazed Dobson Trail departs to the right on a narrow path. After some time, the path crosses a new woods road.

At 20.5 km (12.7 mi) the main trail descends to Woodmouse Brook and follows it for a while. Smith Road is reached at 22.4 km (13.9 mi). The trail turns right and follows this dirt road. After about 200 m/yd a very wide dirt road joins from the right. Continue straight for 3.2 km (2 mi) all the way down to Berryton. Some points offer scenic views onto opposite hills across valleys. At 25.4 km (15.8 mi) the trail reaches the paved Turtle Creek Road at the hamlet of Berryton. Turn right and soon after cross a bridge across the West Branch Turtle Creek. Just before you cross the bridge, you may want to turn off the road to the right down the embankment to the river. There is a good place to rest and to replenish your supply of **drinking water**.

Section 4: Berryton to Rosevale-Prosser Brook Road

Walk across the Berryton bridge and immediately turn left (the left of two dirt roads), parallel to Berryton Brook. The trail soon reaches what used to be a gravel pit. Turn sharply to the left and follow this pleasant trail through woods. There is a steep descent, which is aided by some installed ropes to a brook (**water supply**), followed by a steep incline. Walking is excellent in this area. This part of the trail crosses a number of small brooks, and there are a few wet spots. Despite some steep dips, hiking through the beech and maple trees is pleasant. Cross a woods road that leads to some recent clear-cut. The trail ascends for some time, then levels off and stays level for a long time. Cross a woods road straight ahead. There are a few old campsites in the area. Along this good trail section, you are rewarded with one sweeping view towards the Prosser Brook ridge and across the wooded Stuart Mountains. This is also a popular spot for four-wheelers and mountain bikers. Eventually the trail reaches the gravelly and wide Rosevale-Prosser Brook Road.

Section 5: Rosevale-Prosser Brook Road to Hayward Pinnacle

The trail crosses the Rosevale-Prosser Brook Road at an angle slightly to the right, where it enters the wood again. The trail steadily gains altitude before dipping down twice to brooks. Apart from many roots and rocks on the trail, the hiking here is

quite good through mostly hardwood ridges.

Cross two overgrown access roads straight on. From here on out, the incessant drone from the wind turbines on the hills is a constant companion on the trail. At 34.9 km (21.7 mi), a narrow footpath branches off to the right at a marked junction. It leads to a hut that provides shelter. Continuing on the main trail, which is an old logging road, walking becomes very

78. Dobson Trail – South

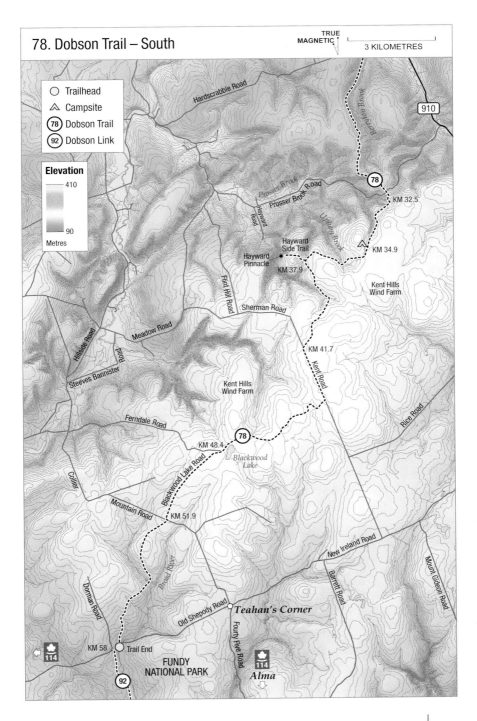

TRUE
MAGNETIC
3 KILOMETRES

Legend
- ○ Trailhead
- △ Campsite
- (78) Dobson Trail
- (92) Dobson Link

Elevation
410
90
Metres

910

Hardscrabble Road

Berylen Brook

(78)
KM 32.5

Prosser Brook

Prosser Brook Road

Hayward Road

Upham Brook

△ KM 34.9

Hayward Side Trail

Hayward Pinnacle
KM 37.9

Kent Hills Wind Farm

Flint Hill Road

Sherman Road

KM 41.7

Kent Road

Meadow Road

Hillside Road

Steeves Bannister Road

Kent Hills Wind Farm

Rice Road

Ferndale Road

Collier

KM 48.4
(78)

Blackwood Lake

Blackwood Lake Road

Mountain Road

KM 51.9

Brook River

New Ireland Road

Barrett Road

Mount Gideon Road

Dorman Road

Old Shepody Road

Teahan's Corner

Forty Five Road

114

KM 58
Trail End

FUNDY NATIONAL PARK

114

Alma

(92)

wet, even in summer. A new path has formed on higher ground to the right of the woods road. Cross a very wide gravel road just in front of power lines and continue straight ahead. After a short distance, cross another dirt road. The trail is level before it dips down to a very large campsite next to a brook. Cross the brook, after which the trail ascends steeply to maple ridges. As the trail reaches a woods road, turn right onto that road for a short distance, then turn left into the woods. Two wind turbines can be seen to the left. Cross two woods roads before the trail reaches a T-junction at 37.9 km (23.6 mi). To the right is the side trail to Hayward Pinnacle; the main trail continues to the left.

The **Hayward Pinnacle side trail** is marked by yellow paint blazes. The short 1 km (0.6 mi) round trip to the hilltop is worthwhile. Follow the woods road for a short distance, cross a woods road, and then the trail ascends fairly steeply. As the trail levels off, there is an open area on the left. Continue through this area and ascend steeply to the Hayward Pinnacle. From the summit, one of the highest elevations in Albert County, you may see parts of Moncton towards the north-northeast and Prosser Brook in a northwesterly direction. However, the views in the other directions are partly obscured by large trees. Return to the T-junction. (Note: the distance for this side trail is not included in that of the Dobson Trail.)

Section 6: Junction of Hayward Pinnacle Side Trail to Blackwood Lake

From the junction at the Hayward Pinnacle side trail, continue on the woods road until 39.2 km (24.4 mi), when the trail leaves the woods road to the right. There are some nice mature softwoods, and the area is beautiful. Turn right at a T-junction onto an old woods road, which immediately crosses Hayward Brook, another **water supply**, on a bridge. The trail briefly follows the old logging road and then turns right into the woods. After a short incline, it crosses a woods road. At 40.8 km (25.4 mi) the trail crosses another woods road and continues for some distance with a large cutover section to its left.

The trail parallels an active woods road and passes a camping and picnic site before it reaches the road. It crosses the road slightly to the right and continues through maples and beeches. As the trail reaches a dirt road, turn left on that road and follow it. Just before the 42 km sign, a gravel road departs to the left. Keep straight at this point. Some distance later, you reach a four-way junction. Again, walk straight. Soon there is another four-way junction with a stop sign. Continue straight. After another 200 m/yd, turn right into the woods on a narrow path.

The wide woods road provides easy hiking but soon gets rocky. There are some nice old fields with tall grass and maples. This section between the lengthy Kent Road section and Blackwood Lake is very scenic, alternating between woods and old fields. Hiking through a hardwood ridge is good. Cross three gravel roads straight on. To the right of the third gravel road, two wind turbines are visible on

above: The view from Hayward Pinnacle; Blackwood Lake (below)

the right. The trail continues on an old, grassy road until it reaches the shores of Blackwood Lake at 48.4 km (30.1 mi). This is a good **camping** and rest area. The lake provides a plentiful supply of **drinking water**.

Section 7: Blackwood Lake to Old Shepody Road at Fundy National Park

The trail continues straight, with Blackwood Lake to its left. At the far end of the lake, the trail crosses a wide dirt road leading to the right. The trail continues straight, becomes grassy, and parallels the wide dirt road. Just beyond the 49 km sign the path swings to the right and again reaches the wide dirt road.

At this point, the trail turns left onto the road. Follow the blue blazes for about 2.5 km (1.6 mi), where the road ends at a T-junction with the Collier Mountain Road. Turn left onto this road for a very short distance and turn right again onto what used to be called the Old Goldmine Road.

Follow the wide road for quite some distance, passing by House #466. Continue straight as a barred road forks off to the right. The now narrower road dips down to a maple sugar operation, whose lines can be seen from the road. This is a pretty area with flaming maples in the fall. Then the blue-blazed path turns off to the left at a clearly marked intersection. Soon it crosses a dirt road straight, but it turns left and parallels the road before turning off into the woods. Cross a brook on a bridge (**water supply**). The rocky trail now ascends steeply, leading into a hardwood ridge. The path then crosses a dirt road slightly to the right. Walk through woods, cross another woods road, and soon the trail leads through tall grass and across small wooden bridges for some distance until it reaches a remarkable small stand of firs before finally descending to the Dobson Trail sign on the Shepody Road at 58 km (36 mi). Directly across the road, there is a gate that marks the starting point of the Dobson Link, a trail that connects the Dobson Trail to the system of trails in Fundy National Park.

This 58 km (36 mi) footpath from Riverview to Fundy National Park is the work of many volunteers under the auspices of the Fundy Hiking Trail Association. As one would expect, a trail of such length offers a wide variety of scenery. This includes a hilltop with a panoramic view, a wilderness lake, cool brooks, beaver ponds, hardwood ridges, stands of softwoods, views, and fields that are reminders of old homesteads with raspberry and blackberry patches as well as a multitude of wildflowers. Wildlife includes all large New Brunswick game animals: deer, moose, and black bears.

79. Irishtown Nature Park

Distance: 3.9 km (2.4 mi)
Type: loop
Difficulty: easy
Ascent: negligible
Hiking time: 1 hr 15 min
Map: 21 I/2 Moncton
Trail condition: The Purple Martin, Dragonfly, and Scout segments are groomed, while John Howard, Scout, and Bunny Hop are footpaths with woodchips. All trail sections are dry with a number of boardwalk sections across wet areas.
Cellphone coverage: Y

Finding the trailhead: From Highway 2, take exit 459A-B (Elmwood Drive). Turn onto Route 115 (Elmwood Drive) north and follow it for 1.6 km (1 mi). There is a large parking lot on the right side of the road. The trailhead starts on the left side of the parking lot next to a building that houses toilets for visitors. The trail is marked by red dots blazes on trees on the Dragonfly and John Howard segments, and purple dots on trees for the Scout part. In addition, there are maps posted at a number of intersections, indicating one's present location.

Trailhead: 46°08'31"N, 64°46'21"W

The hike: This first part is referred to as the Purple Martin Trail. It ends at post number 1. Continue straight on the Dragonfly segment of the trail. The wide trail continues for some distance to the right at a T-junction (the Gerhardt Trail leads to the left) until it eventually reaches post 3. At that point, it continues to the right for a very short distance until a narrow path called John Howard departs to the left; take it. This section parallels the Irishtown Road Reservoir and offers occasional glimpses of it as well as a few spurs directly to the water's edge. At a T-junction, the trail continues to the right (the left is a short spur to the reservoir) until it eventually reaches the wide Bouctouche Line Trail. Continue straight onto the purple-blazed Scout Trail, which ends at post 2 at a dam near a very tall white pine. Turn right onto the Bunny Hop Trail, which returns to post 1. At this point, turn left and return to the parking lot.

80. Pink Rock Trail

Distance: 5 km (3.1 mi) rtn
Type: linear
Difficulty: easy
Ascent: 10 m (33 ft)
Hiking time: 1 hr 30 min

Maps: 21 J/15 Hillsborough and 21 H/10 Alma
Trail condition: some wet spots
Cellphone coverage: P

Finding the trailhead: On Highway 2, take exit 482 to Memramcook Centre and Dorchester. Follow this road for 16.8 km (10.4 mi) to Dorchester and the junction with NB 935. Turn right onto NB 935/Dorchester Cape Road south and follow it for 16.1 km (10 mi). At this point, NB 935 makes a ninety-degree turn to the left. Continue straight on Pink Rock Road for another 300 m/yd, where parking for a few vehicles is possible on the left side of the old woods road. There are no trail markings, but the trail is an old woods road and a beach.

Trailhead: 45°46'03"N, 64°31'01"W

The hike: The trail follows an old woods road/ATV track to the beach. Just before reaching the beach, there are remnants of an old dam on the left. Turn left at the beach and follow the Maringouin Flats for some distance to a dilapidated jetty and pink rock formations. The main attractions of this trail are the access to the beach at the Maringouin Flats, an old dam near the beach at Shepody Bay, an old jetty, and a number of geological features on the beach, such as sandstone cliffs and occasional (often grey) dikes.

Sandpipers

Each year, roughly during the last two weeks of July and the first two weeks of August, large numbers of semi-palmated sandpipers congregate in the upper part of the Bay of Fundy to prepare for the flight to their winter quarters in Guyana and Suriname. As a matter of fact, it has been estimated that up to 75 percent of all living sandpipers make their way south by stopping over in the Upper Bay of Fundy. It is an impressive sight: for a couple of hours before and after high tide, tens of thousands of the birds can be seen roosting and, most impressively, in flight. Preparing for their seventy-two-hour non-stop flight, the birds bulk up so that they almost double their weight. Their main food is Corophium volutator, a tiny shrimp-like amphipod that is found only in the Bay of Fundy  and the Gulf of Maine. Each of these tiny, fat-filled amphipods is the size of a grain of rice, and each sandpiper eats almost thirty thousand of them per day. When roosting, the birds stay close together: you will typically see about one hundred birds per square metre (ten birds per square foot). The main enemies of the sandpipers are peregrine falcons, which dive onto their prey at up to 320 km/h (200 mph). In order to avoid being "sitting ducks," sandpipers will occasionally rise and fly in large groups, which makes for an impressive spectacle. In addition to the semi-palmated sandpipers found here, there are also least sandpipers and semi-palmated plovers.

81. Sackville Waterfowl Park

Distance: various, up to 3.5 km (2.2 mi) rtn
Type: loop
Difficulty: easy
Ascent: negligible

Hiking time: up to 1 hr rtn
Map: 21 H/16 Amherst
Trail condition: dry, some boardwalk
Cellphone coverage: Y

Finding the trailhead: Take exit 504 (Main Street) on Highway 2 near Sackville. Turn onto Main Street (NB 940) towards the town of Sackville and follow that road for 0.8 km (0.5 mi). There is a large parking lot on the right. The trailhead is opposite the parking lot at a large entrance gate to the park. There are no trail markings, but the trail network is easy to follow.

Trailhead: 45°54'07" N, 64°22'24" W

The hike: The gravelly walkway beyond the entrance gate is the main artery through the park. To its left there are marshes with boardwalks and an observation tower close to Highway 2. There are boardwalks on the right side also, as well as views of a church and fine old houses near Mount Allison University. The diverse and rich life in the marshes ranges from beavers and muskrats to marsh birds and wetland plants. The park is a birder's paradise, featuring more than 150 bird species.

82. Westcock Marsh

Distance: 5.3 km (3.3 mi)
Type: loop
Difficulty: easy
Ascent: negligible

Hiking time: 1 hr 30 min
Map: 21 H/16 Amherst
Trail condition: dry
Cellphone coverage: Y

Finding the trailhead: Take exit 504 (Main Street) on Highway 2 near Sackville. Turn onto Main Street (NB 940) towards the town of Sackville and follow the road south for 1.5 km (0.9 mi) to a traffic light. Continue straight for another 0.8 km (0.5 mi) to a T-junction. Turn right onto Queens Road/Route 106 west and follow that road for 1.6 km (1 mi). Turn left onto NB 935 towards Wood Point and follow that road for 1.5 km (0.9 mi), crossing railroad tracks along the way. Here, turn off the highway onto the Old Hospital Loop Road, a dirt road, and follow it for 2 km (1.2 mi). Park just before the dike on the side of the road. There are no trail markings, but the trail is obvious.

Trailhead: 45°51'45" N, 64°20'54" W

The hike: On the dike, turn left and continue along it. Note Fort Beauséjour towards the east at the edge of the Fort Cumberland Ridge. At low tide, you can see the remarkable red clay of the Cumberland Basin with its tidal inlets. At 2.4 km (1.5 mi), a trail departs to the left, next to a barn. Continue on the dike for another 1.4 km (0.9 mi), then leave the dike to the left at another barn. Continue until you reach a T-junction. Turn left, and in 1 km (0.6 mi) you reach the trailhead. The trail features include some fine views across the fields, marshes, and Fundy tidal flats.

99. Coastal Trail

FUNDY NATIONAL PARK

Fundy National Park, founded in 1950, is located on the Bay of Fundy, south-southwest of Moncton. The park is heavily forested, ranging from windswept coastal softwoods to beautiful hardwoods in its interior. The altitude ranges from sea level to about 365 m (1,200 ft), its surface measures 206 km² (80 sq mi), and there are some 100 km (62 mi) of hiking trails in the park.

Various types of accommodation are available in the park, including a motel, chalets, and five campgrounds. In addition to tenting or RV camping, the park offers unique accommodation in yurts, oTENTiks, and the tiny, one- or two-person Goutte d'Ôs, which resemble water droplets. In addition, there are eight wilderness campsites located at Goose River, Marven Lake, Tracey Lake, and Chambers Lake. To reserve a backcountry site, call 506-887-RESERVE or via the internet at www.pc.gc.ca/fundy. Many details about all aspects of the park can be found in the park's brochure, *Salt & Fir*, which is available at park headquarters near the southern entrance of the park. The nearby town of Alma also offers accommodation and other amenities.

Fundy National Park can be reached from Highway 1 by taking exit 211 towards Fundy National Park. Follow Route 114 for 21.1 km (13.1 mi) to the northwestern entrance of Fundy National Park. A park map is available online at https://www.pc.gc.ca/en/pn-np/nb/fundy/visit/cartes-maps, and it is also included in *Salt & Fir*.

Note: Fundy National Park has recently undertaken work to redesign and reroute some trails. Every effort has been made to ensure the information presented here is correct but we suggest getting an up-to-date map from the park prior to hiking.

Alma

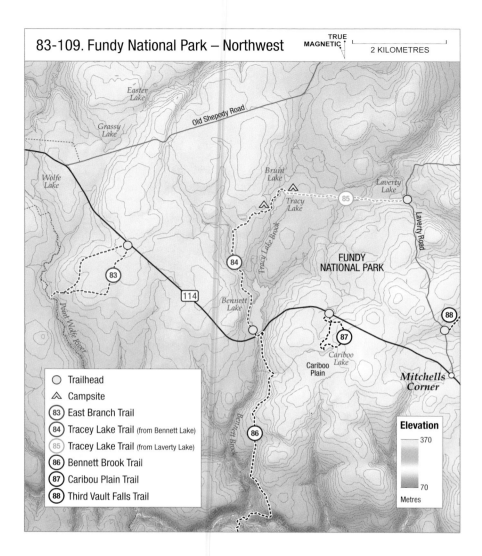

83-109. Fundy National Park – Northwest

TRUE
MAGNETIC

2 KILOMETRES

Easter Lake

Grassy Lake

Old Shepody Road

Wolfe Lake

Bruin Lake

Laverty Lake

Tracy Lake

85

Tracy Lake Brook

FUNDY
NATIONAL PARK

Laverty Road

83

84

114

Bennett Lake

88

Point Wolfe River

87

Cariboo Lake

Cariboo Plain

Mitchells Corner

○ Trailhead
⌂ Campsite
83 East Branch Trail
84 Tracey Lake Trail (from Bennett Lake)
85 Tracey Lake Trail (from Laverty Lake)
86 Bennett Brook Trail
87 Caribou Plain Trail
88 Third Vault Falls Trail

Bennett Brook

86

Elevation
370

70
Metres

83. East Branch (see map p. 206)

Distance: 5.6 km (3.5 mi)
Type: loop
Difficulty: easy
Ascent: 70 m (230 ft)
Hiking time: 1 hr 30 min

Map: 21 H/11 Waterford (or, better, the map in the *Salt & Fir* brochure)
Trail condition: groomed, a few wet spots
Cellphone coverage: P

Finding the trailhead: From the northwest entrance of Fundy National Park at Wolfe Lake, follow Route 114 for 3.3 km (2.1 mi). Turn right and follow the dirt road for a short distance to the parking lot. The marked trailhead is located at the far end of the small parking lot. On the trail, there are some olive-and-yellow signs with a hiker, but most markings consist of blue metal blazes displaying a hiker.

Trailhead: 45°38'36" N, 65°06'56" W

The hike: The trail immediately enters the woods and reaches a junction at 0.2 km (0.1 mi). Take the left path and follow the olive-and-yellow signs. The trail leads through nice, shady hardwood ridges. There are some wet spots, but most of the time, boardwalk sections lead across them. At 2.8 km (1.7 mi), turn left at a T-junction and continue downwards for some 300 m/yd to the remains of an old logging dam at the East Branch Point Wolfe River. Even though there are no benches, this is an excellent place for a rest. Return to the junction and continue straight along an old wide hauling road for about 2.2 km (1.4 mi). The trail keeps to the left and returns to the parking lot. The major attraction of the trail is an old logging dam and yard at the East Branch Point Wolfe River, a reminder of the lumbering era on the Fundy Coast in the nineteenth century. Logs were floated from the dam down the river to the sawmill at Point Wolfe. Some small waterfalls can be seen across the dam and the lake.

People of the Salt and Fir

Life in Pointe Wolfe, today part of Fundy National Park, was hard but prosperous in the 1800s. Author Maimie Steeves called its residents the people of "the salt and fir" because they depended on fishing and lumbering for their livelihood.

When England desperately needed wood for its naval fleet, it turned to its North American colonies for supplies. Saint John merchants saw the wealth in the forested hills of the Fundy Coast, and in 1826, Pointe Wolfe entered the Atlantic timber trade and supplied Britain with lumber.

Merchant John Ward of Saint John quickly built log dams, wharves, and a sawmill spanning the Pointe Wolfe River. Exhaustive cutting of the virgin forest of tall red spruce and fir began. Traditionally, the lumbermen cut logs in the winter. During the spring freshet, they drove them down the rivers to the sawmill at Pointe Wolfe to be cut into boards and then shipped. The economy in Pointe Wolfe and the Alma Parish boomed until the early 1900s, when steel ships replaced wooden ships and the fisheries declined. It was then that the wealth vanished and the people moved on. With the creation of Fundy National Park, the forests and the salmon, once diminished greatly, have been making a comeback.

84. Tracey Lake Trail (from Bennett Lake) (see map p. 206)

Distance: 8.4 km (5.2 mi) rtn
Type: linear
Difficulty: easy to moderate
Ascent: 30 m (100 ft)
Hiking time: 2 hrs 30 min rtn

Map: 21 H/11 Waterford (or, better, the map in the *Salt & Fir* brochure)
Trail condition: some rocks and roots, wet spots
Cellphone coverage: P

Finding the trailhead: From the northwest entrance of Fundy National Park at Wolfe Lake, follow Route 114 for about 7.1 km (4.4 mi). A large parking lot is located on the left side of the road next to Bennett Lake. Follow the paved path at the far right (northeast) end of the parking lot to the restrooms, continue to the beach, and turn left. The trailhead is located at the gate next to a sandy beach. There are occasional yellow metal disks displaying a hiker.

Trailhead: 45°37'32" N, 65°04'49" W

The hike: The trail proceeds with Bennett Lake on the right before swinging off to the left, where it gently ascends. At some point, the trail crosses Kelly Brook on rocks. Beyond this crossing, the trail becomes rocky and rooty. At 3.3 km (2.1 mi) the trail reaches Tracey Lake, where it turns sharply to the left. This is also the location of a campsite with a picnic table and a pit toilet. The trail follows Tracey Lake through open forest, crosses a tiny creek by means of a boardwalk, and reaches the northern edge of Tracey Lake. There are campsites #12 and #13 here, as well as an excellent spot for a picnic. At this point, a short side trail along an old woods road leads to Bruin Lake. Return to the Tracey Lake Trail, or alternatively, you may continue on the Tracey Lake Trail to Laverty Lake, another 5.6 km (3.5 mi) return (see the trail description on p.210). This pleasant trail winds through open forest along two lakes. Moose are sometimes seen at peaceful Tracey Lake, where two picnic sites are located. There are three wilderness campsites at Tracey Lake.

85. **Tracey Lake Trail** (from Laverty Lake) (see map p. 206)

Distance: 5.6 km (3.5 mi) rtn
Type: linear
Difficulty: easy to moderate
Ascent: 30 m (100 ft)
Hiking time: 2 hrs rtn

Map: 21 H/11 Waterford (or, better, the map in the *Salt & Fir* brochure)
Trail condition: large wet spots
Cellphone coverage: P

Finding the trailhead: From the northwest entrance of Fundy National Park at Wolfe Lake, follow Route 114 for some 11.8 km (7.3 mi). Turn left onto Laverty Road and follow it for 4 km (2.5 mi). A parking lot is located next to Laverty Lake on the left; the trailhead is at the parking lot. There are some square blue metal signs, showing the symbol of a hiker.

Trailhead: 45°39'05" N, 65°02'15" W

The hike: This narrow trail follows the southern side of Laverty Lake for a while before continuing through the woods. At 1.1 km (0.7 mi) the trail crosses a creek, and there are several other wet and boggy spots that can be crossed on logs. The trail arrives at an excellent picnic site on Tracey Lake at 2.8 km (1.7 mi). There are two campsites in this area, both equipped with picnic tables, barbecue pits, a wood supply, and a nearby pit toilet. From here, you can either return to Laverty Lake or explore nearby Bruin Lake on a short, wide woods road before heading back. You can also continue the hike to Bennett Lake, which adds another 8.2 km (5.1 mi) return to the trip (see the trail description on p. 209). The trail connects two scenic lakes. There is a peaceful picnic site with a view of Tracey Lake at the end of the trail. Moose can frequently be seen at Laverty Lake.

86. Bennett Brook Trail (see map p. 206)

Distance: 15.4 km (9.6 mi) rtn
Type: linear
Difficulty: easy, but strenuous on both sides of the river; moderate overall
Ascent: 120 m (400 ft)
Hiking time: 4 hrs 45 min rtn

Map: 21 H/11 Waterford (or, better, the map in the *Salt & Fir* brochure)
Trail condition: dry, but two fords are required; near the river, the trail is rocky and rooty
Cellphone coverage: P

Finding the trailhead: From the northwest entrance of Fundy National Park at Wolfe Lake, follow Route 114 for about 7.1 km (4.4 mi). Turn left at Bennett Lake into the parking area. The trailhead is located on the right side, close to the dam. The first part of the trail is unmarked but cannot be missed. Beyond the end of the logging road, the narrow path is well defined. Signs show the places where Bennett Brook and Point Wolfe River must be forded. Some blue blazes with a hiker show the trail between Point Wolfe River and Marven Lake Trail where the path is not obvious.

Trailhead: 45°37'27" N, 65°04'42" W

The hike: Cross the dam at Bennett Lake and follow the wide gravel trail to Route 114. Cross the highway and continue on the other side next to the end of the guardrail. The trail descends, then leads through Siberian dogwood and alders for a short distance. It begins to ascend to the left of a gate but soon levels off somewhat. The trail then leads through a forest where trilliums blossom in May. At 1.2 km (0.7 mi), the trail joins an old logging road. Turn right and follow this old road for about 3 km (1.9 mi). At about 4.2 km (2.6 mi), the road ends at a small turnaround.

At the far right corner of the turnaround, a path descends in steep switchbacks. The path then levels off, crosses a brook, and after a while descends steeply to the bottom of a gorge. Immediately to the right flows Bennett Brook, which joins the Point Wolfe River a short distance downstream. At this point it is necessary to ford Bennett Brook. Once across, a path follows the Point Wolfe River upstream for about 50 m/yd. Here the river must be forded. The trail continues almost straight ahead on the other side of the river and is marked by a sign displaying a hiker.

For the next 1.7 km (1.1 mi), the trail ascends a steep and rocky hill and is strenuous. At 7.1 km (4.4 mi), the trail leaves the woods and ends at a wide, grassy cart road. This is the Marven Lake Trail (see the trail description on p. 244). Turning right leads to Chambers and Marven Lakes a short distance away; turning left leads eventually to the Point Wolfe parking lot.

87. Caribou Plain Trail (see map p. 206)

Distance: 3.4 km (2.1 mi)
Type: loop
Difficulty: easy
Ascent: 20 m (65 ft)
Hiking time: 45 min

Map: 21 H/11 Waterford (or, better, the map in the *Salt & Fir* brochure)
Trail condition: dry, partly boardwalk
Cellphone coverage: P

Finding the trailhead: From the northwest entrance of the Fundy National Park at Wolfe Lake, follow Route 114 for about 9 km (5.6 mi). There is a parking lot on the right side of the road. The trailhead is located on the right side of the road, just as it enters the parking lot. There are no trail markings, but the trail is obvious. There is a shorter, wheelchair-accessible loop all on boardwalk. This loop of about 1 km (0.6 m) is part of the entire trail. The trail described here always keeps to the right.

Trailhead: 45°37'42" N, 65°03'29" W

The hike: This interpretive nature trail starts on a boardwalk. It passes a beaver dam and skirts a beaver lake. Keep right at a junction at 1.2 km (0.7 mi) and continue straight across a boggy area with an observation point and some benches at a small lake. This is a marvellous spot in the middle of a raised bog. At dawn and dusk, moose may be seen at the lake. Back on the main trail, the walk leads through a nice hardwood ridge with beech, maple, and hobblebush. The trail first continues through forest before it returns to the parking lot on an old carriage road and over a boardwalk section across the beaver pond. This popular interpretive trail features a multitude of plants and various types of "bog bonsai," plants that grow very slowly in the bog on account of its acidity. Moose, deer, and red fox might be seen on the trail. The major feature here is the raised bog with its sphagnum moss and the lakes. Certain spots called "flarks" act like quicksand; a moose drowned at one flark in this bog a number of years ago.

88. Third Vault Falls Trail

88. Third Vault Falls Trail (see map p. 219)

Distance: 7.4 km (4.6 mi) rtn
Type: linear
Difficulty: moderate
Ascent: 150 m (490 ft)
Hiking time: 2 hrs 15 min rtn
Map: 21 H/11 Waterford (or, better, the

map in the *Salt & Fir* brochure)
Trail condition: dry, steep with some wooden steps and rocks towards the end
Cellphone coverage: P

Finding the trailhead: From the northwest entrance of Fundy National Park at Wolfe Lake, follow Route 114 for about 11.8 km (7.3 mi). Turn left onto Laverty Road (a dirt road in good condition) and follow it for 1 km (0.6 mi) to the parking lot. The trailhead is located next to the toilet building. There are no trail markings, but the trail is easy to follow.

Trailhead: 45°37'29"N, 65°01'33"W

The hike: For the first part, the surface of the trail is gravel. Beyond that, it becomes a regular forest trail with some rocky spots. For its entire length, the trail lies in partial shade, which makes hiking pleasant in the summer. Except for the last 0.8 km (0.5 mi), the trail is flat. Towards the end it descends steeply, in part on wooden stairs. Once Upper Vault Brook is reached, a narrow path follows the brook and then crosses it on a few rocks. The falls can be seen at the trail end on the left, where the impressive waterfall plunges into a round pool. The main attraction of this trail is the waterfalls. At 16 m (53 ft), these are the highest falls in the park.

Dragonfly

89. The Forks Trail (see map p.219)

Distance: 6.8 km (4.2 mi) rtn
Type: linear
Difficulty: moderate
Ascent: 275 m (900 ft)
Hiking time: 2 hrs 30 min rtn
Map: 21 H/11 Waterford (or, better, the map in the *Salt & Fir* brochure)
Trail condition: dry; some streams must be crossed, which can usually be done by boulder hopping
Cellphone coverage: P

Finding the trailhead: From the northwest entrance of Fundy National Park at Wolfe Lake, follow Route 114 for 11.7 km (7.3 mi), then turn left onto Laverty Road. After 4.9 km (3 mi) on this gravel road, the road makes a sharp right turn. Continue for another 1.4 km (0.9 mi) to a turnaround. The parking lot here accommodates about thirty vehicles. The combined trailhead of the Moosehorn and The Forks Trails is straight ahead next to the toilets; the Laverty Falls Trail begins on the far left. The trail is marked by blue metal blazes displaying a hiker.

Trailhead: 45°39'27" N, 65°00'52" W

The hike: From its trailhead, the trail descends to a fork at 0.2 km (0.1 mi) and continues straight ahead (the left fork leads down the Moosehorn Trail). The Forks Trail first leads through a nice stand of hardwoods and soon descends rather steeply. On its way down it passes a rocky, seasonal pond on its left. The trail gets wider and rocky, continues in an old streambed, and makes its way down in wide switchbacks until it finally reaches its end at the Broad River. Here, the river has remarkably deep pools, which provide a rest stop for spawning salmon. From here, you can ford the Broad River and then the Forty Five River, each with the help of fixed ropes, to connect with the Upper Salmon River Trail (see description on p.229). The main feature is the narrow gorge at the end of the trail. The Broad River has some deep holes here, and Atlantic salmon can be observed when they arrive to spawn in the fall. Fly fishing for salmon is allowed, provided you have a National Parks fishing permit.

90. **Moosehorn Trail** (see map p. 219)

Distance: 4.8 km (3 mi) one-way to the Dobson Link junction
Type: linear
Difficulty: moderate
Ascent: 215 m (705 ft)
Hiking time: 1 hr 45 min one way (note that the trail is best combined to loop with the Laverty Falls Trail for a total of 3 hours)
Map: 21 H/11 Waterford (or, better, the map in the *Salt & Fir* brochure)
Trail condition: dry, rocky, and rooty
Cellphone coverage: P

Finding the trailhead: From the northwest entrance of Fundy National Park at Wolfe Lake, follow Route 114 for 12 km (7.5 mi), then turn left onto Laverty Road. After 5 km (3.1 mi) on this gravel road, the road makes a sharp right turn. Continue for another 1.4 km (0.9 mi) to a turnaround. The parking lot here accommodates about thirty vehicles. The combined trailhead of the Moosehorn and The Forks Trails is straight ahead next to the toilet; the Laverty Falls Trail begins on the far left. The trail is marked by blue metal signs with a hiker and some orange flags. The first part of the trail to the Broad River is obvious and easy to follow. There is some rock scrambling along the river, but the path is not difficult to find.

Trailhead: 45°39'27"N, 65°00'52"W

The hike: The Moosehorn Trail descends right away to a fork at 0.2 km (0.1 mi). Turn left. (The Forks Trail continues straight ahead; see the trail description on p. 216). The path leads through mixed forest. At 1.8 km (1.1 mi) the gentle downward grade steepens considerably. At a fork, a short side trail departs to the left to the foot of a waterfall. The main trail continues straight and reaches Broad River with a signboard. This ends the first section of the trail.

From here, the trail turns to the left and follows Broad River along its western shore. At this point, we have to negotiate some boulders and rooty sections; the trail then alternates between stretches of alder-lined riverbanks and gravelly stream sides. It continues along a now very tame river. In a gravelly area at the confluence of the Broad River and Haley Brook, the trail turns left (westward) and follows Haley Brook until it eventually reaches its end at a junction with the Dobson Link, which crosses Haley Brook to the right (north), and its continuation along the Laverty Falls Trail straight ahead. Rather than turning back, it is highly recommended that you continue to follow the 2.5 km (1.6 mi) long Laverty Falls Trail (see trail description on p. 218) to the parking lot. The trail features nice mixed forest, a waterfall, and access to the midsection of the Broad River with its cold pools and swimming holes and scenic eroded boulders.

91. Laverty Falls Trail (see map p. 219)

Distance: 5 km (3.1 mi) rtn
Type: linear
Difficulty: easy to moderate
Ascent: 185 m (605 ft)
Hiking time: 2 hrs rtn

Map: 21 H/11 Waterford (or, better, the map in the *Salt & Fir* brochure)
Trail condition: wet spots, rooty
Cellphone coverage: P

Finding the trailhead: From the northwest entrance of Fundy National Park at Wolfe Lake, follow Route 114 for 12 km (7.5 mi), then turn left onto Laverty Road. After 5 km (3.1 mi) on this gravel road, the road makes a sharp right turn. Continue for another 1.4 km (0.9 mi) to a turnaround. The parking lot here accommodates about thirty vehicles. The trailhead of the Laverty Falls Trail is located on the far left of the parking lot. The trail is obvious and easy to follow. The trail is marked by blue metal signs with a hiker.

Trailhead: 45°39'28" N, 65°00'53" W

The hike: The trail descends gently but steadily through nice hardwoods, mostly beech and maple. At 2.3 km (1.4 mi) the trail turns sharply to the right. A small lookout straight ahead overlooks the head of Laverty Falls. A short distance farther along, a side trail departs to the left. It leads to the foot of the falls (a nice place for a rest). The main trail continues to a fork at the confluence of Haley and Laverty Brooks. Here you may continue straight across the Broad River to the Dobson Link (see the description on p. 220) or turn right along the Broad River to the Moosehorn Trail, which makes a nice loop (although it is better hiked in the reverse direction). The trail is notable for the beautiful hardwoods it leads through as well as the many wildflowers found here, especially in spring. The Laverty Falls are remarkable, as are the unspoiled Haley and Laverty Brooks at the end of the trail.

83-109. Fundy National Park – Northeast

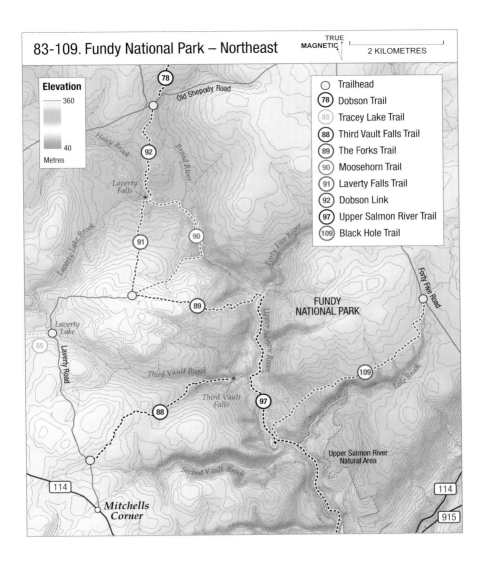

Elevation

360

40

Metres

TRUE
MAGNETIC

2 KILOMETRES

Old Shepody Road

Haley Brook

Broad River

Laverty Falls

Laverty Lake Brook

Forty Five River

FUNDY NATIONAL PARK

Forty Five Road

Laverty Lake

Laverty Road

Upper Salmon River

Third Vault Brook

Third Vault Falls

Lake Brook

Upper Salmon River Natural Area

Second Vault Brook

Mitchells Corner

114

114

915

○ Trailhead
78 Dobson Trail
85 Tracey Lake Trail
88 Third Vault Falls Trail
89 The Forks Trail
90 Moosehorn Trail
91 Laverty Falls Trail
92 Dobson Link
97 Upper Salmon River Trail
109 Black Hole Trail

92. Dobson Link (see map p.219)

Distance: 5 km (3.1 mi) rtn
Type: linear
Difficulty: easy to moderate
Ascent: 50 m (165 ft)
Hiking time: 1 hr 30 min

Map: 21 H/11 Waterford (or, better, the map in the *Salt & Fir* brochure)
Trail condition: one ford required; a few wet spots, rooty
Cellphone coverage: N

Finding the trailhead: From the northwest entrance station to Fundy National Park, follow Route 114 for 1.4 km (0.9 mi), the turn left onto Shepody Road. Follow this somewhat rough gravel road for 10.5 km (6.5 mi) to a gate on the right side marked Dobson Link. This is the trailhead, located directly opposite the southern terminus of the Dobson Trail. The trail is marked by blue metal blazes with a hiker.

Trailhead: 45°41'52"N, 65°00'31"W

The hike: Follow the trail through some mossy areas, where it descends slightly. After some time, the path follows Haley Brook until the path ends at the brook. At this point, Haley Brook must be forded, which may or may not be possible by boulder hopping depending on the season. Once the other side is reached, continue straight on the Laverty Falls Trail or to the left on the Moosehorn Trail. There are some nice stretches along the quiet Haley Brook and some open areas with Irish moss.

Ghost Pipe

This waxy, white plant that grows on the floor of the cool coastal forest is easy to spot. Its slim white stems, flimsy white leaves, and drooping clay pipe flowers are caused by a lack of chlorophyll (very little sunlight permeates to the forest floor). It is also known by the folk names "corpse plant" or "Indian pipe"; botanists call it Monotropa uniflora. Its mode of survival lies in a unique symbiosis with other plants. The ghost pipe feeds off a fungus, which, in turn, feeds on a host tree to which it has attached itself. In case the fungus does not provide sufficient food, the pipe will take food directly from the tree. Thus, the beautiful ghost pipe is a parasite of both the fungus and the tree.

93. Black Horse Trail (see map p. 225)

Distance: 4.4 km (2.7 mi)
Type: loop
Difficulty: easy
Ascent: 60 m (195 ft)
Hiking time: 1 hr

Maps: 21 H/10 Alma and 21 H/11 Waterford (or, better, the map in the *Salt & Fir* brochure)
Trail condition: dry
Cellphone coverage: P

Finding the trailhead: From the northwest entrance of Fundy National Park at Wolfe Lake, follow Route 114 for 14 km (8.7 mi), then turn right onto Hastings Road. The trailhead is 100 m/yd ahead on the right side. There is space for about twelve cars. There are no trail markings, but the trail cannot be missed.

Trailhead: 45°36'17" N, 65°00'12" W

The hike: This multi-use trail (watch for bicycles!) first follows a narrow path through a field. Keep right at a fork. Beyond the fork, the trail widens and fields and woods alternate, although woods later dominate. At some point, there is an open field with a view of the Bay of Fundy in the distance. A walk through the woods and later a field returns to the parking lot. A pleasant field with a view of the bay is the main feature of this trail.

94. **Kinnie Brook Trail** (see map p. 225)

Distance: 2.8 km (1.7 mi) rtn
Type: linear
Difficulty: easy to moderate
Ascent: 80 m (260 ft)
Hiking time: 1 hr

Map: 21 H/10 Alma (or, better, the map in the *Salt & Fir* brochure)
Trail condition: dry
Cellphone coverage: N

Finding the trailhead: From the northwest entrance of Fundy National Park at Wolfe Lake, follow Route 114 for 14.6 km (9.1 mi). The trailhead is on the left side of the road at a parking lot next to a picnic area. The trail is clearly defined and cannot be missed.

Trailhead: 45°36'23" N, 64°59'55" W

The hike: This interpretive trail leads through a moderately shady forest. At 0.8 km (0.5 mi), a short trail to a campground departs to the right. The main trail continues straight and on the level for some time before descending. Notice the steep gorge on the left. At one point, wooden stairs lead down and up again before the trail finally descends a long flight of stairs to Kinnie Brook on the valley floor. On its downward path, the trail passes an imposing rock on the right. The trail ends at a wooden platform overlooking the brook, where an interpretive sign explains some features of the brook. The stream at the bottom of the steep-walled gorge disappears at times. Its banks are densely overgrown, and Siberian dogwood, ferns, and cow parsnip grow on the floodplain.

95. Whitetail Trail (see map p. 225)

Distance: 6.4 km (4 mi) rtn
Type: loop
Difficulty: easy (from South Chignecto Campground)
Ascent: 240 m (790 ft)

Hiking time: 2 hrs 30 min
Map: 21 H/10 Alma (or, better, the map in the *Salt & Fir* brochure)
Trail condition: dry
Cellphone coverage: N

Finding the trailhead: From the northwest entrance of Fundy National Park at Wolfe Lake, follow Route 114 for 15.5 km (9.6 mi) to the South Chignecto Campground. Turn right towards the campground, park alongside the road, and start your hike at the first or second gravel road on the left. The trail is marked by blue metal blazes (and also yellow metal blazes) displaying a white hiker as well as some olive-yellow signs.

Trailhead: 45°36'10"N, 64°59'07"W

The hike: This trail shares the first 800 m/yd with the Tippen Lot Trail before it turns off to the left (the right fork is Tippen Lot (North)). The slightly rocky trail soon crosses two creeks and then swings to the right, keeping the brook to its right in a valley below. The trail descends through beautiful hardwood trees before leading down in switchbacks. It crosses two brooks via bridges and a junction and continues straight to the Salt and Fir Centre and a tennis court. The Whitetail Trail features scenic sections along a gully.

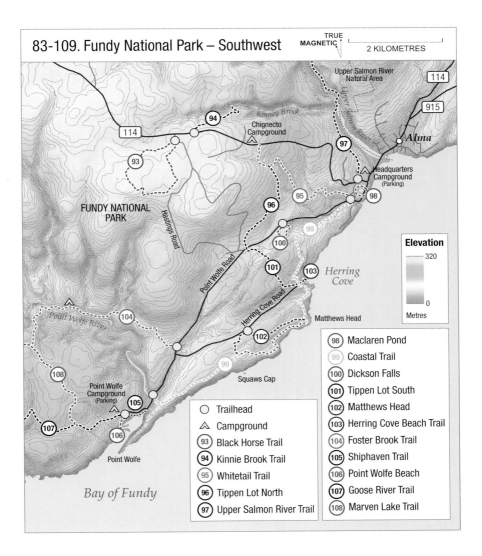

83-109. Fundy National Park – Southwest

TRUE
MAGNETIC

2 KILOMETRES

Upper Salmon River Natural Area

114

915

Kinney Brook

94

Chignecto Campground

97

Alma

114

93

Headquarters Campground (Parking)

FUNDY NATIONAL PARK

95

98

Hastings Road

96

99

Elevation

320

0

Metres

100

Point Wolfe Road

101

103

Herring Cove

104

Point Wolfe River

Herring Cove Road

Matthews Head

102

99

Squaws Cap

108

Point Wolfe Campground (Parking)

105

107

106

Point Wolfe

Bay of Fundy

○ Trailhead

△ Campground

93 Black Horse Trail

94 Kinnie Brook Trail

95 Whitetail Trail

96 Tippen Lot North

97 Upper Salmon River Trail

98 Maclaren Pond

99 Coastal Trail

100 Dickson Falls

101 Tippen Lot South

102 Matthews Head

103 Herring Cove Beach Trail

104 Foster Brook Trail

105 Shiphaven Trail

106 Point Wolfe Beach

107 Goose River Trail

108 Marven Lake Trail

Crossing a River

Most trails in this guide have small wooden bridges to safely lead the hiker over wilderness rivers and brooks. Others provide lined-up rocks that allow rock hopping to the other side. But some trails, particularly along the Fundy Coast, may require you to ford a river or tidal delta. Although fording can be a refreshing experience, it can also be a dangerous backcountry hazard. It is a very good idea to obtain tide tables (available online; before you go, be sure to consult http://www.waterlevels.gc.ca/eng/find/region/5). Once you are at a river, here are some tips on how to cross it safely:

- Use trekking poles or sticks to balance and probe.
- Keep your boots dry by wearing river sandals or Crocs.
- Always cross a river at its widest point as narrow spots are deeper and faster.
- Always step on the lowest rocks; that way, there are fewer places to slip down to.
- Look for alternatives. Do not cross if the water reaches above your knees. Scout downstream if you encounter rapids or obstacles such as deadfall.
- Face fast-flowing water upstream. Move sideways, leaning into the flowing water and bracing with your poles. If there is a steel cable, it is also best to ford on the downstream side. Note that ropes provide less support than you think!
- Before you ford fast-moving rivers, unbuckle your hip belt. If you fall, work with the current. Remove your pack if it constrains you.

96. Tippen Lot (North) (see map p. 225)

Distance: 4.6 km (2.9 mi) one way
Type: linear trail
Difficulty: easy to moderate (from South Chignecto Campground)
Ascent: 240 m (790 ft)
Hiking time: 1 hr 30 min

Map: 21 H/10 Alma (or, better, the map in the *Salt & Fir* brochure)
Trail condition: rocky, rooty, some wet spots
Cellphone coverage: N

Finding the trailhead: From the northwest entrance of Fundy National Park at Wolfe Lake, follow Route 114 for 15.5 km (9.6 mi) to the South Chignecto Campground. Turn right at the first gravel road to the left. Park alongside this road. The trail starts here. The trail is first unmarked, then later marked by blue metal blazes displaying a white hiker.

Trailhead: 45°36'10" N, 64°59'07" W

The hike: This trail shares the first 800 m/yd with the Whitetail Trail, before it turns off to the right (the left fork is the Whitetail Trail). The trail descends through beautiful hardwoods that provide semi-shade while fern covers the forest floor. The trail is narrow and in good condition in this area. The path then crosses wet areas on some boulders and descends. A brook is crossed on some rocks, and then the trail ascends again. There are boardwalk sections and some muddy spots. The mossy trail leads through tall softwoods before ending at the Point Wolfe Road. A small parking lot is located slightly to the right on the other side of the road. The trail through semi-shade and large softwoods and moss at the end is rather scenic.

97. Upper Salmon River Trail (see maps pp. 219, 225)

Distance: 8.8 km (5.5 mi) one way
Section 1: Headquarters to Black Hole: 4.7 km (2.9 mi), 2 hrs, 2 fords
Section 2: Black Hole to The Forks Trail: 4.1 km (2.5 mi), 1 hr 30 min, 2 fords
Type: linear
Difficulty: strenuous
Ascent: 180 m (590 ft)

Hiking time: 3 hrs 30 min one way
Map: 21 H/10 Alma (or, better, the map in the *Salt & Fir* brochure)
Trail condition: dry, some very narrow stretches, river fords with ropes, and some boulder scrambling
Cellphone coverage: P

Finding the trailhead: From the northwest entrance of Fundy National Park at Wolfe Lake, follow Route 114 for 18.9 km (11.7 mi) to the park headquarters parking lot. The trailhead is located a short distance away, along the spur towards the campground on the left side of the road. The trail is generally easy to find except for some portions along the riverbank, which are, however, marked by a hiker painted on rocks.

Trailhead: 45°35'46" N, 64°57'11" W

Note: The two linear sections of the Upper Salmon River Trail can be combined with the Black Hole Trail or The Forks Trail. You can leave a second vehicle at the trailhead of the chosen hiking trail (see map).

The hike:

Section 1: Headquarters to Black Hole

The well-groomed trail leads through mixed forest across some boardwalk sections. At one point, another trail from the campground joins from the right. The trail starts to ascend with a deep gully on the right, then descends. It ends at a gravel road with a cabin on the right. Cross the gravel road straight ahead and ford Kinnie Brook right beyond. This is usually possible by boulder hopping. The trail continues a short distance, keeping the Upper Salmon River to its right, and at 2.3 km (1.4 mi), it makes a sharp turn to the right and ends at the bank of the river. At this point, it is necessary to ford the Upper Salmon River. A fixed rope has been installed to help hikers in the task. Once the river has been forded, the path turns left and follows the east bank of the Upper Salmon River. The trail soon narrows and ascends, and it gets rocky and rooty. It alternates between the gravelly riverbank and the woods near the river. The narrow path follows a fixed installed rope on the right, as there is a steep drop-off on the left towards the river. Cross a landslide and continue right into the woods. Here, Lake Brook must be forded, which is usually possible by boulder hopping. Continue along the beach, where a ranger cabin becomes visible on the right at Black Hole.

Atlantic salmon rest in the Black Hole pool in the fall before swimming upstream to spawn. In summer, this spot serves as a refreshing pool for humans.

Section 2: Black Hole to The Forks

At a sign, the trail turns right off the river, gets into the woods for some 100 m/yd, and turns left at a pit toilet. (At this point, the Black Hole Trail continues to the right.) The short spur leads towards a vista point overlooking the river. Just before it reaches this dead end, the trail turns off to the right. The trail continues close to the Upper Salmon River, where it crosses several small creek beds that are usually dry. Note the cascading Upper Vault Brook at 6.7 km (4.2 mi) across the Upper Salmon River. Continue through mixed forest on the stony but mostly level trail. Just before reaching the confluence of the Forty Five and Broad Rivers at 8.8 km (5.5 mi), the trail scrambles over several boulders. At this point, you can either ford the Forty Five River or retrace your steps to the trailhead. The trail can be forded with the help of a fixed rope. Turning left on the other side, the trail immediately reaches the Broad River with its huge boulders and salmon pools. Ford the Broad River with the help of another fixed rope and continue to ascend the Forks Trail to the Laverty Falls parking lot.

98. MacLaren Pond Trail (see map p.225)

Distance: 0.5 km (0.3 mi)
Type: loop
Difficulty: easy
Ascent: negligible
Hiking time: 20 min

Map: 21 H/10 Alma (or, better, the map in the *Salt & Fir* brochure)
Trail condition: dry
Cellphone coverage: Y

Finding the trailhead: From the northwest entrance of Fundy National Park at Wolfe Lake, follow Route 114 for 19 km (11.8 mi) to the junction at park headquarters. Turn right onto Point Wolfe Road and follow it for 100 m/yd. Parking is on the left side of the road, and the pond is located to the right side of the road. There are some signs, but the trail is obvious.

Trailhead: 45°35'37" N, 64°57'05" W

The hike: The trail leads around the lake in a counter-clockwise direction. The main feature of this trail is the beaver lodge on the northwestern side of the pond. Beaver can frequently be seen. There are some wooden plaques explaining the medicinal and spiritual symbols of First Nations.

99. Coastal Trail (see map p. 225)

Distance: 10.1 km (6.3 mi) one way
Section 1: Swimming pool to Herring Cove: 3.2 km (2 mi) one way
Section 2: Herring Cove to Point Wolfe parking lot: 6.9 km (4.3 mi) one way
Type: linear
Difficulty: moderate
Ascent: 150 m (490 ft)

Hiking time: 3 hrs 15 min one way
Maps: 21 H/10 Alma and 21 H 11 Waterford (or, better, the map in the *Salt & Fir* brochure)
Trail condition: a few wet spots along the middle section, rooty
Cellphone coverage:

Finding the Trailhead:
Section 1 Access: From the northwest entrance of Fundy National Park at Wolfe Lake, follow Route 114 for 19 km (11.8 mi) to the junction at park headquarters. Turn right onto Point Wolfe Road and follow it for 500 m/yd to an old stone bridge leading to the swimming pool. There is a parking lot next to the stone bridge on Point Wolfe Road. Walk to the trailhead by crossing the bridge and see the trailhead immediately on the right.

Section 2 Access: At park headquarters, turn right onto Point Wolfe Road and follow it for 3.8 km (2.4 mi). Turn left and reach the Herring Cove parking lot after 1.9 km (1.2 mi).

The Coastal Trail is an interesting trail to hike in its entire length from the swimming pool to the Point Wolfe parking lot. In order to avoid having to hike back, you need to arrange a pick-up or leave a second vehicle at the other end. Some 4" x 4" blue metal blazes displaying a hiker mark the trail.

Trailhead: 1) 45°35'28"N, 64°57'15"W
2) 45°34'27"N, 64°58'09"W at Herring Cove

The hike:

Section 1: Swimming Pool to Herring Cove
The trail ascends steeply for a short distance and then crosses a paved road. It continues to climb for quite some time, but more gently now through a predominantly softwood forest. The trail then descends rather steeply to a T-junction at 2.8 km (1.7 mi). At this point, the Tippen Lot Trail turns right whereas the Coastal Trail continues straight/left, leading to the Herring Cove parking lot. A nice seaward lookout with some interpretive displays awaits the visitor here. From the picnic site with a toilet, a short path leads down to the beach at Herring Cove.

Section 2: Herring Cove to Point Wolfe parking lot

The trail continues straight across the parking lot and picnic site to the right of a shelter. It dips down to a creek and crosses it. Keep right at a fork; the left fork leads to Herring Cove Beach. Beyond a lookout across the bay, the trail starts ascending through very pretty hardwoods. Beyond a plateau, the trail descends through mixed woods and reaches Matthews Head at 5 km (3.1 mi). There is a good view across the bay at this point, with a small cove immediately to the left and the town of Alma straight ahead in the distance. The trail continues to the right and at 200m/yd turns left at a junction with the Matthews Head Trail, while the Matthews Head Trail departs to the right.

The trail crosses two short boardwalks before the bay becomes visible again. From this point on, the trail is quite level, with the bay visible from time to time. The trail traverses a meadow in the woods on a boardwalk section, where there are some wet spots. Beyond the meadow, the trail leads to an excellent lookout over the bay. From here, you can see Squaws Cap, a flowerpot rock in the bay. The trail then descends, crosses a small brook, and continues through mixed forest. At another junction with the Matthews Head Trail, continue straight and follow the forest trail for 3.2 km (2 mi). The level trail starts sloping down at 9.5 km (5.9 mi), swings in a westerly direction, and descends steeply. The trail terminates at the Point Wolfe Road across from a parking lot and picnic site at the Point Wolfe River. From here, turn left and follow the road to the covered bridge for 500 m/yd, and just behind the bridge, turn left onto the 0.5 km (0.3 mi) long Shiphaven Trail and follow it to the parking lot at Point Wolfe.

100. Dickson Falls (see map p. 225)

Distance: 1 km (0.6 mi)
Type: loop
Difficulty: easy
Ascent: negligible
Hiking time: 30 min

Map: 21 H/10 Alma (or, better, the map in the *Salt & Fir* brochure)
Trail condition: dry, boardwalk
Cellphone coverage: Y

Finding the trailhead: From the northwest entrance of Fundy National Park at Wolfe Lake, follow Route 114 for 19 km (11.8 mi) to the park headquarters. Turn right onto Point Wolfe Road and follow it for 2 km (1.2 mi). There is a large parking lot with a fine viewpoint at its end. The trailhead is located to the right of the lookout. There are no trail markings, but the trail is well groomed and easy to follow.

Trailhead: 45°35'13" N, 64°58'26" W

The hike: The trail descends; at a junction, take the left path to begin the loop. Soon you'll reach the cascading Dickson Brook with its mossy rocks. Climb up along the shady creek on wooden stairs and boardwalks to get a close-up view of the plunging Dickson Falls at 0.5 km (0.3 mi). Take the scenic left trail at a junction (the right is a shortcut to the parking lot) and walk along the banks of the brook. The trail climbs into a nice stand of hardwoods before it returns to the parking lot. The major attraction of this popular trail is Dickson Falls.

101. Tippen Lot (South) (see map p. 225)

Distance: 1.9 km (1.2 mi) one way
Type: linear trail
Difficulty: moderate
Ascent: 140 m (460 ft)
Hiking time: 1 hr one way

Map: 21 H/10 Alma (or, better, the map in the *Salt & Fir* brochure)
Trail condition: rocky, rooty, some wet spots
Cellphone coverage: N

Finding the trailhead: From the northwest entrance of Fundy National Park at Wolfe Lake, follow Route 114 for 18.9 km (11.7 mi) to the park headquarters. Turn right onto Point Wolfe Road and follow it for 3 km (1.9 mi) to a parking lot on the left side of the road. There is parking for about ten vehicles. The trailhead is located a short distance east of the parking lot on the south side of the road (the same as the parking lot).

Trailhead: 45°34'56" N, 64°59'03" W

The hike: The trail descends to a beautiful beaver pond in the middle of the woods. From this point on, it ascends steeply through softwoods. It then levels off before starting its fairly gentle descent with some steeper sections interspersed. The trail ends at the Coastal Trail. Turn right onto the Coastal Trail and follow it to the Herring Cove parking lot a short distance beyond. The main feature is the quiet beaver pond in the forest.

102. Matthews Head (see map p. 225)

Distance: 4.5 km (2.8 mi)
Type: loop
Difficulty: easy to moderate
Ascent: 100 m (330 ft)
Hiking time: 1 hr 30 min

Map: 21 H/10 Alma (or, better, the map in the *Salt & Fir* brochure)
Trail condition: rooty, dry
Cellphone coverage: P

Finding the trailhead: From the northwest entrance of Fundy National Park at Wolfe Lake, follow Route 114 for 19 km (11.8 mi) to the junction at the park headquarters. Turn right onto Point Wolfe Road and follow it for about 5.9 km (3.7 mi), then turn left onto Herring Cove Road. Follow it for 1.6 km (1 mi), then turn right into the parking lot. There are about ten parking places at the trailhead. The trail is marked by some blue metal blazes showing a hiker.

Trailhead: 45°33'56" N, 64°59'04" W

The hike: This trail follows an old wagon road that gradually descends through soft-woods. At 1.2 km (0.7 mi) it passes by the remains of an old homestead settled by Thomas and Ellen Matthews in the 1860s. At a junction at 1.4 km (0.9 mi), continue straight/left for another 200 m/yd, where you reach Matthews Head. This outcrop offers a beautiful view of the Bay of Fundy. You can see the town of Alma from here as well as a cave and a small bay with a sandy beach to the left of Matthews Head. Return to the junction, turn left onto the Coastal Trail, and follow the path along the coast, as it continues up, down, and level to reach Squaws Cap Overlook. Soon beyond the lookout, the trail swings inland, ascends, then levels off and reaches

a junction at 3.3 km (2.1 mi). Leave the Coastal Trail and complete the loop by taking the right path marked Parking. The trail ascends through woods until it reaches a small field with pine trees. It turns right and then crosses a large field, which is abundant with wildflowers, bunchberries, blueberries, and rasp-berries in season, before it continues on a grassy road to the parking lot.

103. **Herring Cove Beach Trail** (see map p. 225)

Distance: 1 km (0.6 mi) rtn
Type: linear
Difficulty: easy
Ascent: negligible
Hiking time: 20 min

Map: 21 H/10 Alma (or, better, the map in the *Salt & Fir* brochure)
Trail condition: dry
Cellphone coverage: P

Finding the trailhead: From the northwest entrance of Fundy National Park at Wolfe Lake, follow Route 114 for 18.9 km (11.7 mi) to the park headquarters. Turn right onto Point Wolfe Road and follow it for 5.8 km (3.6 mi). Turn left onto Herring Cove Road and follow it to its end at a large parking lot. The trailhead is straight ahead past the outhouse next to the viewing platform. There are no trail markings, but the trail is easy to follow and cannot be missed.

Trailhead: 45°34'32" N, 64°58'09" W

The hike: The trail provides access to one of the major sandy beaches in Fundy National Park.

104. Foster Brook Trail (see map p.239)

Distance: 4.4 km (2.7 mi) one way to Marven Lake Trail [3 km (1.9 mi) one way to the Point Wolfe River crossing]
Type: linear
Difficulty: moderate to strenuous
Ascent: 210 m (690 ft)

Hiking time: 1 hr 45 min one way [to Point Wolfe River 1 hr 15 min rtn]
Map: 21 H/11 Waterford (or, better, the map in the *Salt & Fir* brochure)
Trail condition: dry, rocky, one ford
Cellphone coverage: N

Finding the trailhead: From the northwest entrance of Fundy National Park at Wolfe Lake, follow Route 114 for 18.9 km (11.7 mi) to the park headquarters. Turn right onto Point Wolfe Road and follow it for 5.8 km (3.6 mi), then turn right again onto a gravel road. Drive up the gravel road to its end for 0.2 km (0.1 mi). There is room for about eight vehicles. The trailhead is located at the far left of the parking lot. The trail is marked by blue metal signs with a hiker.

Trailhead: 45°33'47" N, 65°00'22" W

The hike: The trail ascends rather steeply for a short distance, then it continues up gentler grades through softwoods. At 1.6 km (1 mi) the trail slopes steeply downwards for some 300 m/yd until it reaches a junction. A short spur provides access to Point Wolfe River. The main trail turns sharply to the right. It crosses Foster Brook and another small brook (both can typically be crossed by boulder hopping) and continues to follow Point Wolfe River for 1.3 km (0.8 mi) to a junction at a wilderness campground. This part of the trail is level and hiking is easy. A short spur to the left leads down to campsites and the river. The main trail continues straight for a short distance before turning sharply to the left and descending to the Point Wolfe River.

Ford the cobblestone riverbed and reach the continuation of the trail directly across at 3 km (1.9 mi). From here, the rooty trail climbs steeply through old-growth red spruce forest, leads through wet sections, and continues to climb before it ascends more gently and levels off. It ends at the Marven Lake Trail at 4.4 km (2.7 mi); see the trail description on p.244. To return to the parking lot, turn left and left again at the junction with the Goose River Trail. From here, return to the parking lot at Point Wolfe.

83-109. Fundy National Park – Southwest

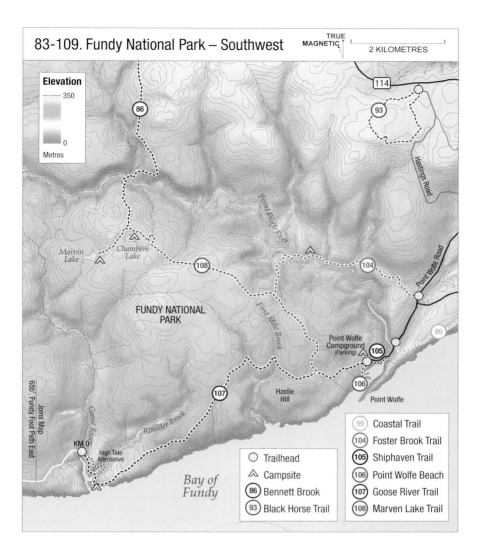

TRUE
MAGNETIC
2 KILOMETRES

Elevation

350

0

Metres

114

93

Hastings Road

86

Point Wolfe River

Marvin Lake

Chambers Lake

108

104

Point Wolfe Road

FUNDY NATIONAL PARK

First Mile Brook

Point Wolfe Campground (Parking)

99

105

Joins Map 68b: Fundy Foot Path East

Goose River

Rossiter Brook

107

Hastie Hill

106

Point Wolfe

KM 0

High Tide Alternative

Bay of Fundy

○ Trailhead

⚑ Campsite

86 Bennett Brook

93 Black Horse Trail

99 Coastal Trail

104 Foster Brook Trail

105 Shiphaven Trail

106 Point Wolfe Beach

107 Goose River Trail

108 Marven Lake Trail

105. Shiphaven Trail <small>(see map p. 239)</small>

Distance: 1 km (0.6 mi) rtn
Type: linear
Difficulty: easy
Ascent: 45 m (150 ft)
Hiking time: 25 min rtn

Map: 21 H/11 Waterford (or, better, the map in the *Salt & Fir* brochure)
Trail condition: boardwalk sections, stairs
Cellphone coverage: N

Finding the trailhead: From the northwest entrance of Fundy National Park at Wolfe Lake, follow Route 114 for 18.9 km (11.7 mi) to the park headquarters. Turn right onto Point Wolfe Road and follow it for 7.7 km (4.8 mi) to its end. The trailhead is well marked and is located at the far end of the parking lot. There are no trail markings, but the short trail cannot be missed.

Trailhead: 45°32'58" N, 65°01'07" W

The hike: This well-groomed, partly boardwalk trail leads through a stand of tall soft-woods. After 100 m/yd, continue straight at a junction (the right fork leads to Point Wolfe Beach). The trail then starts to descend, keeping the mouth of the Point Wolfe River to its right. There are some fine views of the inlet and the surrounding cliffs. The trail terminates at the western end of the covered bridge across the Point Wolfe River. The original bridge was accidentally destroyed by workers in late December 1990. From the platform you can see the back side of the new covered bridge (built in 1992), remnants of an old dam, part of an earlier sawmill operation, and the scenic Point Wolfe estuary.

Shiphaven: The Legacy of Logging

In the 19th and early 20th centuries, logging was one of the main industries in New Brunswick. Near the site of the covered bridge, the logging companies once built a dam and a mill, which was driven by the water of the Point Wolfe River. The ability to process wood did, however, come at a price. The sawdust, which was an unusable by-product at the time, was dumped into the water. Furthermore, the dam blocked access for fish, most prominently salmon that swim upstream to spawn. The fishing industry, another

important generator of employment and wealth in the province, complained about these detrimental effects as early as the mid-1800s. As the mill was shut down and Fundy National Park was established in 1948, the dam was also removed, thus allowing the salmon to swim upriver as they used to.

106. Point Wolfe Beach (see map p.239)

Distance: 0.8 km (0.5 mi) rtn
Type: linear
Difficulty: easy
Ascent: 135 m (445 ft)
Hiking time: 30 min rtn

Map: 21 H/11 Waterford (or, better, the map in the *Salt & Fir* brochure)
Trail condition: boardwalk, steps
Cellphone coverage: N

Finding the trailhead: From the northwest entrance of Fundy National Park at Wolfe Lake, follow Route 114 for 18.9 km (11.7 mi) to the park headquarters. Turn right onto Point Wolfe Road and follow it for 7.7 km (4.8 mi) to its end at a parking lot. There are no trail markings, but the trail is obvious and cannot be missed.

Trailhead: 45°32'58" N, 65°01'07" W

The hike: Start in the far left corner of the parking lot at the trailhead that the Point Wolfe Beach Trail shares with the Shiphaven Trail. Follow the trail for a short distance, then turn off to the right at a well-marked junction. The path leads directly to Point Wolfe Beach. You pass by an old growth of red spruce forest. The gravelly beach features an old dam, some remaining pilings from an old wharf, and a variety of sea life.

107. **Goose River Trail** (see map p. 239)

Distance: 15.8 km (9.8 mi) rtn
Type: linear
Difficulty: moderate
Ascent: 165 m (540 ft)
Hiking time: 4 hrs 30 min rtn

Map: 21 H/11 Waterford (or, better, the map in the *Salt & Fir* brochure)
Trail condition: dry, gravelly
Cellphone coverage: N

Finding the trailhead: From the northwest entrance of Fundy National Park at Wolfe Lake, follow Route 114 for 18.9 km (11.7 mi) to the park headquarters. Turn right onto Point Wolfe Road and follow it for 7.7 km (4.8 mi) to its end. The trailhead is well marked and is located at the far end of the parking lot. The trail is unmarked, but
it follows an old cart road and cannot be missed.

Trailhead: 45°32'57"N, 65°01'10"W

The hike: Not far from the trailhead, the trail joins a wide, old cart road, which provided access to the tiny settlement of Goose River in the last century. The trail soon turns left, and for the next 0.9 km (0.6 mi) it ascends steadily until it reaches the well-marked junction with the Marven Lake Trail. Continue straight and cross Mile Brook at 3.7 km (2.3 mi). Some overgrown clearings on both sides of the trail indicate the sites of old settlements. At 7.7 km (4.8 mi) the trail reaches wilderness campsite #4, located on a high bluff overlooking the rocky coastline. Below campsite #4 on the right side of the trail, there is a turnoff onto a trail that connects the Goose River Trail with the Fundy Footpath. This narrow path can be used during high tides. The trail passes campsite #5, then swings sharply to the right and descends steeply to the beach with two additional campsites near the Bay of Fundy and the mouth of the meandering Goose River. The yellow-blazed National Trail connects the Goose River Trail with the Fundy Footpath during low tide (see the trail description on p. 165). Note that this trail is presently being rerouted.

108. Marven Lake Trail (see map p. 239)

Distance: 16 km (9.9 mi) rtn
Type: linear
Difficulty: easy to moderate
Ascent: 210 m (690 ft)
Hiking time: 4 hrs 15 min rtn
Map: 21 H/11 Waterford (or, better,

the map in the *Salt & Fir* brochure)
Trail condition: dry, often rocky, wide old road. There are some wet spots near Marven Lake.
Cellphone coverage: N

Finding the trailhead: From the northwest entrance of Fundy National Park at Wolfe Lake, follow Route 114 for 18.9 km (11.7 mi) to the park headquarters. Turn right onto Point Wolfe Road and follow it for 7.7 km (4.8 mi) to its end. The trailhead is well marked and is located at the far end of the parking lot. There are no trail markings, but the trail cannot be missed.

Trailhead: 45°32'57" N, 65°01'10" W

The hike: The first part of the Marven Lake Trail duplicates the Goose River Trail. From the trailhead, a path leads through a small forest and very soon reaches an old wagon road, which turns left and rises steeply at times. At 1 km (0.6 mi), keep right at a fork. The trail here follows another wide and mostly level road with a few gentle ascents. At 3.4 km (2.1 mi), the Foster Brook Trail departs to the right. Continue straight on the wide road. It is lined with young growth and makes for an easy hike. At 6.4 km (4 mi), the original trail is often flooded due to beaver activity. Just before that spot is reached, an unmarked detour departs to the right. It gives the area a wide berth, crosses a small brook on a wooden bridge along the way, and rejoins the main trail a short distance above the flooded area. At 7.2 km (4.5 mi), Bennett Brook

Trail departs to the right, and the main road makes a sharp left turn. Just beyond the turn, a short side trail to the left leads down to quiet Chambers Lake and a backcountry campsite. The main trail continues for a short distance, passes two wilderness campsites, and ends at boggy Marven Lake. The trail gives access to Chambers and Marven Lakes, which are dark with acids from their boggy edges.

109. Black Hole Trail  (see map p. 219)

Distance: 11 km (6.8 mi) rtn
Type: linear
Difficulty: easy to moderate
Ascent: 210 m (690 ft)
Hiking time: 2 hrs 30 min rtn

Map: 21 H/10 Alma (or, better, the map in the *Salt & Fir* brochure)
Trail condition: dry, rocky, wide cart road
Cellphone coverage: P

Finding the trailhead: From the northwest entrance of Fundy National Park at Wolfe Lake, follow Route 114 to the park exit at Alma. Continue on Route 114 for 3.4 km (2.1 mi) and then turn left onto Forty-Five Road. Follow this road for 2.1 km (1.3 mi) to a fork. Keep left towards Forty-Five Bridge. After 1.6 km (1 mi), this rough gravel road enters Fundy National Park. Just beyond the sign for the park, turn left into a parking lot about 100 m/yd from the road. The trailhead can be found at the end of the parking lot. There are no trail markings, but the trail is easy to follow.

Trailhead: 45°39'22"N, 64°56'07"W

The hike: After a short distance, the trail passes through a gate. It then leads through mixed forest with some raspberry bushes along the way. Later the trail passes through a beautiful stand of young hardwoods, mostly maple and beech. This part is very scenic. Beyond a small creek, the trail gently slopes downward. At 4.8 km (3 mi) the trail drops sharply until it reaches a T-junction next to a pit toilet on the right. To the right, there is a spur to a vista point that overlooks the Upper Salmon River, and to the left, there is a ranger cabin. Continue straight. A short distance below, the trail ends at the Upper Salmon River. The main feature of the trail is the Black Hole pool in the Upper Salmon River. In late summer and fall, Atlantic salmon linger here awhile before they move upstream to spawn.

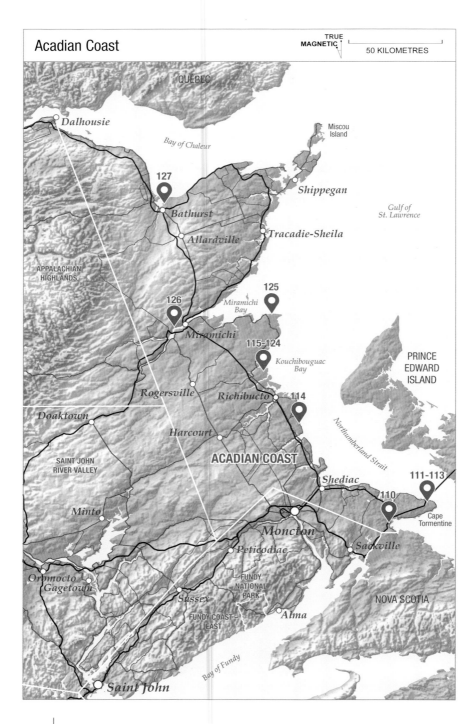

Acadian Coast

TRUE
MAGNETIC
50 KILOMETRES

QUÉBEC

Dalhousie

Bay of Chaleur

Miscou
Island

127

Bathurst

Shippegan

Allardville

Tracadie-Sheila

Gulf of
St. Lawrence

APPALACHIAN
HIGHLANDS

126

125

*Miramichi
Bay*

Miramichi

115-124

*Kouchibouguac
Bay*

PRINCE
EDWARD
ISLAND

Rogersville

Richibucto

114

Doaktown

Northumberland Strait

Harcourt

ACADIAN COAST

SAINT JOHN
RIVER VALLEY

Shediac

111-113

110

Minto

Cape
Tormentine

Moncton

Sackville

Oromocto
Gagetown

Peticodiac

FUNDY
NATIONAL
PARK

NOVA SCOTIA

Sussex

Alma

FUNDY COAST –
EAST

Bay of Fundy

Saint John

ACADIAN COAST

New Brunswick's Acadian Coast is composed of a number of distinct areas. Shediac is located on the eastern shores of the Northumberland Strait, which boasts the warmest saltwater beaches north of Virginia. The small town of Bouctouche is the birthplace of industrialist K.C. Irving, who was one of the richest men in the world before his death in 1992. The nearby Irving Eco-Centre preserves one of the remaining sandbars on the northeastern coast of North America. Renowned Acadian author Antonine Maillet was born in Bouctouche. At the northern end of the Northumberland Strait is Kouchibouguac National Park, which features sandy beaches and lagoons, salt marshes and bogs.

At the city of Miramichi, where river meets ocean, wood products are shipped for the international market. Irish and Scots residents celebrate their heritage each summer with fiddles and bagpipes. Newspaper magnate and benefactor Lord Beaverbrook (Sir Max Aitken), shipping magnate Joseph Cunard, and R.B. Bennett, the only Canadian prime minister born in New Brunswick, were all residents of Miramichi.

The coastal forest bog, with its black spruce and stunted larches, is characteristic of the northern tip of the Acadian Peninsula. Peat moss operations and fisheries are the mainstays of the economy. Near Caraquet, the Acadian Historical Village depicts the life of settlers in the eighteenth century. The northern communities of Caraquet, Bathurst, and Dalhousie are strung along the miles of sandy beaches of Chaleur Bay. It was in this bay that the last naval battle for the possession of Canada between the British and the French took place in 1760.

110. Red-Winged Blackbird Trail

Distance: 2 km (1.2 mi) rtn
Type: loop
Difficulty: easy
Ascent: negligible

Hiking time: 30 min
Map: 21 I/1 Port Elgin
Trail condition: dry
Cellphone coverage: Y

Finding the trailhead: On Highway 2, take exit 513B and follow Highway 16 towards PEI. After 19.2 km (11.9 mi), the road reaches a fork with Route 970. Keep right and drive through Baie Verte. Follow this road for 1.6 km (1 mi) to the white St. James United Church on the right. Directly opposite, there is a small parking lot for about ten vehicles. The trailhead is located here, next to a small observation tower at Goodwin Park. This wide trail cannot be missed.

Trailhead: 46°01'01" N, 64°06'08" W

The hike: Follow the wide grassy track to the right of the observation tower. Some spurs depart to the left; they either lead to picnic sites, observation sites, or into the marshes. At some point, there is a spur to the right to Stan's Tower, an observation tower that overlooks the marshes. In general, the trail keeps first, Goodwins Pond and later, Klass's Pond to its left. It ends at a T-junction with Coburg Road, a wide and straight trail. Turn left and follow Coburg Road to its end at Route 970. Turn left and follow the road back to the parking lot. Birding is excellent in this area at just about any time of the year.

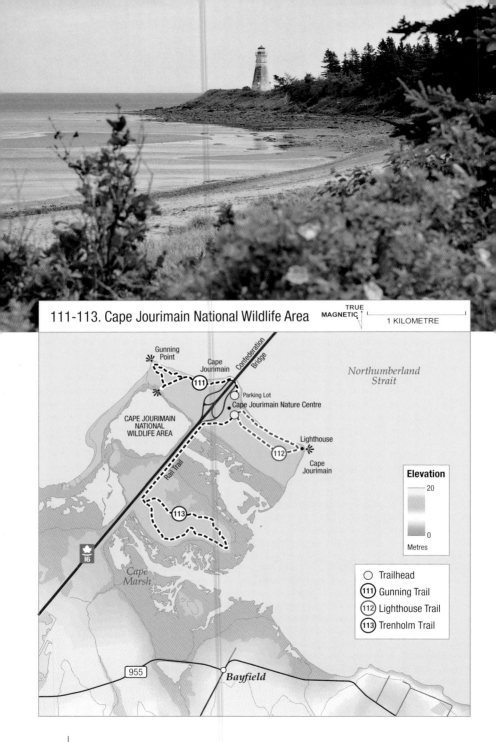

111-113. Cape Jourimain National Wildlife Area

TRUE
MAGNETIC
1 KILOMETRE

Gunning
Point

Cape
Jourimain

Confederation
Bridge

111

*Northumberland
Strait*

Parking Lot
Cape Jourimain Nature Centre

CAPE JOURIMAIN
NATIONAL
WILDLIFE AREA

Lighthouse

112

Cape
Jourimain

Rail Trail

Elevation

20

113

0

Metres

I6

*Cape
Marsh*

○ Trailhead

111 Gunning Trail

112 Lighthouse Trail

113 Trenholm Trail

955

Bayfield

111-113. Cape Jourimain National Wildlife Area

Until 1917, iceboat services at Cape Jourimain were Prince Edward Island's only link to the mainland in the winter. When the impressive 12.4 km (7.7 mi) Confederation Bridge across the Northumberland Strait was completed in 1997, 640 hectares (1,580 acres) near Cape Jourimain were designated as a National Wildlife Area to protect the diverse ecosystem. The area is designated for conservation and protected by the federal government under Environment Canada's Protected Areas Network. An on-site Nature Centre explains the ecological and historical aspects of Cape Jourimain. The following three footpaths invite hikers to explore this unique area. For more information, call 1-506-538-2220 or check the website at www.capejourimain.ca.

Finding the trailhead: On Highway 2, take exit 513B and follow Highway 16 towards PEI. After 25 km (15.5 mi), you reach a traffic circle. Continue straight towards the Confederation Bridge to Prince Edward Island. After another 25.2 km (15.7 mi), take exit 51 (the last exit before the bridge) to the Cape Jourimain Nature Centre. There is a parking lot directly in front of the centre.

111. Gunning Trail

Distance: 2.5 km (1.6 mi)
Type: loop
Difficulty: easy
Ascent: negligible

Hiking time: 45 min
Map: 11 L/4 Cape Tormentine
Trail condition: dry
Cellphone coverage: Y

Finding the trailhead: The trailhead is at the far end of the parking lot directly in front of the Cape Jourimain Nature Centre. The trail is unmarked, but it cannot be missed.

Trailhead: 46°09'46" N, 63°48'53" W

The hike: The trail starts at the far end of the parking lot. It enters the woods, turns left, and continues underneath the Confederation Bridge. The wide, grassy trail passes a signboard with some information and follows the shoreline for some distance. As it swings to the left into the woods, a very short spur leads towards the beach and offers a good view of the shoreline and the bridge. At a boardwalk section, keep to the right at a fork. Follow the trail to Gunning Point with a viewing platform and continue to a T-junction. A spur to the right leads to another observation platform that allows views across a brackish marsh, but the main trail turns to the left. After some distance, it reaches the fork and returns from there. Benches invite hikers to enjoy views across the Northumberland Strait and the Confederation Bridge crossing it and vistas across a brackish marsh as well as beautiful wild roses along the trail.

112. Lighthouse Trail

Distance: 2 km (1.2 mi) rtn
Type: loop
Difficulty: easy
Ascent: negligible

Hiking time: 30 min
Map: 11 L/4 Cape Tormentine
Trail condition: dry
Cellphone coverage: Y

Finding the trailhead: The trailhead is located right behind the Nature Centre. There are no trail markings, but the trail cannot be missed.

Trailhead: 46°09'41" N, 63°48'52" W

The hike: The trail follows the Northumberland Strait to a lighthouse and continues from there in clockwise fashion. The Jourimain Lighthouse, views across the Northumberland Strait and the Confederation Bridge, and birding are the main attractions of the trail. The trail provides access to a sandy beach and allows reasonably close access to an osprey nest.

113. Trenholm Trail

Distance: 5.5 km (3.4 mi) rtn
Type: linear + loop
Difficulty: easy
Ascent: negligible

Hiking time: 1 hr 30 min rtn
Map: 11 L/4 Cape Tormentine
Trail condition: dry
Cellphone coverage: Y

Finding the trailhead: Walk through the Entrance Pavilion and the Nature Centre behind it. The trailhead is located right behind the Nature Centre. There are no trail markings, but the trail is obvious and cannot be missed.

Trailhead: 46°09'41"N, 63°48'52"W

The hike: The trail starts behind the Cape Jourimain Nature Centre. Walk straight for a short distance and keep right at a fork. Cross a wide woods road and follow the signs to an osprey nest. Keep right at a fork and follow the grassy trail lined with wild roses. Eventually, the trail hits the road and a wide rail trail that parallels it. Walk on the rail trail for 0.9 km (0.6 mi) with a salt marsh to the left, then turn left into the woods at a signboard. Keep to the right at a fork and follow the loop through softwoods in a counter-clockwise direction. The trail returns to a point near the rail trail, on which hikers will return to the visitor centre. The trail features good views of salt marshes, an osprey nest, and a blind for bird observations.

Iceboat Crossings, Jourimain to PEI

Since 1829 and running for ninety years, there was a unique connection between the mainland and Prince Edward Island in the winter. So-called iceboats, i.e., flat-bottomed boats with runners, would start at Cape Jourimain to make the 18 km (10 nautical mile) trip to PEI. On that trip, they hauled passengers and freight. The most important freight was mail, which also explains why the service had government support. Passengers were expected to help push the boats over the ice, whenever necessary, unless they paid the premium fare. The crossing was not only hard work, but it was also dangerous, and some passengers and guides lost their lives during the crossing.

---

114. Bouctouche Sandbar
(Irving Eco-Centre: La Dune de Bouctouche)

Distance: 22.6 km (14 mi) rtn
Type: linear
Difficulty: easy to moderate
Ascent: negligible
Hiking time: 5 hrs 15 min rtn

Maps: 21 I/10 Richibucto and 21 I/7 Bouctouche
Trail condition: boardwalk, dry, sandy
Cellphone coverage: Y

Finding the trailhead: From Moncton, follow Highway 15 east to Shediac, then turn onto Highway 11 north towards Miramichi. Take exit 32A towards Bouctouche. Turn right at the T-junction, and after 1.1 km (0.7 mi), Route 134 swings to the left, whereas NB 475 continues straight. Follow NB 475 for 8.9 km (5.5 mi), then turn left into a parking lot. On the other side of NB 475 is a reception centre with information displays, an observation tower, and a boardwalk that marks the beginning of the trail. The trail follows first a boardwalk, then skirts the beach. It cannot be missed.

Trailhead: 46°31'58" N, 64°41'39" W

The hike: The trail begins at the visitor centre. For the first 0.8 km (0.5 mi), it follows the meandering boardwalk that overlooks the beach and the Northumberland Strait. Along the boardwalk, a spur departs to the right: it leads down to a path through Acadian forest back to the trailhead. Back on the boardwalk, it continues until it ends at the beach. The trail then continues along the

beach, passing the pilings of a defunct jetty. At 10.8 km (6.7 mi), the beach turns sharply to the right (west). After a short distance a lighthouse marks the end of the trail. From here, there are some fine vistas across the Bay of Bouctouche. Shorebirds can be seen along the beach. Some shells, crabs, and an occasional sand dollar may also be found. A severe storm in 2010 moved the shifting sand and destroyed much of the boardwalk. A new, shorter boardwalk was built in 2013, and marram grass was planted to stabilize the dune.

114. Bouctouche Sandbar

TRUE
MAGNETIC
2 KILOMETRES

○ Trailhead
114 Bouctouche Sandbar

Elevation
20

0
Metres

Chemin Renaud

Interpretation Centre
(Parking)

*Northumberland
Strait*

*Village
-Ste-Croix*
Chemin Perry

*Fond
de la Baie*

*Buctouche
Baie*
475

114

Chemin de Roches

*Baie de
Buctouche*

Bouctouche

134

*Dixon
Point*
535

Lighthouse

115-124. Kouchibouguac National Park

Kouchibouguac National Park, one of New Brunswick's two national parks, was established in 1969. With its 240 km² (92 sq mi), it is the largest park in the province. The name "Kouchibouguac" derives from a Mik'maq word meaning "river of the long tides." Unlike Fundy National Park, Kouchibouguac is flat, and its major attractions are salt marshes, saltwater lagoons, sand dunes, bogs, and beaches, with their marine environment. Due to the Labrador Current, the water in the Northumberland Strait is quite chilly; in contrast, the water temperature in shallow lagoons may reach 20°C (68°F) in July and August.

The park offers a wide variety of outdoor recreation, most prominently biking, hiking, canoeing, and swimming. Birdwatching is also excellent along the shore and in the marshes. More than two hundred bird species have been recorded. Interpretive programs, dune walks by moonlight, Aboriginal celebrations, and outdoor theatre are offered throughout the summer. In the winter, the park is popular for cross-country skiing. Animals that are frequently sighted include various amphibians as well as deer, bear, moose, mink, lynx, bobcats, coyotes, river otters, flying squirrels, and black terns.

Kouchibouguac National Park is reached from Moncton by taking Highway 15 to Shediac, then following Highway 11 north for 91.2 km (56.7 mi). Turn right onto NB 480, cross Route 134, and enter the park. Continue straight to a junction with the visitor centre located on the right. The trailheads of all trails in the park are described from this junction.

At the visitor centre you can pick up a free visitor guide and map of the park. Information is also available by calling 1-888-773-8888 or online at https://www.pc.gc.ca/en/pn-np/nb/kouchibouguac.

Note: Kouchibouguac National Park has recently undertaken work to redesign and reroute some trails. Every effort has been made to ensure the information presented here is correct but we suggest getting an up-to-date map from the park prior to hiking.

115. Tweedie Trail (see map p. 261)

Distance: 1.2 km (0.7 mi)
Type: loop
Difficulty: easy
Ascent: negligible
Hiking time: 20 min

Map: 21 I/14 Kouchibouguac (or, better, in the *Kouchibouguac National Park Visitor Guide*)
Trail condition: dry
Cellphone coverage: Y

Finding the trailhead: From the junction at the visitor centre, continue straight on Route 117 north for about 3.3 km (2.1 mi). The trailhead is located on the right side of a parking lot. Keep right at any forks.

Trailhead: 46°47'51" N, 65°00'50" W

The hike: The main features of this trail are a saline marsh, a cattail marsh, wildflower fields, and open views across the Kouchibouguac River. This is a great place to observe waterfowl. It is advisable to stay on the gravel trail, as poison ivy grows among the raspberries, thistles, and fireweed.

Salt Marshes

Salt marshes are wetlands that exist in areas flooded by tides. Their soils are typically muddy, often containing peat-like material formed by decomposing and rotting plants (hence their rotten stench) and possess a very low level of oxygen (hypoxia). Salt marshes provide shelter for salt-tolerant plants, protect inland areas from high wind and water erosion by establishing a buffer zone, and provide wildlife with shelter from harsher conditions that exist outside the marsh. The salinity of salt marshes is about 15-18 ppt (parts per thousand), i.e. 1.5-1.8%, as compared to the ocean's average of 3.5%.

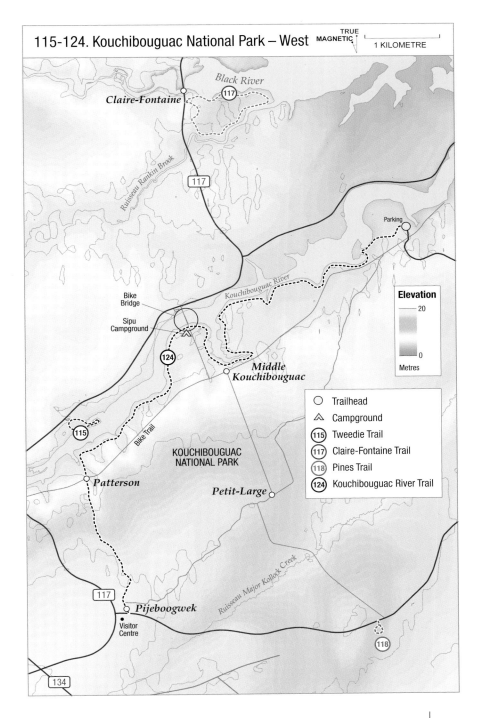

115-124. Kouchibouguac National Park – West

TRUE
MAGNETIC
1 KILOMETRE

Black River

Claire-Fontaine

117

117

Ruisseau Rankin Brook

Parking

Kouchibouguac River

Bike
Bridge

Sipu
Campground

Elevation
— 20

0
Metres

124

Middle
Kouchibouguac

○ Trailhead

△ Campground

115 Tweedie Trail

117 Claire-Fontaine Trail

118 Pines Trail

124 Kouchibouguac River Trail

115

Bike Trail

KOUCHIBOUGUAC
NATIONAL PARK

Patterson

Petit-Large

Ruisseau Major Kollock Creek

117

Pijeboogwek

Visitor
Centre

118

134

116. Osprey Trail (see map p. 263)

Distance: 5.1 km (3.2 mi) including side trail
Type: loop
Difficulty: easy
Ascent: negligible
Hiking time: 1 hr 30 min including spur

Map: 21 I/15 Pointe Sapin (or, better, in the *Kouchibouguac National Park Visitor Guide*)
Trail condition: usually dry
Cellphone coverage: P

Finding the trailhead: From the visitor centre, continue north on Route 117 for about 6.6 km (4.1 mi), then turn right onto North Kouchibouguac Road towards the Loggiecroft/Côte-à-Fabien shore. Follow this road for 3.8 km (2.4 mi), then turn left to the Côte-à-Fabien shore campsite. After 300 m/yd the road makes a sharp right turn. Parking is available on the side of the road as it widens. The trailhead is reached just beyond a gate on the left. There are occasional signs showing a black hiker on a white background. The trail is obvious.

Trailhead: 46°50'10" N, 64°56'22" W

The hike: Pass the gate and turn right after a very short distance. Once the trail reaches the Kouchibouguac Lagoon, it turns sharply to the left and soon enters the woods, with the lagoon always visible on the right. Walk around an inlet with a logjam, and at 1 km (0.6 mi) keep right at a junction towards Black River Point. At 1.6 km (1 mi) a side trail to the right leads to a sandy beach at Black River Point. Many sea- and shorebirds can be observed in this area. Back at the T-junction, the trail continues to the left along the Kouchibouguac Lagoon through a small stand of tall softwoods until, at 3.9 km (2.4 mi), it reaches the junction where the loop began. From here, retrace your steps to the trailhead at Cote-à-Fabien. The main feature of this trail is the many shorebirds that can be observed along the beach. Particularly prominent are the great blue herons and ospreys, and the abundant terns.

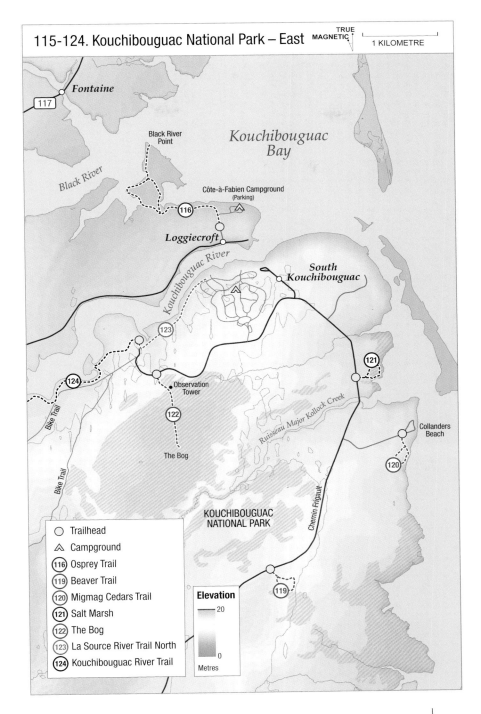

115-124. Kouchibouguac National Park – East

TRUE
MAGNETIC

1 KILOMETRE

Fontaine

117

Kouchibouguac Bay

Black River Point

Black River

Côte-à-Fabien Campground
(Parking)

116

Loggiecroft

Kouchibouguac River

South Kouchibouguac

123

124

Bike Trail

Observation Tower

122

Bike Trail

The Bog

121

Ruisseau Major Kollock Creek

Collanders Beach

120

Chemin Frigault

KOUCHIBOUGUAC NATIONAL PARK

○ Trailhead

△ Campground

116 Osprey Trail

119 Beaver Trail

120 Migmag Cedars Trail

121 Salt Marsh

122 The Bog

123 La Source River Trail North

124 Kouchibouguac River Trail

Elevation

20

0

Metres

119

117. Claire-Fontaine Trail (see map p. 261)

Distance: 3 km (1.9 mi)
Type: loop
Difficulty: easy
Ascent: negligible
Hiking time: 55 min

Map: 21 I/15 Pointe Sapin (or, better, in the *Kouchibouguac National Park Visitor Guide*)
Trail condition: dry
Cellphone coverage: Y

Finding the trailhead: From the junction at the visitor centre, continue on Route 117 north for 8.9 km (5.5 mi). There is a small parking lot on the right just before you cross the Black River. The trailhead is located at the far end of the parking lot. There are no trail markings, but the trail is obvious.

Trailhead: 46°50'11"N, 64°59'28"W

The hike: Beyond the gate, cross a bike trail and continue for a short distance along sheep laurels. Keep right at a fork. Here, the trail is lined with sweet fern, bayberries, and blueberries. The forest gets gradually denser. At about 0.9 km (0.6 mi), Rankin Brook can be seen to the right of the trail. Following the brook, the trail reaches the tip of the peninsula and returns along the south bank of the Black River. At 1.6 km (1 mi), the trail leaves the river and swings to the left. Shortly after, it leads through tall grass and raspberry bushes before returning into the woods. Back at the fork, turn right and return to the parking lot. This forest trail offers views across Rankin Brook and the delta of the Black River.

118. Pines Trail (see map p. 261)

Distance: 0.8 km (0.5 mi)
Type: loop
Difficulty: easy
Ascent: negligible
Hiking time: 15 min

Map: 21 I/15 Pointe Sapin (or, better, in the *Kouchibouguac National Park Visitor Guide*)
Trail condition: dry
Cellphone coverage: Y

Finding the trailhead: Turn right at the visitor centre and follow that road for 3.2 km (2 mi).The trailhead is at the parking lot on the right side of the road. The trail is marked by small red metal blazes.

Trailhead: 46°46'17" N, 64°57'43" W

The hike: This is a short pleasant "open book" nature trail through the woods, with a fine stand of eastern white pines, among them an impressive 40 m (130 ft) tall white pine.

119. Beaver Trail (see map p. 263)

Distance: 1.6 km (1 mi)
Type: loop
Difficulty: easy
Ascent: negligible
Hiking time: 25 min

Map: 21 I/15 Pointe Sapin (or, better, in the *Kouchibouguac National Park Visitor Guide*)
Trail condition: dry
Cellphone coverage: Y

Finding the trailhead: Turn right at the visitor centre towards Beaches and follow that road for about 6.4 km (4 mi). Parking is available at a turnaround at the trailhead.

Trailhead: 46°47'30" N, 64°55'54" W

The hike: As the name of this self-guiding nature trail suggests, the work of the beaver is its main feature. An inactive beaver pond is at the centre of the raised boardwalk trail. Frogs may be heard and partridges are frequently seen.

120. Migmag Cedars Trail (see map p. 263)

(see map p. 263)

Distance: 1.3 km (0.8 mi)
Type: loop
Difficulty: easy
Ascent: negligible
Hiking time: 20 min

Map: 21 I/15 Pointe Sapin (or, better, in the *Kouchibouguac National Park Visitor Guide*)
Trail condition: dry, boardwalk
Cellphone coverage: Y

Finding the trailhead: Turn right at the visitor centre towards Beaches and follow that road for 8.5 km (5.3 mi), then turn right onto a dirt road towards Callanders Beach. After 0.8 km (0.5 mi) the road ends in a loop, circling a picnic area. The trailhead is on the right side of the road where it reaches the loop. There is some parking space at the trailhead on the right. There are no trail markings, but the trail is obvious.

Trailhead: 46°48'29" N, 64°54'31" W

The hike: The trail crosses the field of the old Callander homestead with two replicas of Mi'kmaq wigwams. The raised boardwalk is lined with cedars and maples. There is a glimpse of the seashore across the lagoon to the long sandbar. Symbols and stories of the Mi'kmaq people are explained on plaques.

121. Salt Marsh (see map p. 263)

Distance: 0.7 km (0.4 mi)
Type: loop
Difficulty: easy
Ascent: negligible
Hiking time: 10 min

Map: 21 I/15 Pointe Sapin (or, better, in the *Kouchibouguac National Park Visitor Guide*)
Trail condition: dry, boardwalk
Cellphone coverage: P

Finding the trailhead: Turn right at the visitor centre towards Beaches and continue on that road for about 9.4 km (5.8 mi). There is a parking lot on the right side of the road.

Trailhead: 46°48'55" N, 64°54'57" W

The hike: An "open book" display explains some of the major features of this salt-marsh nature trail. Of particular interest are the different types of grass that grow close to or farther away from the waterline, depending on their salt tolerance. Great blue herons may be seen in the marsh.

122. The Bog (see map p. 263)

Distance: 1.9 km (1.2 mi) rtn
Type: linear
Difficulty: easy
Ascent: negligible
Hiking time: 30 min rtn

Map: 21 I/15 Pointe Sapin (or, better, in the *Kouchibouguac National Park Visitor Guide*)
Trail condition: dry
Cellphone coverage: P

Finding the trailhead: Turn right at the visitor centre towards Beaches and follow that road for about 13.4 km (8.3 mi). A parking lot is located to the left of the road. The trailhead is at the far end of the turnaround.

Trailhead: 46°48'59" N, 64°57'10" W

The hike: After a short distance through Acadian forest, the trail reaches an observation tower. The spiral-staircase tower provides a very good view across the ancient bog. From the tower, the trail continues on a lengthy boardwalk section to its end at an observation platform. Among other plants, bakeapple (also called cloudberry), pitcher plants, cotton grass, and black spruce are rather prominent.

123. La Source River Trail North (see map p. 263)

Distance: 2 km (1.2 mi) rtn
Type: linear
Difficulty: easy
Ascent: negligible
Hiking time: 40 min rtn

Map: 21 I/15 Pointe Sapin (or, better, in the *Kouchibouguac National Park Visitor Guide*)
Trail condition: dry
Cellphone coverage: P

Finding the trailhead: Turn right at the visitor centre towards Beaches and follow that road for 14 km (8.7 mi) to its end at La Source. Parking is available at a picnic site. The trailhead is located at the far right of the parking lot, and the trail leads into the woods after crossing a bike trail. The wide, groomed trail is marked by small red metal blazes and cannot be missed.

Trailhead: 46°49'14" N, 64°57'13" W

The hike: The trail features include a large field where once an old homestead was located. There are also some good views across the Kouchibouguac River, where benches invite you to stay awhile. Of special interest is the hanging red pine tree at Sandstone Gardens. Some distance beyond, the trail ends at a bike trail that parallels this footpath. Here, you may retrace your steps or return on the bicycle trail.

124. Kouchibouguac River Trail (see map p. 261)

Distance: 9.7 km (6 mi) one way
Type: linear
Difficulty: moderate
Ascent: negligible
Hiking time: 2 hrs 30 min
Maps: 21 I/14 Kouchibouguac and

21 I/15 Pointe Sapin (or, better, in the *Kouchibouguac National Park Visitor Guide*)
Trail condition: some wet spots, rooty, somewhat slippery on pine needles
Cellphone coverage: P

Finding the trailhead: Turn right at the visitor centre towards Beaches and follow that road for 13.8 km (8.6 mi) to its end. Parking is available at a picnic site. The trailhead is located on the left side of the parking lot behind the kitchen shelter and water pump. At the beginning and the end of the trail there are small red metal blazes, while in the middle there are orange metal triangles. In any case, the trail is generally easy to follow.

Trailhead: 46°49'11" N, 64°57'15" W

The hike: The path crosses a bike trail and leads into softwoods. The trail soon reaches the Kouchibouguac River, which it follows for almost its entire length. At a T-junction, a short side trail to the right leads to a bench overlooking the river, while the main trail turns left. The trail crosses a number of wooden bridges; note the many signs of beaver activity in this area. The path passes a marshy inlet, and at 5.8 km (3.6 mi) it reaches a T-junction at Middle Kouchibouguac. The left fork connects to a bike trail; the right fork continues the hiking trail. After some distance, the footpath crosses a wide bike trail, which, to the right, leads over a new bridge across the Kouchibouguac River. Continue straight ahead; at 7.8 km (4.8 mi) the trail reaches the open Sipu wilderness campground, which is accessible only on foot or by boat. Some distance beyond Sipu, keep right at a fork, which is not hard to miss. Once out of the softwoods, the trail leads through raspberry patches that provide a welcome snack in season. Then the trail turns sharply to the left, leaves the Kouchibouguac River, and soon reaches a wide bike trail at Patterson. This is the end of the Kouchibouguac River Trail. At this point, you can either retrace your steps, turn left onto the bike trail and follow it for 5.8 km (3.6 mi) back to the trailhead, or turn right onto the bike trail and follow it for 2 km (1.2 mi) to Pijeboogwek near the park headquarters and information centre.

Escuminac Disaster

On June 19 and 20, 1959, a huge storm, remnants of a hurricane, blew up in the Northumberland Strait. However, the weather forecast had been good, and as there were expected to be large schools of salmon in the area, many fishermen set sail and went about their work. The lack of radio equipment on many boats spelled disaster. When the storm hit the region, there were about forty-five boats in the Northumberland Strait. The storm produced 15 m (50 ft) waves that killed thirty-five fishermen and destroyed one-third of the salmon boats in Miramichi and half of the lobster traps. A memorial by Claude Roussel in memory of those who lost their lives was erected in Escuminac in 1969.

125. Point Escuminac Beach Trail

Distance: 12.4 km (7.7 mi) rtn
Type: linear
Difficulty: easy
Ascent: negligible

Hiking time: 2 hrs 30 min rtn
Map: 21 P/2 Point Escuminac
Trail condition: depends on tide
Cellphone coverage: Y

Finding the trailhead: Take Highway 11 from Moncton in a northerly direction. From Kouchibouguac National Park, follow Route 117 to Escuminac. At a T-junction in Escuminac, turn right onto Escuminac Point Road and continue for 3.1 km (1.9 mi) to the Escuminac Beach and Family Park. A parking fee is charged for non-campers. There are no trail markings, but the trail follows the beach and cannot be missed.

Trailhead: 47°04'45" N, 64°52'23" W

The hike: Park at the large parking lot and take the boardwalk to the beach at the wide Miramichi Bay. Turn right (east) and follow the wide sandy beach. A little farther, the sand dunes to the right of the beach change to peat moss "cliffs." As the trail progresses, the beach gets narrower and more gravelly, and the peat moss bluffs become higher, reaching impressive heights of up to 5 m (16 ft). Along the way, in the shelter of little coves, it is possible to see broken lobster traps, buoys, pieces of rope, netting, and shells that the tides have deposited. Just below the modern Point Escuminac Lighthouse, the shore turns into a plateau of shale. The trail ends at the lighthouse. Beachcombing is good in the coves formed by these cliffs. Also note the many holes in the upper reaches of the peat moss cliffs that lead to swallow nests. The 22 m (72 ft) high Point Escuminac Lighthouse is a prominent landmark. The present lighthouse was constructed in 1966 and was fully automated in 1989. It is visible for about 18 nautical miles.

126. French Fort Cove

TRUE
MAGNETIC

500 METRES

○ Trailhead
(126) French Fort Cove

Elevation
— 100

0
Metres

Beaverbrook Road

Nordin Ridge

Canadian National Railway

Creaghan Gulch

French Fort Cove Brook

(126)

French Fort Cove

Old King George Highway

Cove Road

Parking

King George Highway

Miramichi River

Newcastle

126. French Fort Cove Trail

Distance: 8 km (5 mi)
Type: loop
Difficulty: moderate
Ascent: 100 m (330 ft)

Hiking time: 3 hrs
Map: 21 P/4 Sevogle
Trail condition: dry
Cellphone coverage: Y

Finding the trailhead: Entering Miramichi from the south on Highway 8, take exit 164 onto King George Highway, drive 6.6 km (4.1 mi), and turn left onto Cove Road just before you reach a large chimney on the right side of the road. On Cove Road, turn right into a parking lot. The trail starts behind a large sign for French Fort Cove. The trail system consists of four trails: the Cove Trail blazed in green, the Fish Quarry Trail blazed in yellow, the Creaghan Gulch Trail blazed in red, and the Nordin Ridge Trail blazed in grey. Hikers can choose to hike the trails separately or combine all four. Although the loops are blazed, some confusion may arise on account of the grey blazes and the yellow blazes, which do not coincide with the maps that are posted along most of the major intersections. This sometimes makes the trail hard to follow, but more adventurous.

Trailhead: 47°01'01"N, 65°33'02"W

The hike: Just past the sign for French Fort Cove, turn left on the wide, groomed trail that immediately leads into the woods. The trail is marked in green. After some time, the trail reaches a gravel road. Cross it and ascend wooden steps. The now narrow path leads through some very pretty stands of beech and birch trees, while a brook can be heard on the right below. The path then enters young softwoods. At a junction, keep right on the yellow trail (the path leading straight ahead is a spur that ends at the railroad tracks). The trail descends very steeply to a brook. It follows the brook for a short distance and then ascends again straight (a spur to the left leads again to the railroad), until the path crosses a tiny bridge. Just beyond the bridge, continue straight on the red trail, which later ascends steeply.

The trail continues through sheep laurel and aspen. At a junction, continue straight on the red trail. (Alternatively, turn left onto the more confusing gray-blazed Nordin Ridge loop: the gray trail ascends steeply, eventually levels off, and reaches a T-junction. Turn right onto a wide woods road. The road dips down to two successive brooks and eventually hits a wide gravelly road. Continue straight for a few metres/yards and turn right onto a narrow path (the #6 bike trail) that descends. Keep to the right at two successive forks and cross the scenic French Fort Cove Brook on a longer boardwalk bridge. Continue through the woods until a wide gravel road is reached. Continue straight ahead at the signboard. After a pleasant walk along a steep-sided ravine, reach a junction with the red trail. Turn left onto the red trail).

The red trail turns right at a junction and continues the loop on this side of the gorge now. Along the trail, there are some spurs to the right, leading to cliffs. One larger spur leads to a solitary rock providing a vista across the deep and densely wooded Creagham Gulch. Continue and turn right at a T-junction. After a while, the yellow trail joins on the right from behind. Continue for a short distance, then turn right at a fork following the signs to a covered bridge. The trail leads downward to a junction. At this point, you can either continue across the covered bridge, or turn left just before reaching the bridge and walk around the French Fort Cove (the green trail). We choose the latter option. After some distance, the trail reaches a long bridge at the end of the cove just below the King George Highway. It swings to the right, ascends and keeps left at a fork, and terminates next to a pavilion adjacent to the parking lot.

127. Daly Point Reserve Nature Trail

Distance: 5 km (3.1 mi)
Type: loop
Difficulty: easy
Ascent: negligible

Hiking time: 1 hr 30 min
Map: 21 P/12 Bathurst
Trail condition: dry, boardwalk, beach
Cellphone coverage: Y

Finding the trailhead: Approaching Bathurst on Highway 8, exit onto Highway 11 south and take exit 300A. Continue on Miramichi Avenue/Route 134 north. Follow this wide road for 1.6 km (1 mi) to a traffic light and turn right onto Bridge Street. Follow it for 2.4 km (1.5 mi), then turn left onto Carron Drive. After another 0.9 km (0.6 mi), the parking lot of the nature reserve is located on the left side of the road. The trails are marked by different theme names as shown on the local trail map that is available at the visitor centre. Follow our combination of the trails clockwise around the circumference of the trail network.

Trailhead: 47°38'17" N, 65°36'33" W

The hike: The trail starts to the left of the visitor centre. This is trail #1, the Field Trail. Just before reaching a field, turn left onto trail #6, the White Pine Trail. Follow the trail through woods to a junction, then turn left onto trail #4, the Chickadee Landing Trail. After a while, at another junction, turn left onto trail #3, the Warbler Trail. After some distance a T-junction is reached. Turn right onto trail #2, the Salt Marsh Trail. Continue on this trail for some distance. At another junction, trail #7, the Coastal Trail leads to the shore of Bathurst Harbour. Turn right back onto trail #1, the Field Trail, to an observation tower. Shortly after, turn left onto trail #7, the Coastal Trail. Continue on that trail and climb some stairs with a vista point on the left. Keep left at a junction with the Gulch Trail. The trail soon swings to the right. At the next fork, turn left onto trail #8, the Gulch Trail. Follow that trail to a T-junction, then turn left onto trail #1, the Field Trail, which leads back to the visitor centre. The park consists of a salt marsh, old fields, and mixed forests. Many plaques on this nature trail identify various local plants and animals. Special attractions include the Canada geese that arrive on their migratory route in the fall and the rare maritime ringlet butterfly.

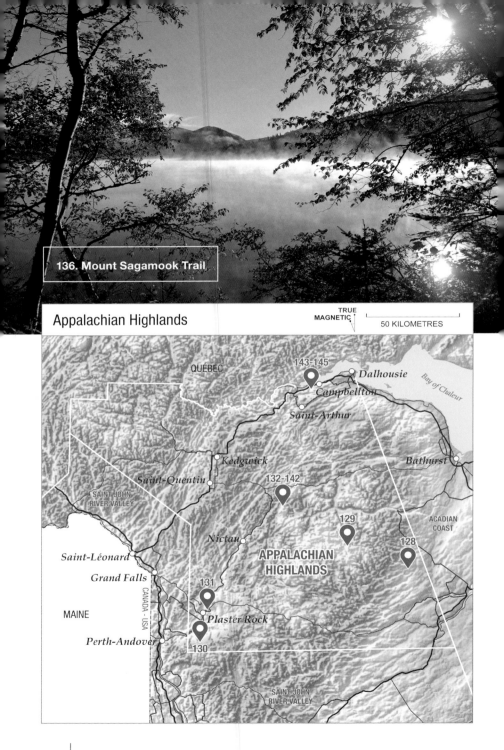

136. Mount Sagamook Trail

Appalachian Highlands

TRUE
MAGNETIC

50 KILOMETRES

QUÉBEC

143-145

Dalhousie

Bay of Chaleur

Campbellton

Saint-Arthur

Kedgwick

Bathurst

Saint-Quentin

132-142

SAINT JOHN
RIVER VALLEY

129

ACADIAN
COAST

Nictau

APPALACHIAN
HIGHLANDS

128

Saint-Léonard

Grand Falls

131

MAINE

CANADA - USA

Plaster Rock

130

Perth-Andover

SAINT JOHN
RIVER VALLEY

APPALACHIAN HIGHLANDS

The Appalachian Highlands (of which New Brunswick's Sugarloaf Mountain and Mount Carleton Provincial Parks are part) are the most remote area of the province. At 820 m (2,690 ft), Mount Carleton is the highest elevation in the Maritimes. The vistas from the top of Mount Carleton, Sagamook Mountain, and Mount Bailey, all in the park, are spectacular. The area around Mount Carleton was described in Charles G.D. Roberts's book *The King of the Mamozekel*. The Restigouche River is famous for its Atlantic salmon.

The colonial history of this area began with a visit from Jacques Cartier to Chaleur Bay in 1534. The French settled along the shore and the mountains in 1690, and during the 1800s, the British came, mostly settlers from Scotland and Ireland.

The region is dominated by miles and miles of densely forested highlands and valleys from Sugarloaf Mountain to Mount Carleton and from Big Bald Mountain to the Christmas Mountains, as the locals aptly call the North Pole Mountain and Mount St. Nicholas in New Brunswick's unpopulated wilderness interior. The forests are the region's riches, and lumbering is one of the major industries here.

In addition, there are a number of maple groves near Kedgwick and Saint-Quentin. The hardy maple tree thrives here, and its sap is collected every spring to produce good-quality maple sugar products.

128. Little Sheephouse Falls Nature Trail

(Developed by United Paper Mills, Miramichi)

Distance: 0.8 km (0.5 mi)
Type: loop
Difficulty: easy
Ascent: negligible

Hiking time: 30 min
Map: 21 O/1 Big Bald Mountain
Trail condition: dry, groomed trail
Cellphone coverage: N

Finding the trailhead: On Highway 8 near Miramichi, take the exit towards Red Bank on NB 415 north and follow this road for 8.8 km (5.5 mi). Turn left onto NB 420, follow the Miramichi River, and after 1.9 km (1.2 mi) turn right onto NB 425 towards Sunny Corner. Cross the bridge across the Miramichi and follow the road straight ahead on Tozer Lane to a stop sign. Turn left onto Northwest Road and follow it for 20.5 km (12.7 mi), then turn left onto NB 430 towards Heath Steele Mines. Continue for 4 km (2.5 mi) to the junction with Fraser Burchill Road, crossing the Northwest Miramichi River on the way. Turn left onto Fraser Burchill Road, where a sign already indicates the trail. Follow this good gravel road for 9.8 km (6.1 mi), and turn left onto Sheephouse Road at a wooden sign. Continue on this road, crossing a small bridge across the North Branch Big Sevogle River until you reach a fork at 4.3 km (2.7 mi). Keep left on Falls Road and proceed for another 2.4 km (1.5 mi). The trailhead is located on the left side of the road at a small picnic site and a large map. There is space for about ten vehicles. There are no trail markings, but the trail cannot be missed.

Trailhead: 47°05'37"N, 66°00'21"W

The hike: This is a groomed nature trail that is easy to follow. This trail has a number of explanatory plaques pointing out features of various softwood species, animal life, facts about glaciation, and the legend of Sheephouse Brook. Of specific interest are the Sheephouse Falls, the Hopewell Falls, and the trunk of a 350-year-old logged white pine near the entrance of the trail.

129. Big Bald Mountain Trail

Distance: 3.2 km (2 mi) rtn
Type: linear
Difficulty: moderate
Ascent: 240 m (790 ft)
Hiking time: 1 hr rtn

Map: 21 O/1 Big Bald Mountain
Trail condition: rough woods road, mostly dry
Cellphone coverage: N

Finding the trailhead: On Highway 8 near Miramichi, take the exit towards Red Bank on NB 415 north and follow this road for 8.7 km (5.4 mi). Turn left onto NB 420, follow the river, and after 1.9 km (1.2 mi) turn right onto NB 425 towards Sunny Corner. Cross the bridge across the Miramichi River, and go straight for 0.4 km (0.2 mi) on Tozer Lane to a stop sign. Turn left onto Northwest Road and follow it for 1.9 km (1.2 mi) to a junction at the sign for Back Road. Turn left, cross the bridge, and at 1.3 km (0.8 mi) from the Back Road junction, leave Back Road and turn right onto the Mullin Stream Road. At 2 km (1.2 mi) the road turns to the left onto a good unnamed dirt road; follow it for 20 km (12.4 mi). Keep right at a fork and continue on the South Branch Sevogle Road. After another 18.8 km (11.7 mi), keep left at a junction, cross over a bridge, and follow this road for 15.8 km (9.8 mi) to a small bridge that crosses the Nepisiguit River. After another 2.6 km (1.6 mi), turn right onto Nepisiguit Road, which soon crosses the river again. At a distance of 1.5 km (0.9 mi) beyond the junction, turn off the main road to the right onto a smaller, unnamed dirt road. Follow it for 1.6 km (1 mi) to a point, at which a steep and rutted dirt road departs to the right. This is the trail. Park the vehicle along the side of the road. There are no trail markings. The trail follows a wide woods road and is easy to follow.

Trailhead: 47°12'28"N, 66°25'44"W

The hike: The very rough dirt road ascends fairly steeply, then levels off. Ahead on the right, the summit of Bald Mountain with a transmission tower and an attached outbuilding can be seen. The trail swings to the right and then it forks. Take the left fork, which first leads to a scenic bald outcrop. The trail then ascends steeply. This last part is very badly eroded and three wide, parallel tracks exist that are made by four-wheelers. The trail ends at the summit. The main feature of this trail is the panoramic view from the top. It makes up for the long access road and the poor condition of the trail. The outcrop just below Big Bald Mountain is scenic, and its water holes (tinajas) are of geological interest.

130. Maggie's Falls

Distance: 1.6 km (1 mi) rtn
Type: linear
Difficulty: easy
Ascent: negligible

Hiking time: 35 min rtn
Map: 21 J/11 Juniper
Trail condition: dry gravel road
Cellphone coverage: N

Finding the trailhead: On Highway 2, take exit 115 and follow Route 109 to Perth-Andover. Cross the bridge and turn left towards Mount Carleton on Route 109. Continue for 17.8 km (11.1 mi) to Arthurette. Turn right onto Birch Ridge Road and follow it for 5.7 km (3.5 mi) to a junction, where a road turns off to the right. The trailhead is located on the left at the junction. Park the vehicle somewhere alongside the road. There are no trail markings, but the trail cannot be missed.

Trailhead: 46°44'16" N, 67°28'25" W

The hike: Walk the level trail to a point, where it makes a ninety-degree right turn just below a house. Continue for a short distance straight down to the Odellach River and Maggie's Falls. You can explore the falls farther down, along a narrow path that follows the stream. The beautiful cascading falls at the end justify the walk on the gravel road.

131. **Sadlers Nature Trail** (Plaster Rock Tourist Park)

Distance: 1.2 km (0.7 mi) short loop, 2.8 km (1.7 mi) long loop
Type: loop
Difficulty: easy
Ascent: negligible

Hiking time: 30 min short loop, 1 hr 10 min long loop
Map: 21 J/14 Plaster Rock
Trail condition: groomed, dry
Cellphone coverage: Y

Finding the trailhead: On Highway 2, take exit 115 to Route 109 east to Perth-Andover. Cross the bridge, turn left, and follow Route 109 north towards Plaster Rock. After 19.4 km (12.1 mi), turn left, cross the Tobique River, and turn right, staying on Route 109. Continue for another 10.2 km (6.3 mi) to the Tourist Park, located on the left side of the road. Turn onto the premises and follow the short dirt road towards the campground straight to the end to a large parking lot at Roulston Lake. The trailhead is located on the left. There are no trail markings, but the trail is easy to find.

Trailhead: 46°53'42" N, 67°23'53" W

The hike: The trail immediately enters the woods and follows the lake for some time, keeping it to its right. Keep right or left at a fork, as the two paths will soon rejoin. Ignore the marked Steeves Trail that departs to the left. The main trail then forks again. At this point, you can either take the right fork that skirts the lake and follow it back to the trailhead (short loop), or you can take the left fork (long loop), which soon leads to a junction with a bench and a dilapidated signboard. Turn left and immediately left again on a smaller path that descends first and levels off after some distance. The trail crosses a service road straight ahead, continues through the woods, then ends at the service road. Turn right onto the dirt road and follow it as it swings to the right, and at some red markers, turn left into the woods. This path eventually swings to the right and crosses a muddy area. After crossing a woods road straight ahead (turning left will lead to the trucker's bypass Route 108), the trail parallels the road for a while, keeping it to its left slightly above. The trail leads across some corduroy sections, ascends, and soon reaches a T-junction with a sign. Turn left, cross a small wooden bridge, and pass by a beautiful picnic site and vista point across the lake. Continue along the northeastern shore of the lake to the end of the trail at a large, covered picnic site.

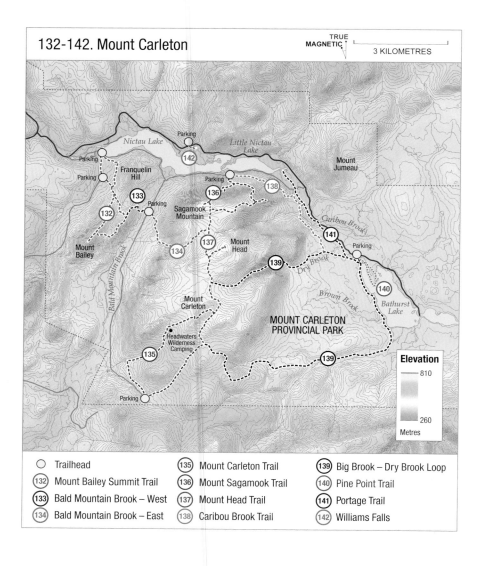

132-142. Mount Carleton

TRUE
MAGNETIC
3 KILOMETRES

Nictau Lake

Little Nictau Lake

Parking

142

Parking

Parking

Franquelin Hill

Mount Jumeau

133

Parking

136

138

132

Sagamook Mountain

Caribou Brook

141

Parking

Mount Bailey

134

137

Mount Head

139

Dry Brook

140

Mount Carleton

Brown Brook

Bathurst Lake

MOUNT CARLETON PROVINCIAL PARK

Bald Mountain Brook

Headwaters Wilderness Camping

135

139

Elevation
810
260
Metres

○ Trailhead

⑬② Mount Bailey Summit Trail

⑬③ Bald Mountain Brook – West

⑬④ Bald Mountain Brook – East

⑬⑤ Mount Carleton Trail

⑬⑥ Mount Sagamook Trail

⑬⑦ Mount Head Trail

⑬⑧ Caribou Brook Trail

⑬⑨ Big Brook – Dry Brook Loop

⑭⓪ Pine Point Trail

⑭① Portage Trail

⑭② Williams Falls

132-142. Mount Carleton Provincial Park

Mount Carleton Provincial Park, with more than 17,000 hectares (42,000 acres), is by far the largest provincial park in the province. At 820m (2,690 ft), Mount Carleton is not only the highest peak in the Provincial Park, but also the highest elevation in the Maritimes. This altitude is also partly responsible for the comparatively harsh climate: snow can be expected from about mid-October to mid-May. Large game such as moose, bear, and white-tailed deer can be spotted in the park sporadically, and beavers, rabbits, and squirrels are common. The park is heavily forested and features numerous rivers, brooks, and lakes.

The park is open from May to mid-October, and the entry gate is open from 8 a.m. to 8 p.m. You have to register at the visitor centre before you enter the park. The park is unserviced, and most roads remain unplowed during the winter. The gates are open in the daytime from January 1 to the end of March for cross-country skiing and ice fishing. Also note that all of the roads in the park are gravel, and some of them are quite rough. While they remain passable for passenger cars, caution is advised.

To access the park from the south of the province, on Highway 2, take exit 115 to Route 109 east to Perth-Andover. Cross the bridge, turn left, and follow Route 109 north towards Plaster Rock. After 19.4 km (12.1 mi), turn left, cross the Tobique River, and turn right, staying on Route 109. Continue for another 10.4 km (6.5 mi) to a junction in Plaster Rock just beyond the Tourist Park. Continue straight, drive along Main Street through Plaster Rock, and turn onto NB 385 north. Follow this road for 75.5 km (46.9 mi), where the entrance station to Mount Carleton Provincial Park is located on the right. All distances in the park are measured from the entrance station and the visitor centre next to it.

Further information concerning the park as well as reservations may be obtained and made at http://www.tourismnewbrunswick.ca/Products/Parks/MountCarletonProvincialPark.aspx, or by calling toll-free 1-800-561-0123 or 506-235-0793 (office) from mid-May to mid-October. Note that campgrounds close earlier, so check the website. The park brochure includes decent maps and is available to pick up from the visitor centre or download at http://friendsofmountcarleton.ca/images/stories/pdf/center-map.pdf.

132. **Mount Bailey Summit Trail**

Distance: 7.4 km (4.6 mi)
Type: loop
Difficulty: moderate
Ascent: 320 m (1,050 ft)
Hiking time: 2 hrs 30 min

Map: 21 O/7 Nepisiguit Lakes or park brochure
Trail condition: dry
Cellphone coverage: P

Finding the trailhead: From the visitor centre, continue on the main road in a southeasterly direction for 2.2 km (1.4 mi), passing roads that depart first to the left and then to the right at a large parking lot and picnic area. Turn right onto a grassy road (formerly called the Old Mamozekel Road and based on Charles G.D. Roberts's book *The King of the Mamozekel*) and follow it for 0.7 km (0.4 mi). The trail is marked by orange diamonds with a reflective ribbon. There are also some of the older blue metal blazes with a white diagonal bar.

Trailhead: 47°25'01" N, 66°55'15" W

The hike: From its head, the trail leads immediately into the woods and ascends at a gentle grade. It continues straight at a junction; turning left leads to the group campground. The trail narrows and keeps right at a fork (the left fork is also marked), then ascends, at times steeply. Turn left at an inconspicuous fork and continue the ascent. The trail continues through open hardwoods. On top of the hill, there is a spur to the left that allows some views. Keep to the right on the main trail. At a junction, the trail continues straight to the vista point at the end of the trail (turning left will lead to the Bald Mountain Brook Trail). At the summit of the 564 m (1,850 ft) high Mount Bailey, there is a picnic table as well as spectacular views towards some ponds of the Bald Mountain Brook deep below in the valley as well as Mount Carleton right across.

Return to the junction, where you can turn to the right towards the Bald Mountain Brook Trail. The trail is still blazed in orange. The trail descends and eventually reaches a fork. Here you have a choice: either keep to the right and take the more exposed cliff trail, which offers wonderful views across the Mountain Brook valley, or take the left and stay in the woods. The two trails will rejoin after some distance. If you take the cliff trail, turn to the left at the end of the cliff section and turn right at a T-junction. After some distance, there is another vista point to the right. Keep left at a fork (the right fork leads to Bald Mountain Brook Trail) and follow the sign towards Bailey Trail and a day-use area. You soon rejoin the wide trail you went up. At a junction, continue straight ahead to the parking lot. Turning right leads through a moose yard, meanders a bit, and eventually ends at a picnic site at the group campground.

The stunning views from the top of Mount Bailey across the mountain range with Sagamook Mountain on the left, Mount Carleton with an old fire tower straight ahead, and Bald Mountain Brook and watershed deep below in the valley make hiking this trail worthwhile. There is also a picnic table at Bailey's peak. Other good vistas are along the alternate cliff section of the trail. Deer and moose are occasionally seen in the watershed below, as are partridges near the cliffs.

Life on the Fire Tower

Until the advent of firefighting airplanes and sensors that are able to detect fires, fire detection was in the hand of workers. The government constructed fire towers on major peaks, which were manned by fire lookouts. If these lookouts saw smoke somewhere, they would contact the operator with the exact direction of the fire from their own site. The operator would then attempt to obtain similar information from lookouts on neighbouring peaks. The report from each fire tower indicated a line on a map, and with two or more reports, the intersections of these lines would indicate the exact location of the fire. Today, the profession of fire lookouts has joined that of lighthouse keepers and others whose jobs have been replaced by technology.

below: the old fire tower atop Mount Carleton

133. Bald Mountain Brook Trail – West

Distance: 2.6 km (1.6 mi) rtn [+ 4 km (2.5 mi) rtn to the summit of Mount Bailey]
Type: linear
Difficulty: moderate
Ascent: 300 m (985 ft)

Hiking time: 2 hrs rtn [+ 2 hrs rtn to the summit of Mount Bailey]
Map: 21 O/7 Nepisiguit Lakes or park brochure
Trail condition: rocky
Cellphone coverage: N

Finding the trailhead: From the visitor centre, continue in a southeasterly direction for 2.2 km (1.4 mi), passing roads that depart first to the left and then to the right. At a junction near a large picnic area on the right, keep to the left along Nictau Lake, following a sign pointing to Mount Carleton. After another 2.9 km (1.8 mi), just beyond the crossing of Bald Mountain Brook, the road to the Mount Carleton trailhead departs to the right. Follow this dirt road for 1.1 km (0.7 mi). The trailhead of the Bald Mountain Brook Trail — West is located on the right side of the road. There are a few parking spaces on the right side of the road. The trail is marked by blue squares/diamonds with a reflective ribbon.

Trailhead: 47°24'26" N, 66°54'05" W (measured in the middle of the trail on the Bald Mountain Brook Road)

The hike: The trail descends gently to a brook, crosses it on a bridge/boardwalk section, and continues along the stream for some distance. It then turns sharply to the left and begins its ascent. First, the grade is steep; the trail passes by a large white pine and then swings to the left. The path continues its ascent on switchbacks through hardwoods. The grade becomes somewhat gentler, and the trail eventually reaches the junction with the Mount Bailey Trail. Here, one can turn left and continue to the summit of Mount Bailey; the trail to the right leads down to the Mount Bailey parking lot. A key feature of this trail is access to one of the major peaks of the park.

134. **Bald Mountain Brook Trail – East**

Distance: 3.4 km (2.1 mi) one way
Type: linear
Difficulty: moderate
Ascent: 366 m (1,200 ft)
Hiking time: 2 hrs one way

Map: 21 O/7 Nepisiguit Lakes or park brochure
Trail condition: wet spots, rocky and rooty
Cellphone coverage: N

This trail links the Mount Carleton Road and the Mount Head Trail.

Finding the trailhead: From the visitor centre, continue in a southeasterly direction for 2.2 km (1.4 mi), passing roads that depart first to the left and then to the right. At a junction near a large picnic area on the right, keep to the left along Nictau Lake, following a sign pointing to Mount Carleton. After another 2.9 km (1.8 mi), just beyond the crossing of Bald Mountain Brook, the road to the Mount Carleton trailhead departs to the right. Follow this dirt road for 1.1 km (0.7 mi). The trailhead of the Bald Mountain Brook Trail – East is located on the left side of the road. A few parking spaces exist on the right side of the road. The trail is marked by blue diamonds with reflective ribbons as well as some older blue metal blazes with a white diagonal bar.

Trailhead: 47°24'26" N, 66°54'05" W

The hike: The trail leads through softwoods in a southeasterly to easterly direction. It first ascends gently and later at a steeper grade. It then turns to the right, descends again, and reaches an old beaver pond. The trail continues in a southerly direction along the edge of the forest. After crossing a number of branches of a brook, the path turns left into the woods, crosses a deep wet spot, and follows the cascading Bald Mountain Brook upstream. After passing a scenic waterfall, the ascent gets steeper. The trail crosses the brook on a rough bridge made of birch logs and continues in a southerly direction, away from the water. After a relatively short but steep climb, the grade gets gentler as the trail leads through a nice stand of birch trees. After a while, the trail crosses the brook again. The trail runs parallel to the brook for a while, then it passes through dense softwoods and later, mixed open forest and a small open field, until it reaches the Mount Head Trail. The trail is notable for its beautiful tumbling waterfalls.

135. **Mount Carleton Trail**

Distance: 9.5 km (5.9 mi)
Type: loop
Difficulty: moderate to strenuous
Ascent: 390 m (1,280 ft)
Hiking time: 4 hrs

Map: 21 O/7 Nepisiguit Lakes or park brochure
Trail condition: rocky, boulders near the top
Cellphone coverage: P

Finding the trailhead: From the visitor centre, continue in a southeasterly direction for 2.2 km (1.4 mi), passing roads that depart first to the left and then to the right. At a picnic area on the right, take the left road along Nictau Lake to Mount Carleton. After 2.9 km (1.8 mi), just beyond the crossing of Bald Mountain Brook, the road to the Mount Carleton trailhead departs to the right. Follow this quite rough dirt road for 7.8 km (4.8 mi) to its end. On the left, there is a large parking lot and a pit toilet, but no drinking water. The trailhead begins beyond the barrier at the end of the dirt road. The trail is marked by green diamonds with a reflective ribbon. There are also some older blue metal blazes with a white diagonal bar. In areas where the trail leads across rocks, there are green and some blue paint blazes on boulders. In general, the trail is easy to follow.

Trailhead: 47°21'10" N, 66°54'07" W

The hike: The trail first follows an old woods road through mixed woods. It is very rocky in parts and gently ascends and levels off shortly before it reaches a junction with the Big Brook - Dry Brook Loop (see the trail description on p. 301). Take the left fork, which immediately ascends rather steeply. Soon the trail passes an open log cabin, a shelter with a picnic table inside. It used to be home to the men who operated Mount Carleton's fire tower until 1968. At a clearing at 4.2 km (2.6 mi), the trail turns left. (Straight across the clearing is the trailhead of the Mount Head Trail; see the trail description on p. 299) After a short, steep ascent over boulders, the trail arrives at the fire tower on the summit of Mount Carleton. On a clear day, there are many fine views from the top, including the Nepisiguit Lakes in an easterly direction.

The trail continues behind the fire tower on a rocky ridge. This area provides the best views along the trail. Follow the ridge to its very end (this requires some rock scrambling where the trail swings sharply to the right). The trail continues to descend to a T-junction, where it meets again with the alternative trail that avoids the boulder-strewn and – in high winds – hazardous ridge. The alternative, a more sheltered trail, continues to the right of the fire tower. It first descends on rocks for 0.4 km (0.2 mi), then levels off with pleasant hiking, joining the ridge trail.

Soon hikers pass the Headwaters wilderness campground, consisting of four separate campsites, two on the right and two on the left side of the trail. The main path first leads along the mossy Mamozekel Brook in the distance, then continues next to its banks. At one point, the trail swings away from the creek by turning left. It ascends steeply for a short distance, then levels off, continues, and eventually reaches the parking lot.

Mount Carleton is the highest peak in the Maritime provinces and, on a clear day, the 360-degree view from there is excellent. Near the Headwaters wilderness campground there are many signs of moose, for this is their winter resting place. A scenic mossy creek on the last part of the loop allows for good resting places. The area also boasts a very large number of fiddleheads in the spring.

136. Mount Sagamook Trail

Distance: 7.4 km (4.6 mi) including side trails
Type: loop
Difficulty: strenuous
Ascent: 580 m (1,900 ft)
Hiking time: 3 hrs 45 min including spurs

Map: 21 O/7 Nepisiguit Lakes or park brochure
Trail condition: rocky and rooty. Just below the top, some rock scrambling is required.
Cellphone coverage: P

Finding the trailhead: From the visitor centre, continue in a southeasterly direction for 2.2 km (1.4 mi), passing roads that depart first to the left and then to the right. At a picnic area on the right, take the left road along Nictau Lake to Mount Carleton. After another 2.9 km (1.8 mi), just beyond the crossing of Bald Mountain Brook, the road to the Mount Carleton trailhead departs to the right. Continue straight at this point and follow the road for another 1.9 km (1.2 mi). The trailhead of the Mount Sagamook Trail (and the Caribou Brook Trail) is located on the right side of the road. There is also a pit toilet in the direct vicinity. Parking spaces are available on both sides of the road for about twelve vehicles. The trail is marked by light blue diamond-shaped blazes with reflective ribbons. Occasionally, there are also some 2" x 2" blue metal blazes with a white diagonal bar. On the rocks near the summit, the trail is marked by light blue paint blazes on the rocks.

Trailhead: 47°25'08"N, 66°52'04"W

The hike: The trail gently ascends on an old, wide logging road for a short distance, where it coincides with the Caribou Brook Trail (see trail 138). Soon the Sagamook Trail turns off sharply to the right, and the path ascends steeply through softwoods. At another fork turn right again, following the sign that reads Mt. Sagamook (the trail later returns on the left fork). As the trail climbs, there are some glimpses of Nictau Lake and the mountain range behind it. The trail turns sharply to the left at a sign. The trail continues to climb through alternating stands of birches and softwoods. As the trail passes a stand of birch trees, note a few white quartz boulders on and along the trail. At a rocky outcrop there are some fine views of the lakes and hills to the north.

After climbing up the rocks for about 200 m/yd, the trail reaches a junction. From here, a 0.6 km (0.4 mi) (return distance) side trail departs to the right. This side trail offers the best views of the chain of lakes far below and is definitely worthwhile. This spur first continues fairly level, then leads to magnificent vistas across the

Nictau and Little Nictau Lakes and the hills behind them, and finally descends very steeply (caution!) on loose rocks to a rocky outcrop.

The main trail continues straight and turns southerly. At a fork, continue straight; the right fork steeply descends to the Mount Head Trail. The main trail soon reaches the top of Mount Sagamook. At the 777 m (2,550 ft) peak you are rewarded with excellent views of the park with Mounts Gordon and Jumeau to the north and northeast, as well as Mounts Head and Carleton to the south. Nictau and Nepisiguit Lakes, however, cannot be seen from here.

Just behind the top of Mount Sagamook, the trail descends steeply in a southeasterly direction. The trail continues to descend, then levels off and eventually reaches a junction where a 1 km (0.6 mi) return side trail departs to the right. It leads to two vista points, one looking north to the lakes (this one is a bit overgrown) and another looking south-southwest towards Mount Head and Mount Carleton. This spur is very steep and, as it is a dead end, it is necessary to hike back up. The main trail starts descending, first gently, later at a steeper grade. The path is rocky and rooty in this area. It crosses a brook, keeps right at a fork, then turns left, and from here returns straight ahead to the parking lot.

A spectacular view from the summit of Sagamook Mountain of Nictau Lake and adjacent mountain ranges makes this demanding hike worthwhile. The old Native name Sagamook refers to the reflections in the water of Nictau Lake, which are nearly perfect on a clear day.

137. Mount Head Trail

Distance: 4.8 km (3 mi) one way [plus 1.6 km (1 mi) rtn for side trail to the summit of Mount Head]
Type: linear
Difficulty: moderate
Ascent: 120 m (400ft)

Hiking time: 1 hr 30 min one way [plus 30 min side trail]
Map: 21 O/7 Nepisiguit Lakes or park brochure
Trail condition: rocky and rooty
Cellphone coverage: P

Finding the trailhead: Note that this trail connects the Sagamook and Mount Carleton Trails. It is not directly accessible by vehicle. Its two trailheads are located at the summit of Sagamook Mountain and at a platform below the rock scramble below Mount Carleton. The description below starts at the summit of Sagamook Mountain (see trail 136). The trail is marked with faint pink diamond blazes with reflective ribbons. There are also older blue metal blazes with a white diagonal bar. Near the summit of Sagamook Mountain, there are blue and some red paint blazes on rocks.

Trailhead: 47°24'30" N, 66°52'35" W

The hike: The trail starts 100 m/yd below the summit of Sagamook Mountain and descends across boulders in a southerly direction. Once the rocks are crossed at a sign indicating 4 km, the trail becomes almost level. The path gently descends through young mixed forest to a junction at 0.8 km (0.5 mi), where the Bald Mountain Brook Trail departs to the right. Continuing straight, level first and gently ascending later, the path reaches another junction, where a 1.6 km (1 mi) return side trail departs to the left to the summit of Mount Head. The side trail soon makes a sharp turn to the left (it is marked) and continues through softwoods. The rocky path continues for some distance, then swings to the right and reaches the summit after a short climb. There are some fine views of Mount Carleton with its fire tower and the Nepisiguit Lakes.

Back on the main trail, the path leads through softwoods on mossy boulders. It is quite rocky in this area. After a long, gentle descent, the trail reaches a mature forest and continues for some time before it dips down to Dry Brook. Just beyond the brook, the trail ascends again and reaches the junction with the Big Brook-Dry Brook Loop (see trail 139). From here, the trail continues straight, ascends, and then swings to the right. The path follows an old cut that is an undeveloped road. The rocky trail passes through mixed forest with a large number of birch trees before it reaches a clearing on a small plateau, just below the steep but short climb to the summit of Mount Carleton, which is marked by green paint blazes on the rocks. The trail connects three of the major summits of the park: Sagamook Mountain, Mount Head, and Mount Carleton. The views from all these peaks are spectacular.

138. **Caribou Brook Trail**

Distance: 10.4 km (6.5 mi) one way to Bathurst Lake
Type: linear
Difficulty: easy to moderate
Ascent: 50 m (165 ft)
Hiking time: 4 hrs 30 min rtn

Map: 21 O/7 Nepisiguit Lakes or park brochure
Trail condition: rooty, overgrown, deadfall
Cellphone coverage: N

Finding the trailhead: From the visitor centre, continue in a southeasterly direction for 2.2 km (1.4 mi), passing roads that depart first to the left and then to the right. At a picnic area on the right, take the left road along Nictau Lake to Mount Carleton. After another 2.9 km (1.8 mi), just beyond the crossing of Bald Mountain Brook, the road to the Mount Carleton trailhead departs to the right. Continue straight at this point and follow the road for another 1.9 km (1.2 mi). The trailhead of the Mount Sagamook Trail (and the Caribou Brook Trail) is located on the right side of the road. There is also a pit toilet in the direct vicinity. Parking spaces are available on both sides of the road for about twelve vehicles. The trail is marked by maroon squares/diamonds with a reflector ribbon.

Trailhead: 47°25'08" N, 66°52'04" W

The hike: For a short distance, this trail coincides with the Mount Sagamook Trail. The latter soon departs to the right, whereas the Caribou Brook Trail continues straight ahead, ascending at a gentle grade. The path leads through nice hardwoods and soon levels off. After a while, the trail crosses a number of small mountain brooks in the mixed forest. The trail descends for some distance, then becomes more open and reaches a forest road on the left, but the trail continues straight. It ascends to an open area with a view, then levels off and ascends again. The trail continues up and down in this area. The trail reaches a sign for the Caribou Brook viewpoint, and the roaring brook can be heard below. Here, the trail makes a sharp right turn and soon enters an area with a lot of deadfall. The trail circumvents the deadfall, crosses a dry brook and later another, and eventually reaches the junction with the Dry Brook Trail. From here, the wide trail leads through raspberry bushes before it then descends into softwoods, crosses a fire road, and continues straight ahead to Bathurst Lake and the parking lot. This trail may be useful as a connector; it may be used to form a long loop that includes the Big Brook Trail, the Mount Carleton Trail with a spur to the summit, the Mount Head Trail, the eastern side of the Mount Sagamook Trail, and the Caribou Brook Trail. However, this trail has suffered from a few years of neglect. Check the trail conditions at the visitor centre before heading out.

139. Big Brook–Dry Brook Loop

Distance: 19 km (11.8 mi)
Type: loop
Difficulty: strenuous
Ascent: 420 m (1,380 ft)
Hiking time: 6 hrs 30 min
Map: 21 O/7 Nepisiguit Lakes or park

brochure
Trail condition: The trail is partially overgrown, so paying close attention to the blazes is a must. Deadfall and wet spots are also present.
Cellphone coverage: N

Finding the trailhead: From the visitor centre, continue in a southeasterly direction for 1.1 km (0.7 mi), then turn left. Cross a bridge and follow the dirt road, keeping to the left at all forks and junctions. After 12.3 km (7.6 mi), a small spur departs to the right. This short access road ends at a gate, where there are parking spaces for maybe three vehicles. Pass by the gate and walk a short distance to Bathurst Lake. The trailhead of Big Brook Trail is located next to the lake on the right side of a grassy area. Right next to the trailhead of Big Brook Trail is also the trailhead of Dry Brook Trail, which is where the trail returns. The trail is marked with black squares/diamonds with reflective ribbons as well as fully reflective white squares with a black disk. There are also some older blue metal blazes with a white diagonal bar.

Trailhead: 47°23'34"N, 66°48'43"W

The hike: The level trail follows the shore of Bathurst Lake through mixed spruce and white birch woods. Cross two branches of Brown Brook, and at 2.3 km (1.4 mi) the trail turns right at a ninety-degree angle and leaves the shoreline. This part of the trail appears to be an old wagon road, and it passes through softwoods with vigorous young growth. After a while, the trail ascends and the roaring Big Brook can be heard (but not seen) on the left below. At 4.8 km (3 mi) the path reaches a junction with an old access road, which departs to the right. It is possible to return to the parking lot on this road.

Continuing straight ahead, the trail soon reaches a fork. Keep to the right at a marked fork; the trail crosses a brook on a wooden bridge and soon rejoins the old woods road at the signed 8 km mark, turning right onto it. Here, the trail climbs for a while and then levels off. Fiddleheads are abundant here in the spring and the trail can be quite muddy. Ascents and level parts alternate in this area. At some point, the trail steeply dips into a valley and climbs immediately after. The path is narrow and overgrown, so watch for blazes! The descent to a brook is slippery; just as the trail reaches the brook, it turns left and follows the stream for some distance. It then crosses the brook at a 12 km sign and ascends steeply. After some distance, the ascent gets gentler and then levels off altogether. The trail then continues in a

rocky streambed, leads through dense softwoods, and eventually reaches the rocky Mount Carleton Trail. Turn right onto this trail.

The trail starts to ascend rather steeply. It soon passes an open log cabin on its right. At a small clearing/plateau, the trail turns right onto the Mount Head Trail, while the steep and rocky 400 m/yd trail to the left leads to the summit of Mount Carleton (see the trail description on p. 293). Continue on the Mount Head Trail, which first leads through mixed forest with a large number of birch trees, then swings to the left and descends farther. Eventually, the path reaches the junction of the Mount Head Trail and the Dry Brook Trail.

The Dry Brook Trail departs to the right and immediately descends steeply, keeping Dry Brook to its left. The trail is seriously overgrown in this area, so watch for the blazes. The path skirts a beaver pond and then turns right into the woods. It then crosses the brook, which remains to the right of the trail for a little while. Note the decorative Siberian dogwood in some of the wet areas. After a while, the trail crosses the brook again. The next part is very steep; caution is strongly advised. As it descends, the trail then drops down and turns left to a waterfall. The creek is crossed a number of times, as the path always keeps close to the brook.

As the trail then levels off, walking gets easier and the trail is easier to follow. After skirting a number of beaver ponds, the trail swings to the right, keeping Dry Brook to its left and following it for a while until only the creek bed remains. This gives Dry Brook its name: the creek disappears in the gravelly streambed. The path continues through mixed and pure hardwood ridges. Beyond the turnoff of the Caribou Brook Trail to the left, the wide trail leads through raspberry bushes before it then descends into softwoods, crosses a fire road, and continues straight ahead to Bathurst Lake and the parking lot.

The main attractions of this trail are found along Dry Brook: a series of tumbling waterfalls, beautiful stands of white birch, and active beaver ponds. The trail has suffered from a few years of neglect, so check the trail condition at the visitor centre. A short spur also provides access to the summit of Mount Carleton.

140. Pine Point Trail

Distance: 2 km (1.2 mi)
Type: loop
Difficulty: easy
Ascent: negligible
Hiking time: 45 min

Map: 21 O/7 Nepisiguit Lakes or park brochure
Trail condition: dry
Cellphone coverage: N

Finding the trailhead: From the visitor centre, continue in a southeasterly direction for 1.1 km (0.7 mi), then turn left. Cross a bridge and follow the dirt road, keeping to the left at all forks and junctions. After 12.3 km (7.6 mi), a small spur departs to the right. This short access road ends at a gate, where there are parking spaces for maybe three vehicles. Pass by the gate and walk a short distance to Bathurst Lake. The trailhead of Pine Point Trail is located next to the lake on the far side of a grassy area just left to the lake access. The trail is marked by white metal blazes.

Trailhead: 47°23'33" N, 66°48'40" W

The hike: Immediately beyond the trailhead there is a fork. Keep to the right (the trail returns on the left fork) and follow the lakeshore trail. This area leads through very pretty red pines. After some distance, the trail swings left and rounds the tip of the peninsula, where hikers can enjoy nice vistas across the lake. From here, the trail ascends gently and returns through softwoods, cutting across the top of this small peninsula. It re-enters the stand of pines and descends to the parking lot. The pure stand of red pines on the eastern shore is a main feature of this trail. It is the result of natural reforestation, following the 1933 forest fire. In addition, a hanging red pine and nice views across Bathurst Lake make walking this short trail very worthwhile. Listen to the cry of the common loon while you round the peninsula.

Ancient Portage

The re-established Portage Trail in Mount Carleton Provincial Park is a witness of ancient times, when Maliseet and Mi'kmaq First Nations travelled through the land by foot and waterways. There were about eighty of those ancient travel routes in New Brunswick, but most water-connecting lands were later used for settlements or simply went dormant. In 2008, Canoe Kayak New Brunswick and other stakeholders restored six of these old portage routes from the Nepisiguit Lakes to the Upsalquitch and the Mackay Brook region, and also from the Salmon-Richibucto River to the Cains-Gaspereau. The recently restored Portage Trail, which for First Nations was once the important connector of Bathurst Lake and Little Nictau Lake, is now a lovely hiking trail and at the same time an experience of Indigenous culture and our provincial heritage.

141. **Portage Trail**

Distance: 8.4 km (5.2 mi) rtn
Type: linear
Difficulty: easy
Ascent: negligible
Hiking time: 2 hrs 30 min rtn

Map: 21 O/7 Nepisiguit Lakes or park brochure
Trail condition: excellent, with boardwalk sections
Cellphone coverage: N

Finding the trailhead: From the visitor centre, continue in a southeasterly direction for 1.1 km (0.7 mi), then turn left. Cross a bridge and follow the dirt road, keeping to the left at all forks and junctions. After 12.3 km (7.6 mi), a small spur departs to the right. This short access road ends at a gate, where there are some parking spaces. Pass through the gate and walk a short distance towards Bathurst Lake. Turn right at a yellow sign on the right side of the trail displaying a canoeist.

Trailhead: 47°23'35" N, 66°48'43" W

The hike: The narrow path leads through woods until it crosses a woods road. It then descends to a dry brook, ascends again, and levels off. It passes an open area with a stand of birch trees and then reaches the road with a beautiful view across a marshy area at Caribou Brook. Turn left and walk on the road for a short distance, cross a bridge, and immediately turn left into the woods. After some distance, the trail becomes grassy and more open with dramatic mountain views on the left. A few boardwalk sections lead across wet parts until you reach a small bridge next to a dirt road, where there is a small parking spot. Cross the road and continue to Little Nictau Lake. The trail ends at the lake. The heritage trail follows an ancient portage used by Maliseet and Mi'kmaq people hundreds of years ago. It also marks a watershed: bodies of water to its west are drained via the Tobique River and the Saint John River into the Bay of Fundy, while those in the east eventually find their way to Chaleur Bay. As well, it provides quick access to beautiful Bathurst Lake and an outlet of Little Nictau Lake with views of some of the major mountains in the park.

142. Williams Falls

Distance: 0.6 km (0.4 mi) rtn
Type: linear
Difficulty: easy
Ascent: negligible
Hiking time: 20 min rtn

Map: 21 O/7 Nepisiguit Lakes or the park brochure
Trail condition: dry, part boardwalk
Cellphone coverage: N

Finding the trailhead: From the visitor centre, continue on the main road in a southeasterly direction for 2.2 km (1.4 mi), then turn left towards Armstrong Brook Campground. Follow this road for 5 km (3.1 mi), passing the campground along the way. The trailhead is located on the right side of the road. There are no trail markings, but the trail is obvious and cannot be missed.

Trailhead: 47°25'36" N, 66°53'03" W

The hike: Follow the short trail all the way down to the platform. The commanding feature of this trail is the picturesque Williams Falls. They can be viewed up close from a wooden bridge and, even better, a platform a few steps farther down, at the end of the trail.

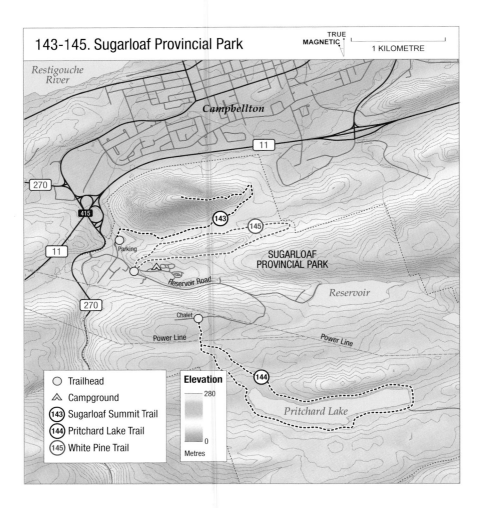

143-145. Sugarloaf Provincial Park

TRUE
MAGNETIC
1 KILOMETRE

Restigouche River

Campbellton

11

270

415

11

Parking

270

Reservoir Road

SUGARLOAF PROVINCIAL PARK

Reservoir

Chalet

Power Line

Power Line

143

145

144

Pritchard Lake

○ Trailhead
△ Campground
(143) Sugarloaf Summit Trail
(144) Pritchard Lake Trail
(145) White Pine Trail

Elevation
280
0
Metres

143-145. **Sugarloaf Provincial Park**

Sugarloaf Provincial Park is located near Campbellton. The park is designed for multiple uses. In addition to a tourist information centre and a picnic area, the park offers lighted tennis courts, an alpine slide, and camping facilities. The rather extensive network of trails is shared by joggers and hikers in summer, and skiers and snowmobilers in winter. The highlight of the park, however, is the summit of Sugarloaf Mountain, from which you have a panoramic view of Campbellton, the Gaspé Peninsula, and Chaleur Bay.

The park is easily reached by taking Highway 2 to exit 58 in Saint-Léonard and turning onto Highway 17, which later turns into Highway 11, towards Saint-Quentin and Campbellton. Take exit 415 and follow the signs to nearby Sugarloaf Provincial Park, keeping left twice. A map of the trails of the park is available at http://parc sugarloafpark.ca/pdf/general_map.pdf.

143. Sugarloaf Summit Trail

Distance: 5.1 km (3.2 mi) rtn
Type: linear
Difficulty: moderate to strenuous
Ascent: 240 m (785 ft)
Hiking time: 1 hr 45 min

Map: 21 O/15 Atholville or park map from website
Trail condition: groomed trail, dry, boulders, ladders
Cellphone coverage: Y

Finding the trailhead: Enter the park and immediately turn left onto Atholville Street. Cross a bridge and turn left again onto Campbellton Street. There is plenty of parking space available. The trailhead is located at the far end of the lot. There are no trail markings, but the trail is well groomed and easy to follow.

Trailhead: 47°59'10" N, 66°41'39" W

The hike: Follow the wide road to a junction with a memorial honouring Terry Fox. Turn right and follow the wide gravel road. After a while, it swings to the left. At 1.5 km (0.9 mi) at a signed fork, turn left onto a wide dirt trail (Trail #9). The trail immediately ascends fairly steeply in a westerly direction. The top of the mountain is reached by means of guardrails and ladders. A breathtaking view towards Campbellton, the bay (Restigouche Harbour), and the Gaspé awaits the hiker. In addition, some plaques highlight the Battle of the Restigouche in 1760 as well as a flag in honour of the fallen RCMP officers in the 2014 Moncton shooting. From here you can return by descending on the wide trail and then either continuing on the loop by turning left at the T-junction or turning right and retracing your steps. The main feature of this trail is the truly amazing view from the 283 m (930 ft) summit of Sugarloaf Mountain. There is a picnic site alongside the first section of the trail.

Battle of the Restigouche

The year was 1760. Britain and France were engaged in a bitter war for parts of the New World. Three French vessels, after capturing a number of British ships, were on their way to Montreal. When the captains learned that the British were already present in the St. Lawrence River, they decided to regroup in Chaleur Bay, where they were joined by some twenty-five Acadian boats. On June 22, an armada of British boats engaged the French in what became known as the last naval battle between France and Britain for dominance in the New World. The battle ended on July 8, by which time the British had destroyed ten French boats. In addition, the French destroyed twenty-two vessels of their own to ensure they would not fall into British hands. The rest of the story is, as they say, history.

143. Sugarloaf Summit Trail

144. Prichard Lake Trail

Distance: 6.4 km (4 mi)
Type: loop
Difficulty: easy to moderate
Ascent: 150 m (490 ft)
Hiking time: 2 hrs 15 min

Map: 21 O/15 Atholville or park map from website
Trail condition: rooty, some wet spots
Cellphone coverage: P

Finding the trailhead: Enter the park and turn left immediately. Cross a bridge and continue straight towards the campground. Pass by the campground, leaving it on the left, continue straight for 1.2 km (0.7 mi), and keep right at a fork onto Atholville Street. Continue for 0.8 km (0.5 mi) to a parking lot at a cabin. Just behind the gate in front of the cross-country ski cabin, take the left path up (trail #5). There is a network of trails, mostly for skiers and snowmobilers in the winter and four-wheelers in the summer. The trail to the lake (#5) can be confusing, but the one around the lake (trail #6), although unmarked, is easy to find.

Trailhead: 47°58'41" N, 66°40'47" W

The hike: Follow trail #5, cross a brook, and continue across a dirt road. Continue underneath power lines and enter the woods again straight ahead (the trail will return from the left at this point). The trail first climbs, descends again, crosses a dirt road, and ascends steeply. At the top, the trail passes the gravestone of a Mr. Prichard. At this point, the trail descends to Prichard Lake with some picnic tables. At the lake, turn right onto trail #6, keeping the lake to your left. The trail skirts the lake. There are some wet spots in this area. Halfway around the lake (at its eastern end), there is another picnic table built on a platform that juts out over the shore of the lake. Just beyond the picnic place, cross the dam and continue on the drier northern side of the lake. Eventually, turn off the lake onto trail #5. The trail crosses three woods roads straight on. Just before reaching the power lines, turn left onto a grassy road and follow it for a short distance. Then turn right, cross the power lines, and continue the same way you came. The trail leads through nice hardwoods and offers some pleasant views of Prichard Lake. There are a number of picnic sites along the lake.

145. **White Pine Trail**

Distance: 3.8 km (2.4 mi)
Type: loop
Difficulty: easy to moderate
Ascent: 30 m (100 ft)
Hiking time: 1 hr

Map: 21 O/15 Atholville or park map from website
Trail condition: dry
Cellphone coverage: P

Finding the trailhead: Enter the park and immediately turn left. Cross a bridge and continue straight to the campground. There are some parking spaces on the side of the road outside the campground. Turn left into the campground behind the gate. The trailhead is straight ahead on the left side of the road; the trail returns next to the gate. The trail is numbered with #7, #10, and #11, which can be confusing at times.

Trailhead: 47°58'58" N, 66°41'28" W

The hike: The trail ascends immediately. Turn left at the first junction and straight to start the loop in a counter-clockwise direction. The trail ascends steeply, then levels off. Continue straight on trail #10 at a junction, then straight at a fork on trails #7/#10, and later on trail #10 (a shortcut trail, #7, turns off to the left). Walking through hardwoods is nice in this area. Go straight at a junction on the #10 trail and turn left onto trail #11 at a subsequent junction. Here, the loop leads back, reaches a sign with the #7 trail, and continues straight on the #7 trail. After a while, at a junction, either keep left and return the way you came or continue straight. In the latter case, after some distance, turn left at a T-junction and return to the parking lot on the lower trail next to the gate at the campground. There are a few nice glimpses across Sugarloaf and Chaleur Bay.

Acknowledgements

It is now our pleasant task to thank all those who have helped in making this book a reality. Our thanks go out to Mr. Dave Ward, who provided us with ideas about new trails and reports on the condition of existing trails. We thank Stephen R. Clayden of the New Brunswick Museum for his detailed description of aspects of the rare flora in Mount Carleton Provincial Park. We also would like to express our gratitude to Pauline Cormier, Sandra Savoie, Anne Faucher, and Theresa Everett at Mount Carleton Provincial Park for taking care of us during our visits to the park. Also at Mount Carleton, there was Robert Doyle, who filled us in on many details concerning the new Portage Trail in the park. Tim Humes and Kevin Silliker from Canoe Kayak New Brunswick provided the bigger picture. Our gratitude goes out to Manuela Lange for the shuttle to the end of the Dobson Trail (may you never run out of gas in the night) and Larry Adair for providing transportation and, most of all, many highly entertaining stories. We much appreciate his help. We also thank our chiropractor Robert Allaby for his enthusiastic account of his hike into the Glen Walton Gorge, which made us explore the area further. Many thanks go out to Gui and Xian of the Glory Inn Downtown Moncton Bed & Breakfast for their patience and their long wait for us. We also thank Gabriele Hoenow for the hot coffee and dinner after our chilly November hike of the Meduxnekeag trails. We'd also like to thank Fritz Grein for taking care of our residence during our frequent absences. Last, but certainly not least, we would like to thank Susanne Alexander and Julie Scriver of Goose Lane Editions for their continued support and encouragement. Thanks are also due to our editor Charles Stuart and proofreader Shelley Egan, who meticulously followed our trails on paper and ensured consistency, and to our production editor Alan Sheppard, who was very helpful with the production of this book, and Jim Todd for his superb maps. Finally, a nod to the general public for their praise, occasional critiques, and the opportunity for impromptu book signings. May your trails be adventurous and smooth, the wildlife friendly, and the weather cooperative. Enjoy New Brunswick's wild areas as much as we did!

H.A. & Marianne Eiselt

Bibliography

New Brunswick Nature Guides

Boland, T. *Wildflowers of New Brunswick: Field Guide*. Portugal Cove-St. Philip's, NL: Boulder Publications, 2015.

Burrows, R., and M.J. Cormier. *Birding in New Brunswick*. Fredericton: Goose Lane Editions, 2010.

Domm, J. *Formac Pocket Guide to Nature: Animals, Plants and Birds in New Brunswick, Nova Scotia and Prince Edward Island*. Halifax: Formac, 2012.

Guitard, N. *Waterfalls of New Brunswick: A Guide*. Fredericton: Goose Lane Editions, 2010.

Stone, Bob. *Heritage Trails and Footpaths of Grand Manan, New Brunswick, Canada*. 9th edition. Grand Manan, NB: Grand Manan Trails Committee, 2012.

Hiking, Backpacking, and Wilderness Medicine

Backpacker Magazine. www.backpacker.com.

Bratman, G., et al. "Nature Experience Reduces Rumination and Subgenual Prefrontal Cortex Activation." *PNAS* 112, no. 28 (July 2015): 8567-8572. https://doi.org/10.1073/pnas.1510459112.

Clelland, M. *Ultralight Backpackin' Tips: 153 Amazing & Inexpensive Tips for Extremely Lightweight Camping*. Nashville, TN: Falcon Guides, 2011.

Explore Magazine. www.explore-mag.com.

Forgey, W. *Wilderness Medicine: Beyond First Aid*. 7th edition. Guilford, CT: Globe Pequot Press, 2012.

Fundy Hiking Trail Association. *Fundy Footpath – Hiker's Guide Book*. http://fundyhikingtrails.com/index.php/explore-the-trails/com_guides/.

Gadd, B. *The Canadian Hiker's & Backpacker's Handbook*. Toronto: Whitecap Books, 2008.

James, P., et al. "Exposure to Greenness and Mortality in a Nationwide Prospective Cohort Study of Women." Environmental Health Perspectives 124, no. 9 (September 2016): 1344-1352. DOI:10.1289/ehp.1510363.

Johnson, R. *The Ultimate Survival Manual Canadian Edition (Outdoor Life): Urban Adventure, Wilderness Survival, Disaster Preparedness.* San Francisco: Weldon Owen, 2013.

Oh, B. et al. "Health and Well-being Benefits of Spending Time in Forests: Systematic Review." *Environmental Health and Preventative Medicine* 22, no. 71 (2017). https://environhealthprevmed.biomedcentral.com/track/pdf/10.1186/s12199-017-0677-9?site=environhealthprevmed.biomedcentral.com.

Schimelpfenig, T., and J. Safford. *NOLS Wilderness Medicine.* Mechanicsburg, PA: Stackpole Books, 2016.

Skurka, A. *The Ultimate Hiker's Gear Guide: Tools and Techniques to Hit the Trail.* 2nd edition. Des Moines, IA: National Geographic Books, 2017.

Stevenson J. *The Complete Idiot's Guide to Backpacking and Hiking.* Indianapolis, IN: Alpha Books, 2010.

Tilton, B. *Knack Hiking and Backpacking: A Complete Illustrated Guide.* Guilford, CT: Globe Pequot Press, 2009.

Townsend, C. *The Backpacker's Handbook.* 4th edition. New York: McGraw Hill, 2011.

Wiseman, J. *SAS Survival Guide: How to Survive in the Wild, on Land or Sea.* Glasgow: Collins Gem, 2015.

Local History

Adney, T., and C.T. Behne. *The Travel Journals of Tappan Adney: Vol. 1, 1887-1890.* Fredericton: Goose Lane Editions, 2016.

Guitard, Nicholas. *The Lost Wilderness: Rediscovering W.F. Ganong's New Brunswick.* Fredericton: Goose Lane Editions, 2015.

Helmuth, K. *Tappan Adney and the Heritage of the St. John River Valley.* Woodstock, NB: Chapel Street Editions, 2017.

Rudin, R. *Kouchibouguac: Removal, Resistance, and Remembrance at a Canadian National Park.* Toronto: University of Toronto Press, 2016.

Outdoor Recreation Clubs and Associations

CanoeKayakNB: http://www.canoekayaknb.com/

Focus Camera Club Moncton: https://www.focuscameraclub.com/

Fredericton Nature Club: http://www.fnc.gbnature.com/

Fredericton Outdoor Enthusiasts Club: http://outdoorenthusiasts.weebly.com/
   contact-us.html

Fundy Hiking Trail Association: http://fundyhikingtrails.com/

Meduxnekeag River Association: https://www.meduxnekeag.org/

Moncton Outdoor Enthusiasts: https://monctonoutdoorenthusiasts.wordpress.com/

Nature Moncton: http://www.naturemoncton.com/

NBTrails: https://www.sentiernbtrail.com/

Photo Fredericton: http://photofredericton.ca/

Saint John Outdoor Enthusiasts Club: https://www.sjoe.ca/

Trans Canada Trail: www.tctrail.ca/

Luna moth

128. Little Sheephouse Falls Nature Trail

Index

(Sidebar page references are listed in bold type)

Over the past 30 years, Marianne and H.A. Eiselt have backpacked the Chilkoot Trail in Alaska and British Columbia; the West Coast Trail in British Columbia; the Grand Canyon in Arizona; the Torres del Paine in Chile; the Annapurna, Manaslu, and Everest treks in Nepal; the Rennsteig in Thuringia, Germany; and many others.

They are presently planning the second part of their fourth pilgrimage to Santiago de Compostela in northern Spain.

They have co-written several books on New Brunswick, including the first three editions of this popular guide.